# Adobe® Photoshop®
## Elements 10
# CLASSROOM IN A BOOK
The official training workbook from Adobe Systems

D0521179

Adobe

Adobe® Photoshop® Elements 10 Classroom in a Book®

Adobe Press books are published by Peachpit, a division of Pearson Education located in Berkeley, California. For the latest on Adobe Press books, go to www.adobepress.com. To report errors, please send a note to errata@peachpit.com. For information on getting permission for reprints and excerpts, contact permissions@peachpit.com.

Printed and bound in the United States of America

ISBN-13:    978-0-321-81100-4
ISBN-10:        0-321-81100-3

9 8 7 6 5 4 3 2

# WHAT'S ON THE DISC

**Here is an overview of the contents of the Classroom in a Book disc**

The *Adobe Photoshop Elements 10 Classroom in a Book* disc includes the lesson files that you'll need to complete the exercises in this book, as well as other content to help you learn more about Adobe Photoshop Elements 10 and use it with greater efficiency and ease. The diagram below represents the contents of the disc, which should help you locate the files you need.

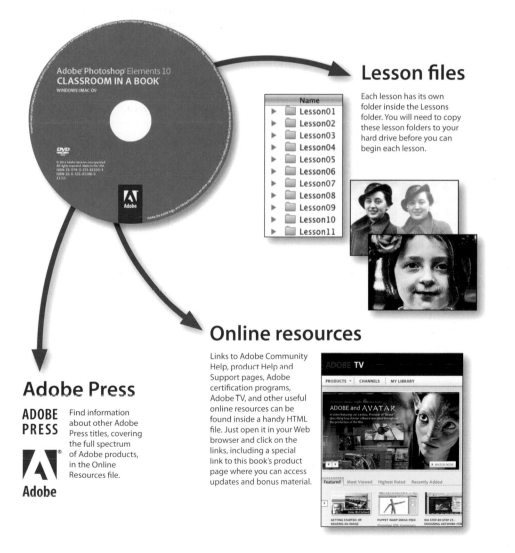

## Lesson files

Each lesson has its own folder inside the Lessons folder. You will need to copy these lesson folders to your hard drive before you can begin each lesson.

| Name |
| --- |
| ▶ 📁 Lesson01 |
| ▶ 📁 Lesson02 |
| ▶ 📁 Lesson03 |
| ▶ 📁 Lesson04 |
| ▶ 📁 Lesson05 |
| ▶ 📁 Lesson06 |
| ▶ 📁 Lesson07 |
| ▶ 📁 Lesson08 |
| ▶ 📁 Lesson09 |
| ▶ 📁 Lesson10 |
| ▶ 📁 Lesson11 |

## Online resources

Links to Adobe Community Help, product Help and Support pages, Adobe certification programs, Adobe TV, and other useful online resources can be found inside a handy HTML file. Just open it in your Web browser and click on the links, including a special link to this book's product page where you can access updates and bonus material.

## Adobe Press

**ADOBE PRESS**

Find information about other Adobe Press titles, covering the full spectrum of Adobe products, in the Online Resources file.

# CONTENTS

**3    ADVANCED ORGANIZING                                    58**

## 5   PRINTING, SHARING, AND EXPORTING                                122

## 6   EASY EDITING                                                     144

## 11  ADVANCED EDITING TECHNIQUES                                              262

## INDEX                                                                        294

# GETTING STARTED

Adobe® Photoshop® Elements 10 delivers image-editing tools that balance power and versatility with ease of use. Whether you're a home user or hobbyist, a professional photographer or a business user, Photoshop Elements 10 makes it easy to produce good-looking pictures, share your stories in sophisticated creations for both print and web, and manage and safeguard your precious photos.

If you've used an earlier version of Photoshop Elements, you'll find that this Classroom in a Book® will teach you advanced skills and provide an introduction to the many new and improved features in this version. If you're new to Adobe Photoshop Elements, you'll learn the fundamental concepts and techniques that will help you master the application.

## About Classroom in a Book

*Adobe Photoshop Elements 10 Classroom in a Book* is part of the official training series for Adobe graphics and publishing software developed with the support of Adobe product experts. Each lesson in this book is made up of a series of self-paced projects that will give you hands-on experience using Photoshop Elements 10.

*Adobe Photoshop Elements 10 Classroom in a Book* includes a CD attached to the inside back cover. On the CD you'll find all the image files used for the lessons in this book, together with additional learning resources.

## Prerequisites

Before you begin the lessons in this book, make sure that you and your computer are ready by following the tips and instructions on the next few pages.

### Requirements on your computer

You'll need about 800 MB of free space on your hard disk—around 250 MB for the lesson files and up to 550 MB for the work files that you'll create as you work through the exercises.

## Required skills

● **Note:** In this book, the forward slash character (/) is used to separate equivalent terms and commands for Windows / Mac OS, in the order shown here.

The lessons in this book assume that you have a working knowledge of your computer and its operating system. Make sure that you know how to use the mouse and the standard menus and commands, and also how to open, save, and close files. Can you scroll (vertically and horizontally) within a window to see content that may not be visible in the displayed area? Do you know how to use context menus, which open when you right-click (Windows) / Control-click (Mac OS) items? If you need to review these basic and generic computer skills, see the documentation included with your Microsoft® Windows® or Apple® Mac® OS X software.

# Installing Adobe Photoshop Elements 10

You must purchase the Adobe Photoshop Elements 10 software separately and install it on a computer running Windows Vista®, Windows® XP, Windows® 7, or Mac® OS X. For system requirements and complete instructions on installing the software, see the Photoshop Elements 10 Read Me file on the application disc and the accompanying documentation.

## Trouble-shooting installation problems

Should you have problems installing Photoshop Elements 10, point your browser to www.adobe.com/support and choose Photoshop Elements from the list of product help and support centers. On the Adobe Photoshop Elements Help And Support page, click Downloading, Installing And Setting Up, under Getting Started & Help.

# Copying the Classroom in a Book files

The CD attached to the inside back cover of this book includes a Lessons folder containing all the digital files you'll need for the lessons. Keep the lesson files on your computer until you have completed all the exercises.

## Copying the Lessons files from the CD

1   Create a new folder named **PSE10CIB** inside the *username/My Documents* (Windows) or *username/Documents* (Mac OS) folder on your computer.

2   Insert the *Adobe Photoshop Elements 10 Classroom in a Book* CD into your CD-ROM drive. For Windows users: if a message appears asking what you want Windows to do, choose Open Folder To View Files Using Windows Explorer, and then click OK. If no message appears, open My Computer and double-click the CD icon to open it.

3   Locate the Lessons folder on the CD and copy it to the PSE10CIB folder you've just created on your computer.

4   When your computer has finished copying the Lessons folder, remove the CD from your CD-ROM drive and put it away.

## Creating a work folder

Now you need to create a folder for the work files that you'll produce as you work through the lessons in this book.

1   In Windows Explorer (Windows) / the Finder (Mac OS) open the Lessons folder that you copied to your new PSE10CIB folder on your hard disk.

2   Choose File > New > Folder (Windows) / File > New Folder (Mac OS). A new folder is created inside the Lessons folder. Type **My CIB Work** as the name for the new folder.

● **Note:** In this book, the forward arrow character (>) is used to denote submenus and commands found in the menu bar at the top of the workspace or in context and options menus; for example, Menu > Submenu > Command. The forward slash character (/) is used to separate equivalent keyboard shortcuts and commands for Windows / Mac OS, in the order shown here.

# About catalog files

Photoshop Elements stores information about your images in a library catalog file, which enables you to conveniently manage the photos on your computer. The catalog file is a central concept in understanding how Photoshop Elements works. Photoshop Elements doesn't actually "import" your images at all; for each image you import Photoshop Elements simply creates a new entry in the catalog that is linked to the source file, wherever it is stored. Whenever you assign a tag or a rating to a photo, or group images as an album, the catalog file is updated. All the work you put into organizing your growing photo library is recorded in the catalog.

As well as digital photographs, a catalog can include video and audio files, scans, PDF documents, and any presentations and layouts you might create in Photoshop Elements, such as slide shows, photo collages, and CD jacket designs.

The first time you launch Photoshop Elements it automatically creates a default catalog file (named My Catalog) on your hard disk. Although a single catalog can efficiently handle thousands of files, you can also establish separate catalogs for different purposes if that's the way you prefer to work.

In the first lesson in this book you'll create and load a new, dedicated catalog into which you'll import the lesson sample images. In this way, it will be easy to keep your own photo library separate from your lesson files.

In the first three lessons, you'll learn a number of different ways to add files to your catalog, together with a variety of techniques for tagging, marking, and organizing your images, and for sorting and searching your catalog. You'll be able to practice these new skills when you import lesson files to your Classroom in a Book catalog at the beginning of each chapter.

# Additional resources

*Adobe Photoshop Elements 10 Classroom in a Book* is not meant to replace the documentation that comes with the program, nor to be a comprehensive reference for every feature; only the commands and options used in the lessons are explained in this book. For comprehensive information and tutorials about program features, please refer to these resources:

**Adobe Community Help** Community Help brings together active Adobe product users, Adobe product team members, authors, and experts to give you the most useful, relevant, and up-to-date information about Adobe products. Whether you're looking for a code sample or an answer to a problem, have a question about the software, or want to share a useful tip or recipe, you'll benefit from Community Help. Search results will show you not only content from Adobe, but also from the community. With Adobe Community Help you can:

- Access up-to-date definitive reference content online and offline

- Find the most relevant content contributed by experts from the Adobe community, on and off Adobe.com

- Comment on, rate, and contribute to content in the Adobe community

- Download Help content directly to your desktop for offline use

- Find related content with dynamic search and navigation tools

**To access Community Help** The Community Help application downloads when you first install Photoshop Elements 10. To invoke Help, press F1 or choose Help > Elements Organizer Help in the Organizer, or Help > Photoshop Elements Help in the Editor. This companion application lets you search and browse Adobe and community content, and to comment on and rate any article just as you would in the browser.

You can also download Adobe Help and language reference content for use offline, and subscribe to new content updates (which can be downloaded automatically) so that you'll always have the most up-to-date content for your Adobe product. You can download the application from www.adobe.com/support/chc/index.html

Adobe content is updated based on community feedback and contributions. You can contribute in several ways: you can add comments to both content and forums—including links to web content, or publish your own content using Community Publishing. You'll find more information about how to contribute at www.adobe.com/community/publishing/download.html

See http://community.adobe.com/help/profile/faq.html for answers to frequently asked questions about Community Help.

**Adobe Photoshop Elements 10 Help and Support**  Point your browser to www.adobe.com/support/photoshopelements/ where you can find and browse Help and Support content on adobe.com.

**Adobe TV**  http://tv.adobe.com is an online video resource for expert instruction and inspiration about Adobe products, including a How To channel to get you started with your product.

**Resources for educators**  www.adobe.com/education includes three free curriculums that use an integrated approach to teaching Adobe software and can be used to prepare for the Adobe Certified Associate exams.

Also check out these useful links:

**Adobe Forums**  http://forums.adobe.com lets you tap into peer-to-peer discussions, and questions and answers on Adobe products.

**Adobe Photoshop Elements 10 product home page**
http://www.adobe.com/products/photoshopel/

**Adobe Labs**  http://labs.adobe.com gives you access to early builds of cutting-edge technology, as well as forums where you can interact with both the Adobe development teams building that technology and other like-minded members of the community.

**Free trial versions of Adobe Photoshop Elements 10 and Adobe Premiere Elements 10**  The trial version of the software is fully functional and offers every feature of the product for you to test-drive (does not include Plus membership). To download your free trial version: http://www.adobe.com/cfusion/tdrc/index.cfm?product=photoshop_elements&loc=en_us

# 1 A QUICK TOUR OF PHOTOSHOP ELEMENTS

## Lesson Overview

This lesson provides an overview of Adobe Photoshop Elements 10.

The exercises will familiarize you with the Photoshop Elements workspace and with many of the tools and procedures you'll use to capture, manage, and edit your digital images.

As you work through the exercises in this lesson you'll be introduced to the following basic skills and concepts:

- Working with the Organizer and the Editor
- Creating and loading Catalogs
- Importing media
- Reconnecting missing files
- Reviewing and comparing photos
- Creating an Adobe ID
- Using Photoshop Elements Help

 You'll probably need between one and two hours to complete this lesson.

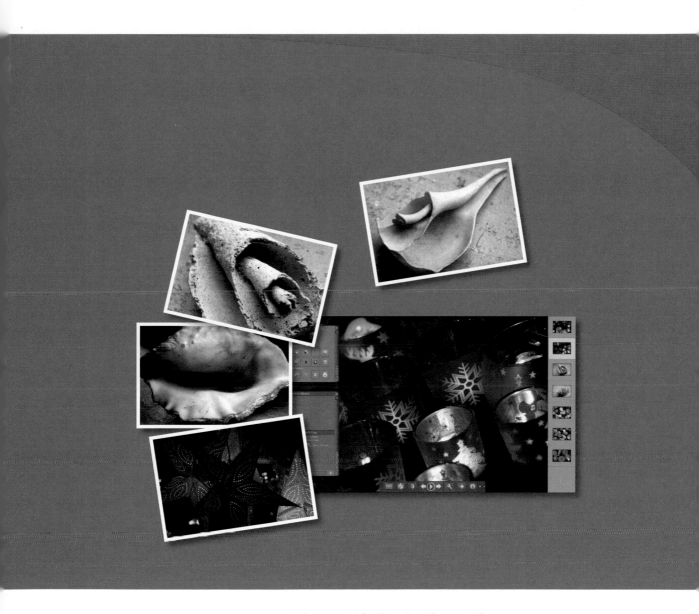

Welcome to Adobe Photoshop Elements! Take a
quick tour and get to know the Photoshop Elements
workspace. You'll find all the power and versatility
you'd expect from a Photoshop application in an easy-
to-use, modular interface that will help you take your
digital photography to a new level.

# How Photoshop Elements works

● **Note:** Before you start working on this lesson, make sure that you've installed the software on your computer from the application CD (see the Photoshop Elements 10 documentation) and that you have correctly copied the Lessons folder from the CD in the back of this book onto your computer's hard disk (see "Copying the Classroom in a Book files" on page 2).

Photoshop Elements has two primary workspaces: the Elements Organizer and the Editor. An easy way to understand these two components is to think of the Organizer as a library and browser for your photo collection, and the Editor as a darkroom and workshop.

You'll work in the Organizer to locate, import, manage, and share your photos and media files, and then use the Editor to edit and adjust your images and to create presentations to showcase them.

## The library catalog file

Photoshop Elements stores information about your images in a library catalog file, which enables you to conveniently manage all the photos and media files on your computer from within the Organizer. A new entry is created in the catalog file for each image you import. Whenever you tag, rate, sort, or group images, the catalog file is updated. All of your work in the Organizer is recorded in the catalog.

As well as digital photographs, a catalog can include video and audio files, scans, PDF documents, and any presentations and layouts you might create in Photoshop Elements, such as slide shows, photo collages, and CD jacket designs.

## Creating a new catalog

The first time you launch Photoshop Elements, a default catalog file (named My Catalog) is automatically created on your hard disk. Although a single catalog can efficiently handle thousands of files, you can also establish separate catalogs for different purposes—if that's the way you prefer to work. In this exercise you'll create and load a new catalog specifically to handle the sample files used for the lessons in this book, making it easy to keep them separate from your own photos.

1 Start Photoshop Elements 10; then, click the Organize button in the Welcome screen to launch the Elements Organizer module. You don't need to be concerned about the prompt to create an Adobe ID; this topic will be covered later in this lesson. If a welcome dialog box appears offering import options, click Cancel.

2 When the Organizer has opened, choose File > Catalog.

**3** In the Catalog Manager dialog box, click New. Don't change the location setting, which specifies who can access the catalog file and where it is stored.

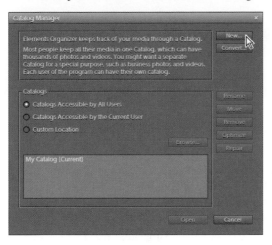

**4** Type **CIB Catalog** in the Enter A Name For The New Catalog dialog box. Disable the option Import Free Music Into This Catalog, if necessary, and then click OK.

Your new catalog is loaded in the Organizer. If you are ever unsure which catalog is currently loaded, you can always check the catalog name displayed in the lower left corner of the Organizer workspace.

Now that you have a catalog created specifically to manage the sample files that you'll use for the lessons in this book, you're ready to put some photos into it.

# Importing media

Before you can view, organize, and edit your photos and other media files in Photoshop Elements, you first need to link them to your catalog by importing them into the Organizer. Bringing your digital files into Photoshop Elements is easy.

## Getting photos from files and folders

You can bring photos into Photoshop Elements from a variety of sources and in a number of different ways.

If your image files are already on your computer hard disk—as is the case for the Classroom in a Book sample photos—you can either drag them directly into the Elements Organizer workspace from Windows Explorer or the Mac OS Finder, or import them from within Photoshop Elements by using a menu command.

1   Choose File > Get Photos And Videos > From Files And Folders.

2   In the Get Photos And Videos From Files And Folders dialog box, navigate to and open the Lessons folder inside your PSE10CIB folder. Click once to select the Lesson01 folder.

3   Make sure that the options Automatically Fix Red Eyes and Automatically Suggest Photo Stacks are disabled; then, click Get Media.

The Getting Media dialog box appears briefly as the photos are imported. Since the imported photos contain keyword metadata, the Import Attached Keyword Tags dialog box appears. You'll learn more about keyword tags in Lessons 2 and 3.

4   In the Import Attached Keyword Tags dialog box, click Select All, and then click OK. Click OK to close any other alert dialog box.

Thumbnails of the imported photos appear in the Organizer's Media Browser pane, marked with orange tags to indicate that the images have attached keywords.

# About keyword tags

Keyword tags are personalized labels, such as "Vacation" or "Beach," that you attach to photos, video clips, audio clips and other creations in the Media Browser to make it easier to organize and find them.

When you use keyword tags, there's no need to manually organize your photos in subject-specific folders or rename files with content-specific names.

In fact, both of the latter solutions confine a given photo to a single group. By contrast, you can assign multiple keyword tags to a photo, allowing it to be included in several different groupings. You can then easily retrieve the selection of images you want by clicking the appropriate keyword tag or tags in the Keyword Tags panel.

For example, you could create a "Beach - Normandy" keyword tag and attach it to every photo you took at that location. You can then instantly find all the photos with the Beach - Normandy keyword tag by clicking the Find box next to that tag in the Keyword Tags panel, even if the photos are stored in different folders on your hard disk.

You can create keyword tags to group your images any way you want. For example, you could create keyword tags for individual people, places and events in your life.

You can attach multiple keyword tags to your photos and easily run a search based on a combination of keyword tags to find a particular person at a particular place or event.

For example, you can search for all "Pauline" keyword tags and all "Sophie" keyword tags to find all pictures of Pauline taken together with her sister Sophie.

Or search for all "Pauline" keyword tags and all "Beach - Normandy" keyword tags to find all the pictures of Pauline vacationing at the beach in Normandy.

Use keyword tags to organize and find photos by their content or any other association. You'll learn more about keyword tags in Lessons 2 and 3.

# The Organizer workspace

In the Organizer, the main work area is the Media Browser pane. This is where you sort, organize, and search your photos and media files, and preview the presentations that you create to showcase and share them. At the right of the Organizer window is the Task Pane, with tabs for the Organize, Fix, Create, and Share modes.

The Elements Organizer is an integral part of both Adobe Photoshop Elements and Adobe Premiere Elements video editing software. You can import, manage, and view both photos and video in the Elements Organizer, which serves as a hub, allowing seamless integration of the two editing applications.

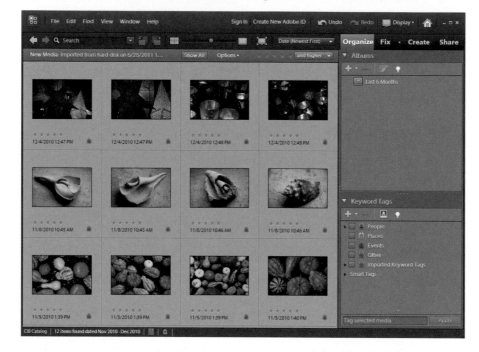

The Media Browser pane can display a single photo or show thumbnails of the files in your catalog arranged in a variety of ways. You can view your images sorted by import batch, folder location, or keywords—or presented in a calendar format in the Date view. The Media Browser makes it easy to browse, preview, organize, and search all the files in your catalog in one comprehensive workspace.

On the Organize tab of the Task Pane are the panels you'll use to sort, search and manage your photos by applying keyword tags and grouping them in albums.

The Fix tab offers tools for some of the most common editing tasks. For more sophisticated editing, you'll switch to one of the three editing modes in the Editor.

On the Create tab you'll find options and guidance for creating projects and presentations—from greeting cards to slide shows.

The Share tab offers a variety of options for sharing your files with your friends, family, clients, or the world at large by burning a CD or DVD, sending your photos as e-mail attachments or photo mail layouts, or publishing an online album.

1   Experiment with the Thumbnail Size slider above the Media Browser pane. Note that when you reduce the thumbnails to a very small size, the orange tags are no longer visible at the lower right of the image cells; reset the thumbnails to a large enough size to see the tags.

2   Hold the pointer over the orange tag below any of the images in the Media Browser; a tool tip appears to show that the image is tagged with the keyword **Lesson 01**. This is the tag that you enabled for import with the image in the last step of the previous exercise.

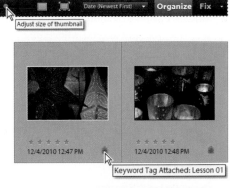

3   In the Keyword Tags panel to the right of the thumbnail view, click the small triangle to expand the Imported Keyword Tags category; you can see that the newly imported **Lesson 01** tag is nested inside, and has been color-coded accordingly.

4   Double-click any thumbnail in the Media Browser. Use the arrow keys on your keyboard to cycle through the photos in the single photo view. When you're done, double-click the enlarged image to return to the thumbnail grid view.

▶ **Tip:** To switch to the single photo view, you can also press Ctrl+Shift+S (Windows) / Command+Shift+S (Mac OS). In single photo view, you can use the controls below the enlarged image to add either a text or audio caption to a photo.

# Reviewing and comparing

Photoshop Elements provides several options for quickly and easily reviewing and comparing your images in the Elements Organizer. Use the Full Screen view to assess your photos in detail, or to effortlessly present a selection of images as an instant slideshow. The Side By Side viewing mode lets you keep one image fixed on one side of a split screen while you cycle through a selection of photos on the other—great for comparing composition and detail or for choosing the best of a series of similar shots. In both Full Screen and Side By Side viewing mode you can apply keywords, add photos to albums, and even perform a range of editing tasks.

## Comparing photos side-by-side

The Side By Side View lets you compare photos at any level of magnification, without the distraction of interface items such as windows, menus and panels.

1 Press Ctrl+Shift+A / Command+Shift+A to ensure that no images are selected in the Media Browser.

2 Click the Display button (■) near the upper right corner of the Organizer window, and choose Compare Photos Side By Side from the menu.

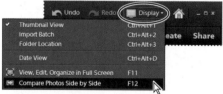

Because we made no selection in the Media Browser, the Organizer treats all the images visible in the Media Browser as the selection. The Film Strip at the right of the screen displays thumbnails of the photos in the selection.

▶ **Tip:** If you don't see the Film Strip at the right of the screen, press Ctrl+F / Command+F on your keyboard or click the button at the left end of the control bar at the bottom of the screen. If you don't see the control bar at the bottom of the screen, move the pointer; the control bar fades from view after a few seconds of inactivity.

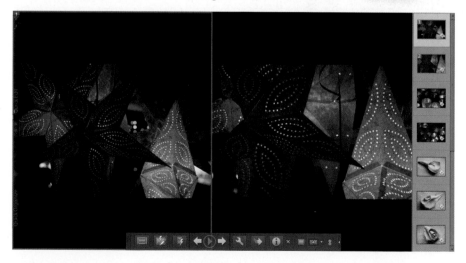

By default, the photo on the left—image #1—is active, as indicated by the blue line surrounding the preview and the highlighted thumbnail in the Film Strip.

**3** With the photo on the left—image #1—still active, scroll down the Film Strip at the right of the screen and click another thumbnail. Your new choice becomes the #1 image in the Side By Side view.

**4** Click image #2—the photo on the right of the split screen—to make it active. Click the forward and back navigation buttons in the control bar at the bottom of the screen, or use the arrow keys on your keyboard, to cycle the #2 preview through all the photos in the filmstrip, while the photo on the left of the screen remains fixed.

**5** Click either image repeatedly to toggle between fit-to-view and 100% magnification. To compare detail at higher magnification, zoom in and out in the active image using the scroll-wheel on your mouse—or by pressing the Ctrl / Command key together with the plus (+) or minus (-) key. Drag the zoomed photo with the hand cursor to see a different portion of the image.

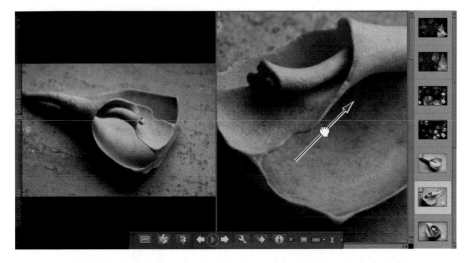

▶ **Tip:** You can sync panning and zooming in the #1 and #2 photos by clicking the chain-link icon at the right end of the extended control bar. If you don't see the chain-link icon, click the triangle at the right end of the control bar to extend it.

As well as the forward and back navigation buttons, the control bar contains buttons that let you show and hide the Film Strip, the Quick Edit pane and the Quick Organize pane, where you can perform common editing tasks and tag images or group them by adding them to an album.

**6** If necessary, click the triangle at the end of the control bar to extend it. Click the triangle next to the Side By Side View button ( ![icon] ) to switch the split-screen arrangement from Side By Side to Above And Below.

**7** Press the Esc key on your keyboard or click the Exit button (x) in the control bar to close the Side By Side view and return to the regular Organizer workspace.

## Choosing files

In the Media Browser, you can select multiple images by simply dragging a selection marquee in the thumbnail view, but for better control, use your mouse together with a modifier key.

1   To select a series of four or five images that are in consecutive order, click the first photo in the series, and then hold down the Shift key as you click the last. All the photos in the range you Shift-clicked are selected.

2   Add three or four non-consecutive photos to the selection by holding down the Ctrl / Command key and clicking the thumbnails you wish to select. Keep your selection active for the next exercise.

## Viewing photos at full screen

1   Click the View, Edit, Organize In Full Screen button, to the right of the Thumbnail Size slider in the bar above the thumbnails view.

<br/>

**Tip:** You'll have the opportunity to change the default slideshow music, or switch it off, in step 3.

2   Press the spacebar or the Play button in the center of the control bar to start the Full Screen view cycling through the selected images in slideshow mode. Experiment with the three buttons at the left of the control bar to show and hide the Film Strip and the Quick Edit and Quick Organize panels.

**Tip:** You can also access Full Screen view by choosing from the menu on the Display button, or by clicking the Full Screen View button on the control bar in Side By Side view. You'll learn more about working in Full Screen view in the next lesson.

3   Try the two buttons to the right of the navigation controls to set Full Screen View and slideshow options and to choose a style for the transitions between slides. When you're done, press the Esc key to return to the Organizer.

## Reconnecting missing files to a catalog

When you bring a photo into Photoshop Elements, the name and location of the image file is recorded in the catalog. If you wish to move, rename, or delete a photo that has already been imported into your catalog, its best if you do it from within the Elements Organizer.

If you move, rename, or delete a file in the Windows Explorer / Mac OS Finder after it has been added to the catalog, Photoshop Elements searches your computer for the missing file automatically, and will usually do a great job finding it—even when the file has been renamed; however, you need to know what to do if the automatic search fails. If a file cannot be located, the missing file icon (🔳) appears in the upper left corner of its thumbnail in the Media Browser to alert you that the link between the file and your catalog has been broken.

▶ **Tip:** To avoid the problem of files missing from your catalog, use the Move and Rename commands from the File menu, and the Edit > Delete From Catalog command to move, rename, or delete files from within Photoshop Elements, rather than doing so outside the application.

1 Switch to the Windows Explorer / Mac OS Finder by doing one of the following:

 • On Windows, minimize the Elements Organizer by clicking the Minimize button (🔳) at the right of the menu bar, or simply click the Elements Organizer application button on the Windows taskbar.

 • On Mac OS, click the Finder icon in the Application Switcher (hold down Command; then press and release the Tab key) or the Dock.

2 Open an Explorer / Finder window, if there's not one already available. Navigate to and open your Lessons folder. Drag the Lesson01 folder out of the Lessons folder to the Recycle Bin / Trash. Do not empty the Recycle Bin / Trash.

3 Switch back to the Organizer and choose File > Reconnect > All Missing Files. Photoshop displays a message to let you know it's busy searching for the missing files. We don't expect the files to be found in the Recycle Bin / Trash, so you can stop the automatic search by clicking the Browse button.

The Reconnect Missing Files dialog box opens, as it would have had you let the search run its course, and Photoshop Elements had not located the missing files.

4 For this exercise, you won't follow the re-linking process through to completion, but you should take this opportunity to inspect the dialog box thoroughly (*see the illustration on the next page*).

At the upper left of the Reconnect Missing Files dialog box is a list of all missing files. Below the list, a preview displays a thumbnail of the currently selected missing file. To the right, you can browse the contents of your computer.

When you select a candidate file on the Browse tab, you'll see a preview thumbnail adjacent to the missing file preview, enabling you to visually verify the photo as a match, even if its name has been changed.

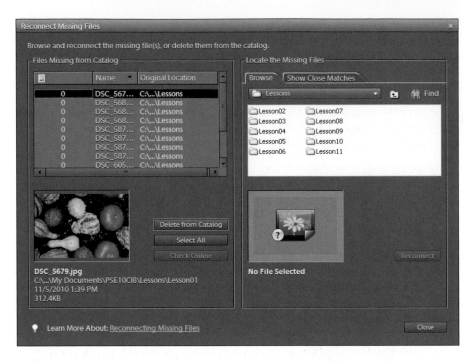

5   Once you've verified a file or files to be reconnected, you can click the Reconnect button. For now, click Close to cancel the operation. Note that all of the thumbnails in the Media Browser now display the missing file icon ([?]).

6   Switch back to the Explorer / Finder; then, drag the Lesson01 folder out of the Recycle Bin / Trash and return it to your Lessons folder.

**Note:** The missing file icons may persist until you next change the view or execute another command.

7   Switch back to the Organizer and choose File > Reconnect > All Missing Files. Photoshop displays a message to let you know that there are no missing files to reconnect. Click OK to dismiss the message.

## Switching between the Organizer and the Editor

Although the Fix tab in the Organizer offers one-step tools for some of the most common editing tasks, for more sophisticated editing you'll switch to the Editor.

1   Select any two photos in the Media Browser.

2   Do one of the following:

-   Choose Edit > Edit With Photoshop Elements Editor.

-   Click the Fix tab in the Task Pane, and then click the Edit Photos button.

-   Right-click / Control-click either of the selected images and choose Edit With Photoshop Elements Editor from the context menu.

Once both the Organizer and the Editor are open, you can move quickly between the two workspaces by using the task bar in Windows or the Dock in Mac OS.

# The Editor workspace

The Editor is where you'll edit, adjust and correct your images, and create projects and presentations to showcase them. You can choose between the default Full Edit mode, with a powerful set of tools for color correction, special effects, and image enhancement, the Quick Edit mode, with simple tools and commands for quickly fixing common image problems, and the Guided Edit mode, which provides easy step-by-step instructions for a range of editing tasks.

In the Editor, the main work area is the Edit pane. This is where you'll work on your photos and the presentations that you create to showcase and share them. Below the Edit pane is the Project Bin, which provides easy access to the images you're working with, no matter how many files you have open. The Edit pane is flanked by the tool bar on the left and the Panel Bin on the right. The Panel Bin has tabs for Edit, Create, and Share modes. At the top of the Edit tab in the Panel Bin, you'll find buttons for switching between the three editing modes.

If you're new to digital imaging, the Quick Edit and Guided Edit modes make a good starting point for fixing and modifying your photos, and provide a great way to learn as you work. The Full Edit mode provides a more powerful and versatile image editing environment, with commands for correcting exposure and color and tools for making precise selections and fixing image imperfections. The Full Edit tool bar also includes painting and text editing tools. You can arrange the flexible Full Edit workspace to suit the way you prefer to work by floating, minimizing, hiding and showing panels, or rearranging them in the Panel Bin.

1  In the Project Bin, double-click each of the thumbnails in turn to bring that photo to the front in the Edit pane, making it the active image.

2  Choose Preferences > General from the Edit / Photoshop Elements Editor menu. On the General tab of the Preferences dialog box, click the check box to activate the option Allow Floating Documents In Full Edit Mode. Click OK.

3  Drag whichever image is foremost by its name tab, away from its docked position to float above the Editor workspace.

**Note:** Once you've activated the option to allow floating document windows, this becomes the default for any image opened in Full Edit mode. Throughout the rest of this book however, it will be assumed that you are working with tabbed image windows that are docked (consolidated) in the Edit pane, unless otherwise specified. When you complete this exercise you'll disable floating document windows so that it'll be easier for you to follow the exercise steps as written.

4  Explore the options for arranging image windows that are available from both the Window > Images menu, and from the menu on the Arrange button (⊞) at the top of the Editor workspace to develop a feel for the way you prefer to work with your images. When you're done, Choose Preferences > General from the Edit / Photoshop Elements menu and disable floating documents. Click OK.

## Using panels and the Panel Bin

In the Full Edit workspace, the Panel Bin provides a convenient location to organize the panels you use most often. By default, the Effects, Content and Layers panels are docked in the Panel Bin; other panels can be opened from the Window menu. All panels can either be kept docked in the Panel Bin or dragged to float in a convenient position above your image as you work. It's a good idea to familiarize yourself with organizing the Full Edit workspace so that you'll always have the controls you need at your fingertips.

1  Try each of the following tips and techniques:

•  To open a panel that you don't see in the workspace, choose its name from the Window menu in the menu bar at the top of the workspace.

- To collapse an open panel so that you see only its header bar, choose its name from the Window menu or double-click its header bar.

- To float a panel above your image in the work area, drag it out of the Panel bin by its header bar. You can also float the Project Bin and the toolbox by dragging them away from their default positions.

- To return a floating panel to the Panel Bin, drag it into the Panel Bin and release the mouse button when you see a blue line indicating the new position. Place the panel between two others, or drag it onto another panel to create a tabbed panel group. Switch between grouped panels by clicking their name tabs. Drag the name tag to move a panel out of a group.

 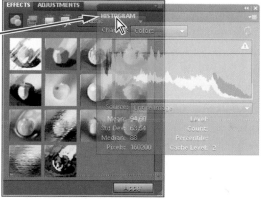

▶ **Tip:** Floating panels can also be grouped in this manner, or snapped together one above the other.

- To collapse a floating panel to an icon, click the two white triangles at the right of the header bar. You can collapse a group of floating panels that are snapped together in the same manner.

- To expand a single panel in a collapsed group, choose its name from the Window menu.

- To close a panel, drag it out of the Panel Bin and click the close button (x) in its header bar (at the right on Windows, at the left for Mac OS) or click the small menu icon at the right of the header and choose Close from the panel's Options menu.

- To adjust the height of panels in the Panel Bin, drag the separator bars between panels up or down. To adjust the size of a floating panel, drag the panel's lower right corner. (Some panels can not be resized.)

- To return the workspace to the default arrangement, you can either choose Window > Reset Panels or click the Reset Panels button (🔄) at the top of the workspace.

**2** Choose File > Close All to close both of the open images. Close the Editor window by clicking the Close button (in the top right corner of the workspace on Windows, at the upper left on Mac OS).

# Creating an Adobe ID

**Note:** Elements Membership services are available only to users registered in the United States.

Photoshop Elements users in the U.S. can create an Adobe ID to register their software and sign up for a free Photoshop.com account. Creating an Adobe ID gives you access to Elements Membership services that are integrated with your software, enabling Organizer-based backup and sharing and other exciting Adobe-hosted services that extend the capabilities of your Photoshop Elements software.

With your free Basic Elements Membership you get your own storage space on Photoshop.com—with a personal Photoshop.com URL—where you can share and showcase your images, and access your photos from anywhere that you can connect to the Internet. You can use your Photoshop.com account to back up your catalog, and even to synchronize your photo library across multiple computers.

Basic membership also enables integrated access to the Inspiration Browser, which offers regularly updated tips, tricks and tutorials related to whatever you're currently working on—providing a powerful way to advance your skill set and helping you to make the most of your photos and creations.

Upgrade to a Plus Membership to get more storage space, access to advanced tutorials in the Inspiration Browser, and regularly updated content—such as project templates, themes, backgrounds, frames, and graphics—delivered directly to your software to help you keep your projects fresh and appealing.

## Signing up from the Welcome screen

1   Start Photoshop Elements or—if Photoshop Elements is already running—click the Welcome Screen button (⌂) at the top right of the workspace.

2   In the Welcome screen, click Create Adobe ID. Enter your name, e-mail address and a password, type a name for your personal Photoshop.com URL, and then click Create Account. An e-mail message will be sent to you to confirm the creation of your account. Follow the instructions in the e-mail to activate your account. If you are asked whether you wish to activate backup and synchronization, click No; you'll learn about using this feature in Lesson 5.

## Signing up from the Organizer or Editor

**Tip:** You don't have to start from the Welcome screen to create an Adobe ID. Links for registering and signing in are conveniently located throughout the Photoshop Elements workspace.

1   In the Organizer or Editor, click the Create New Adobe ID link in the menu bar.

2   Enter your personal details in the Create Your Adobe ID dialog box, and then click Create Account. Follow the instructions in the confirmation e-mail to activate your account. Don't activate backup and synchronization yet.

## Signing in to your Photoshop.com account

Once you've created an Adobe ID, you may still need to sign in if you or another user has signed out of your account.

1  Make sure your computer is connected to the Internet, and then start Adobe Photoshop Elements.

2  In the Welcome screen, enter your Adobe ID and password, and click Sign In.

If you didn't sign in at the Welcome screen, you can always click the Sign In link at the top of either the Organizer or Editor workspace.

# Using Help

Help is available in several ways, each one useful in different circumstances:

**Help in the application**  The complete user documentation for Adobe Photoshop Elements is available from the Help menu, in the form of HTML content that displays in the Adobe Community Help application. This documentation provides quick access to information on using the various features in Photoshop Elements.

**Help on the Web**  You can also access the most comprehensive and up-to-date documentation on Photoshop Elements via your default browser. Point your browser to http://help.adobe.com/en_US/photoshopelements/using/index.html

**Help PDF**  Help is also available as a PDF document, optimized for printing; you can download the document by clicking the View Help PDF link in the top right corner of any Help page.

**Links in the application**  Within the Photoshop Elements application there are links to additional help topics, such as the hot-linked tips associated with specific panels and tasks, and the tips and tutorials links that appear below the Task pane in both the Organizer and the Editor.

● **Note:** You must be connected to the Internet at least once to download the Help content to your computer. Once you've downloaded the Help content, you can access it even when you're not connected to the Internet. However, with an active Internet connection, you can access the latest updates as well as community-contributed content.

## Navigating Help

Depending on which module you're working in, choose Help > Elements Organizer Help or Help > Photoshop Elements Help, or simply press the F1 key. Once you've downloaded the Help content the Adobe Community Help application will open to the front page of the respective Help documentation, even if you are not currently connected to the Internet.

Click a topic heading in the table of contents. Click the plus sign (+) to the left of a topic heading to see its sub-topics. Click a topic or sub-topic to display its content. In Community Help, choose View > Show Search Panel. Type a search term in the Search text box at the top of the Search panel, choose search options, and then press Enter on your keyboard.

▶ **Tip:** If you search for a phrase, put quotation marks around the phrase. Make sure that your search terms are spelled correctly. If a search term doesn't yield results, try searching a synonym; for example "photo" instead of "picture."

## Links to help in the application

You'll find links to additional task-specific help at various places in the Photoshop Elements workspace. Clicking these links will either take you to the corresponding topic in Help or—in the case of the links shown here—open the Elements Inspiration Browser.

## Hot-linked tips

Hot-linked tips, marked with a light bulb icon, are scattered throughout Adobe Photoshop Elements. These tips either display information in the form of a typical tip balloon or link you to the appropriate topic in Help.

## Additional resources

*Adobe Photoshop Elements 10 Classroom in a Book* is not meant to replace the documentation that comes with the program, nor to be a comprehensive reference for every feature. Additional resources are listed in detail at the end of the Getting Started chapter in this book; please refer to these resources for comprehensive information and tutorials about program features.

You've reached the end of the first lesson. Now that you know how to import photos, understand the concept of the catalog, and are familiar with the essentials of the Photoshop Elements interface, you're ready to start organizing and editing your photos in the next lessons.

Before you move on, take a few moments to read through the review questions and answers on the next page.

# Review questions

**1** What are the primary workspaces and working modes in Adobe Photoshop Elements?

**2** What is a catalog file?

**3** What are keyword tags?

**4** How can you select multiple thumbnail images in the Media Browser?

# Review answers

**1** Photoshop Elements has two primary workspaces: the Elements Organizer and the Editor. You'll work in the Organizer to locate, import, manage, and share your photos, and use the Editor to adjust your images and to create presentations to showcase them. The Editor offers three editing modes: Full Edit, Quick Edit, and Guided Edit. Both the Organizer and the Editor provide access to the Create and Share modes.

**2** A catalog file is where Photoshop Elements stores information about your images, enabling you to conveniently manage the photos on your computer from within the Organizer. For each image you import, Photoshop Elements creates a new entry in the catalog file. Whenever you assign a tag or a rating to a photo, or group images in an album, the catalog file is updated. All your work in the Organizer is recorded in the catalog.

As well as digital photographs, a catalog can include video and audio files, scans, PDF documents, and any presentations and layouts you might create in Photoshop Elements such as slide shows, photo collages, and CD jacket designs. A single catalog can efficiently handle thousands of files, but you can also create separate catalogs for different types of work.

**3** Keyword tags are labels with personalized associations that you attach to photos, creations, and video or audio clips in the Media Browser so that you can easily organize and find them.

**4** To select images that are in consecutive order in the Media Browser, click the first photo in the series, and then hold down the Shift key and click the last. All the photos in the range that you Shift-clicked will be selected. To select multiple non-consecutive files, hold down the Ctrl / Command key as you add files to the selection.

# 2 BASIC ORGANIZING

## Lesson Overview

As you capture more and more images with your digital camera, it becomes increasingly important that you have effective ways to organize and manage your pictures on your computer so that those valuable memories are always accessible.

Adobe Photoshop Elements makes it easy to import your photos and other media files from a variety of sources and provides an array of powerful tools for sorting and searching your collection.

This lesson will get you started with the essential skills you'll need to import images and keep track of your growing photo library:

* Opening Adobe Photoshop Elements 10 in Organizer mode

* Importing images from folders on your computer

* Importing photos from a digital camera

* Switching between viewing modes in the Media Browser

* Working in the Date and Folder Location views

* Creating, organizing, and applying keyword tags

* Searching for files by keyword

* Finding and tagging faces in your photos

You'll probably need about one and a half hours to complete this lesson.

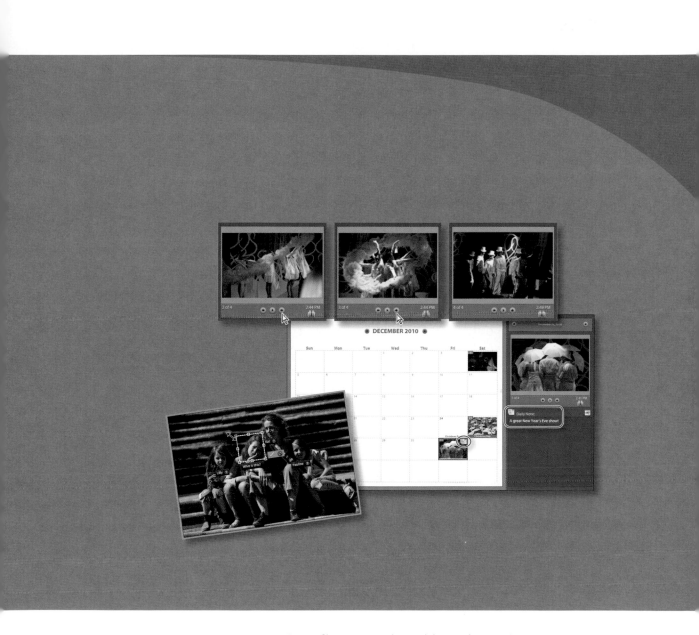

Import files to your catalog, and then explore a variety of ways to view and sort them. Learn how tagging and rating your photos can help you find just the pictures you want, just when you want them—easily and quickly. Once they share a keyword tag, a group of related photos can be retrieved with a single click, no matter how big your catalog, or across how many folders those images are scattered.

# Getting started

● **Note:** Before you start working on this lesson, make sure that you've installed the software on your computer from the application CD (see the Photoshop Elements 10 documentation) and that you have correctly copied the Lessons folder from the CD in the back of this book onto your computer's hard disk (see "Copying the Classroom in a Book files" on page 2). You should also have created a working catalog (see "Creating a new catalog" on page 8).

For the exercises in this lesson you'll be working in the Elements Organizer.

1  If the Organizer is still open from the previous exercise, skip to step 3; if not, start Photoshop Elements by doing one of the following:

- On Windows, either double-click the shortcut on your desktop, or choose Start > All Programs > Adobe Photoshop Elements 10.

- On Mac OS, either click the Photoshop Elements 10 icon in the Dock or choose Photoshop Elements 10 from the Apple > Recent Items > Applications menu.

2  In the Welcome screen, click the Organize button at the left, and then wait while the Elements Organizer opens.

3  Hold the pointer over the Elements Organizer icon (▦) at the upper left of the Organizer workspace window to see the name of the currently loaded catalog displayed in a tooltip. Note that the catalog name is also displayed in the lower left corner of the Organizer workspace.

4  If the CIB Catalog that you created in Lesson 1 is not currently loaded, choose File > Catalog. Select the CIB Catalog from the list in the Catalog Manager dialog box, and then click Open.

# Getting photos

The Elements Organizer provides a workspace where you can view, sort and organize your media files. Before you process, print, or share your photos, the first step is to assemble them in the Organizer. In the following exercises you'll import the images for this lesson into your new catalog using a variety of different methods.

Perhaps the most direct and intuitive way to bring media files into the Organizer and add them to your catalog is to use the familiar drag-and-drop method.

## Dragging photos from Windows Explorer

1  Minimize the Organizer by clicking the Minimize button (▬) at the right of the Organizer menu bar, or simply click the Elements Organizer application button on the Windows taskbar.

**2** Open the My Computer window in Windows Explorer; either double-click a shortcut icon on your desktop, or choose My Computer from the Start menu.

**3** Locate and open the Lessons folder that you copied to your hard disk. Open the Lesson02 folder, and then the sub-folder named Import.

**4** Inside the Import folder you'll find two sub-folders: drag the BATCH1 subfolder and hold it over the Elements Organizer application button on the Windows taskbar.

**5** Wait until the Organizer becomes the foreground application; then, drag the BATCH1 folder onto the Media Browser pane in the Organizer and release the mouse button. Skip to "Importing attached keyword tags" on the next page.

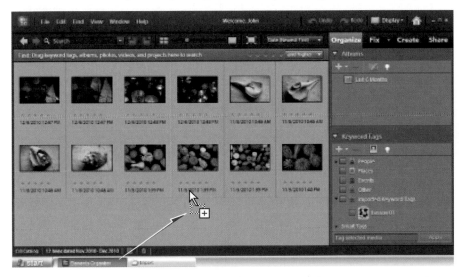

▶ **Tip:** If you can arrange the Windows Explorer window and the Organizer application window on your screen so that you can see both at once, you can simply drag the folder (or individual media files) directly from the Windows Explorer window into the Organizer, rather than going via the Windows taskbar.

## Dragging photos from the Mac OS Finder

**1** There are several ways to switch to the Finder on Mac OS. For this exercise, we'll use the Application Switcher. Hold down the Command key; then, press and release the Tab key. Continuing to hold down the Command key, click the Finder icon; then, release the Command key.

**2** In the Finder, press Command+N to open a new Finder window. Navigate to and open the Lessons folder that you copied to your hard disk. Open the Lesson02 folder, and then the sub-folder named Import.

**3** Inside the Import folder are two sub-folders: BATCH1 and BATCH2. If necessary, move the finder window enough to see the Elements Organizer workspace behind it; then, drag the BATCH1 subfolder onto the Media Browser pane and release the mouse button.

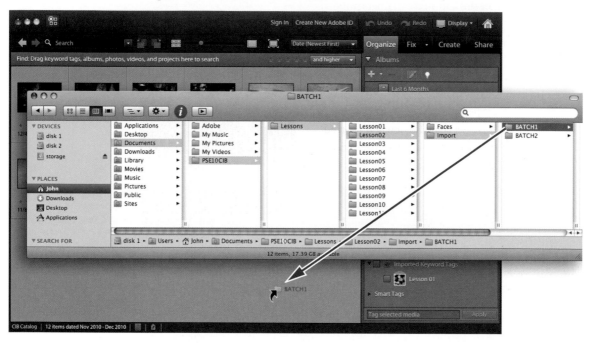

**4** Photoshop Elements briefly displays a dialog box while searching inside the BATCH1 folder for files to import; then, the Import Attached Keyword Tags dialog box opens. Click the Organizer workspace to bring it back to the front.

## Importing attached keyword tags

Whenever you import photos that have already been tagged with keywords, the Import Attached Keyword Tags dialog box will appear, giving you the opportunity to specify which tags you wish to import with your images.

**1** In the Import Attached Keyword Tags dialog box, click Select All; then, click OK.

**2** The Getting Media dialog box appears briefly as the Organizer imports the images from your BATCH1 folder. If a message appears telling you that only the newly imported items will be visible in the Media Browser, click OK. Thumbnails of the images you just imported appear in the Media Browser.

**3** Each thumbnail is displayed with an orange tag icon indicating that the image has keywords attached. Hold the pointer over the tag icon at the lower right of any image cell in the Media Browser to see a tooltip listing attached keywords.

**4** If necessary, click the small triangle to expand the Imported Keyword Tags category in the Keywords Tags panel to the right of the Media Browser; you can see that the newly imported **Lesson 02** tag is nested inside, together with the keyword that you imported in the previous lesson.

▶ **Tip:** If you don't see a tag icon associated with each thumbnail in the Media Browser, use the Thumbnail Size slider above the Media Browser to increase the size of the thumbnails.

## Searching for photos to import

This import method is useful when you're not sure exactly where on your hard disk you've stashed your photographs and other media files over the years.

You could run a search of your entire hard disk, or just search your My Documents folder, but for the purposes of this exercise, you'll limit the search to just a small branch of your folder hierarchy.

**1** In the Organizer, choose File > Get Photos And Videos > By Searching. Under Search Options in the Get Photos And Videos By Searching For Folders dialog box, choose Browse from the Look In menu.

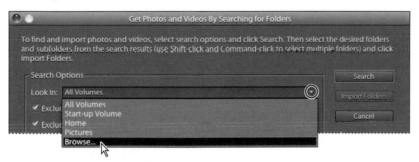

**2** In the Browse For Folder / Select Folder For Search dialog box, locate and select your Lessons folder, and then click OK.

**3** Under Search Options in the Get Photos And Videos By Searching For Folders dialog box, make sure the Automatically Fix Red Eyes option is disabled; then, click the Search button located at the upper right of the dialog box.

**4** The Search Results box lists all folders inside the Lessons folder. Select the folder **Lessons/Lesson02/Import/BATCH2**. The preview pane at the right shows thumbnails of the contents of the selected folder. Click Import Folders.

▶ **Tip:** When you already know the location of the images you wish to import into Photoshop Elements, you can do so by using the menu command File > Get Photos And Videos > From Files And Folders, as you did in Lesson 1. You'll use this method again in the next exercise.

Get Photos and Videos By Searching for Folders

To find and import photos and videos, select search options and click Search. Then select the desired folders and subfolders from the search results (use Shift-click and Command-click to select multiple folders) and click Import Folders.

Search Options

Look In: /Users/John/Documents/PSE10CIB/Lessons/

Search

Import Folders

✔ Exclude System Folders

Cancel

✔ Exclude Files Smaller Than: 100 KB

☐ Automatically Fix Red Eyes

✔ Preview

Search Results

/Users/John/Documents/PSE10CIB/Lessons/Lesson01/
/Users/John/Documents/PSE10CIB/Lessons/Lesson02/Faces/
/Users/John/Documents/PSE10CIB/Lessons/Lesson02/Import/BATCH2/

**5** In the Import Attached Keyword Tags dialog box, click Select All, and then click OK. Click OK to close any other alert dialog box.

## Automatically fixing red eyes during import

The term "red eye" refers to the phenomenon common in photos taken with a flash, where the subject's pupils appear red instead of black. This is caused by the flash reflecting off the retina at the back of the eye. In most cases, Photoshop Elements can successfully remove the red eye effect automatically during the import process, saving you the effort of further editing.

**1** If you don't see the image file names displayed below the thumbnails in the Media Browser, choose View > Show File Names.

**2** Double-click the photo RedEyes.jpg to see the enlarged single image view. As you can see, the red eye effect is very pronounced in this flash photograph.

**3** Double-click the enlarged image to return to the thumbnail display in the Media Browser. With the image RedEyes.jpg still selected, choose Edit > Delete From Catalog. In the confirmation dialog box, make sure that the option Also Delete Selected Item(s) From The Hard Disk is disabled, and then click OK.

**4**  Choose File > Get Photos And Videos > From Files And Folders. In the Get Photos And Videos From Files And Folders dialog box, navigate to and open the BATCH2 folder; then, click once to select the image RedEyes.jpg. Activate the option Automatically Fix Red Eyes, and then click Get Media. In the Import Attached Keyword Tags dialog box, select the Lesson 02 tag; then, click OK. Dismiss any other alert dialog box.

A thumbnail of the newly imported image appears in the Media Browser. Photoshop Elements has stacked the corrected photo with the original in a Version Set, with the edited version on top; the filename has been extended to indicate that the photo has been edited.

You can identify a Version Set by the badge in the upper right corner of the thumbnail and the label below the lower right corner. You'll learn more about working with Version Sets in Lesson 3.

▶ **Tip:** For some images, the automatic red eye fix may not be so effective; more tools and techniques for correcting the effect are discussed in Lesson 7.

**5**  Click the arrow at the right of the thumbnail once to expand the Version Set, and again to collapse it.

**6**  Double-click the edited photo to see it enlarged in the single image view.

**7**  To display all of the images that you've imported during this lesson, click the find box beside the Lesson 02 tag listed under Imported Keyword Tags in the Keyword Tags panel.

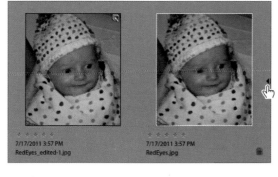

## Importing from a digital camera

If you have a digital camera or memory card at hand with your own photos on it, you can step through this exercise using those images. Alternatively, you can skip to the next section of this lesson and return to this exercise when you are prepared.

**1**  Connect your digital camera or card reader to your computer, following the manufacturer's instructions. If you're working on Mac OS, skip to step 3.

**2**  On Windows, the Auto Play dialog box may appear. You could choose the option Organize And Edit Using Adobe Elements Organizer 10, but for the purposes of this lesson, simply click Cancel to dismiss the dialog box. If the Photo Downloader dialog box appears automatically, you can skip to step 4; otherwise, continue to step 3.

**3** Choose File > Get Photos And Videos > From Camera Or Card Reader.

**4** In the Photo Downloader dialog box, choose the name of your connected camera or card reader from the Get Photos From menu.

**5** Accept the default target folder listed beside Location, or click Browse / Choose to designate a different destination for the imported files.

**6** From the Create Subfolder(s) menu, choose Today's Date (yyyy mm dd) as the folder name format; the Location path reflects your choice.

**7** Choose Do Not Rename Files from the Rename Files menu. From the Delete Options menu, choose After Copying, Do Not Delete Originals. If you're working on Windows, deactivate the Automatic Download option.

**8** Click the Advanced Dialog button. In advanced mode, the Photo Downloader Dialog displays thumbnail previews of all the photos on your camera's memory card, and also offers options for processing, tagging, and grouping your images.

**9** If there is a photo on your camera that you wish to exclude from the selection to be imported, click the check box below its thumbnail to remove the check mark.

● **Note:** If you choose one of the Advanced Options that deletes the original images from your camera after copying, only those images selected to be imported will be deleted from the camera; those excluded from the selection will not be deleted.

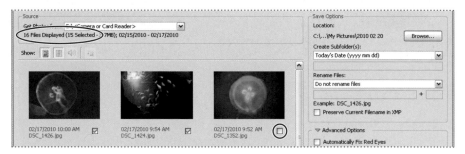

**10** If you see a photo that needs to be rotated, select its thumbnail, and then click the appropriate Rotate button in the lower left corner of the dialog box.

**11** Under Advanced Options, make sure that the Automatically Fix Red Eyes, Automatically Suggest Photo Stacks, Make 'Group Custom Name' A Tag, and Import Into Album options are disabled.

**12** Click Get Media. The selected photos are copied from the camera to the specified folder on your hard disk. By default, images imported from a camera will be copied to your My Pictures / Pictures folder.

**13** In the Files Successfully Copied dialog box, click Yes. Click OK to close any other alert dialog box.

The imported photos appear in the Media Browser, already rotated where specified.

## Using watched folders on Windows

*Watched folders are not supported for Mac OS; if you're working on Mac OS, you can skip to "Viewing photo thumbnails in the Organizer" on the next page.*

On Windows, you can simplify and automate the process of keeping your catalog up to date by using watched folders. Designate any folder on your hard disk as a watched folder and Photoshop Elements will automatically be alerted when a new file is placed in (or saved to) that folder. By default, the My Pictures folder is watched, but you can set up any number of additional watched folders.

You can either choose to have any new files that are detected in a watched folder added to your catalog automatically, or have Photoshop Elements ask you what to do before importing the new media. If you choose the latter option, the message "New files have been found in Watched Folders" will appear whenever new items are detected. Click Yes to add the new files to your catalog or click No to skip them.

In this exercise you'll add a folder to the watched folders list.

**1** Choose File > Watch Folders.

**2** Under Folders To Watch in the Watch Folders dialog box, click Add, and then browse to your Lesson02 folder.

**3** Select the Lesson02 folder and click OK.

The Lesson02 folder now appears in the Folders To Watch list. To stop a folder from being watched, select it in the list, and then click Remove.

**4** Ensure that the Notify Me option is activated, and then click OK to close the Watch Folders dialog box.

# Viewing photo thumbnails in the Organizer

In the Organizer, there are several ways to view the images in your catalog. You can switch between the various viewing modes to suit different stages in your workflow or to make it easier and more efficient to perform specific organizing tasks.

## Using the Media Browser views

Up to this point, you've been working in the default Media Browser view: the Thumbnail View, where your images are arranged by capture date and time. You can reverse the display order by choosing either Date (Oldest First) or Date (Newest First) from the menu to the right of the Thumbnail Size slider.

Let's look at some of the other display options in the Organizer.

**1** In the Keyword Tags panel, click the find box beside the Lesson 02 tag, if it's not already activated; then, use the Thumbnail Size slider above the Media Browser pane to reduce the size of the thumbnails so that you can see all of the images that you've imported during this lesson.

**2** Click the Display button (▣) near the upper right corner of the Organizer window, and then choose Import Batch from the menu to see the lesson images organized in groups according to their separate import sessions.

**3** In the Import Batch view, a divider bar marked with a film canister icon (🎞) and an import session date separates each group of thumbnails. Click any of the divider bars to select all of the images that were imported in that session.

**4** Another way to work with the Import Batch view is to use the timeline. Choose Window > Timeline. The timeline shows a series of bars representing the separate import sessions that account for all the images in this catalog.

● **Note:** The white bar represents images imported for Lesson 1, and therefore not currently displayed in the Media Browser.

The height of each bar in the timeline indicates the relative number of images in each import batch. In this illustration, the timeline represents four imports spread across a few hours. Your bars may be arranged differently, especially if you've completed the preceding exercises over several days.

**5** Choose Edit > Deselect, and then use the Thumbnail Size slider to increase the size of the thumbnails until you see only a subset of your Lesson 2 images.

**6** Click each of the bars in the timeline in turn. As you click, the view in the Media Browser jumps to show the corresponding import batch and the first image in that batch is temporarily highlighted by a green border and a flashing capture date.

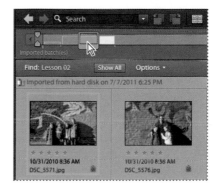

**7** Select any photo in the Media Browser; then, click the Display button (🖥) near the upper right corner of the Organizer window and choose Folder Location to see the image file's location in the folder hierarchy on your computer. The bars in the timeline now represent the three folders that contain images that are being managed by your CIB Catalog; hold the pointer over any of the three bars to see the corresponding folder's path-name displayed in a tooltip. The bar across the top of the Media Browser now displays a Managed Folder icon (📁) and shows the path-name of the folder containing the image you selected.

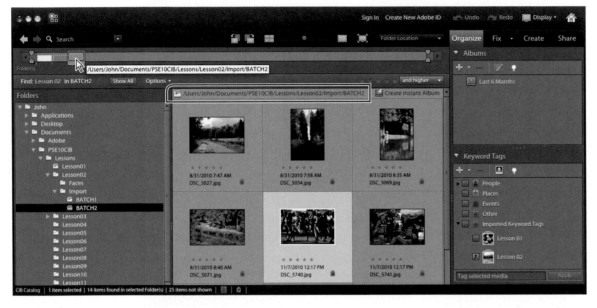

● **Note:** Watched folders are not supported on Mac OS.

In the Folders panel at the left of the Media Browser, you can see at a glance which folders contain images that have been imported to the Lesson2 catalog; these folders are marked with the Managed Folder icon (📁). On Windows, you'll also be able to spot your watched folders: look for the Watched Folder icon (📁).

At this point, you're working with a catalog that contains very few images, so it may not be instantly apparent that a single folder may contain multiple import batches and a single import batch may include files from multiple folders.

▶ **Tip:** You can move entire folders on your hard disk in the same way, making it easy to manage your photo library from within the Organizer. Right-click / Control-click any of your managed folders and note the commands that are available in the context menu.

**8** In the Folders panel, drag the selected image from the Media Browser to the PSE10CIB folder. The CIB catalog is updated to record the new location of the moved photo; in the Folders panel, the PSE10CIB folder is now marked with a Managed Folder icon. Choose Edit > Undo Move.

**9** Click the header bar across the top of the Media Browser to select all the photos in the folder you're viewing.

**10** Choose Window > Timeline to hide the timeline from view, and then choose Edit > Deselect. Click the Display button (🖥) near the upper right corner of the Organizer window and choose Thumbnail View from the menu.

## Using the Date View

The Date View can be a great way to browse and search your images, particularly once you're working with a large collection of photos that span a number of years.

1   From the Media View Arrangement menu (to the right of the Thumbnail Size slider above the Media Browser), choose Date (Oldest First); then, click the Display button (⬛) and choose Date View from the menu.

2   If the Date View opens to display other than a full year calendar, click the Year view button (⬛ Year) below the calendar display.

You can see at a glance that your CIB catalog contains photographs taken on eight separate dates during 2010. The earliest entry, August 31, is already selected on the calendar. A thumbnail preview of the first image captured on that date appears at the right of the Organizer window; an image count at the lower left of the preview pane indicates that there are four files in your catalog that share this creation date.

**Note:** Photoshop Elements automatically adjusts dates from different time zones; as a result, you may see different dates highlighted on your calendar page.

**Tip:** Dates shown in red are holidays; in the Date View pane of the Organizer preferences you can specify which holidays are marked.

3   Click the Find This Photo In The Media Browser button (▦) below the preview thumbnail to see the currently previewed photo in the Media Browser, where it's already selected, ready for action.

4   In the Media Browser, click the Back To Previous View button (◀) near the upper left corner of the Organizer window to return to the Date View.

Find this photo in the Media Browser

**5** Click the Month view button (⊞ Month ) below the calendar pane; then, click the name of the month at the head of the calendar page and choose December from the months menu. Alternatively, move one month at a time by clicking four times on the Next Month button to the right of the month name.

● **Note:** Photoshop Elements automatically adjusts dates from different time zones; as a result, you may see different dates featured on your calendar page.

**6** The December page opens with the 4th selected. the earliest date in December for which there are photos in your catalog. The Month view conveniently displays photo thumbnails for the daily entries.

**7** Click the entry for December 31. Click in the Daily Note box below the preview pane and type **A great New Year's Eve show!** Click the entry for December 31 on the calendar page; a note icon appears on the thumbnail for that day.

**8** The counter in the preview pane shows that there are four photos in the catalog corresponding to this date. Use the Next Item On Selected Day button (●) below the preview image to see the other images captured on the same day.

**9** Click the Start Automatic Sequencing button (●) under the preview image to view all the photos taken on the same day as a mini slide show.

**10** To return to the Media Browser in thumbnail view, either click your way back using the Back To Previous View button (◀) near the upper left corner of the Organizer window or click the Media Browser button below the calendar page.

# Working with star ratings and keyword tags

Most of us find it challenging to organize our files and folders efficiently. It can be so easy to forget which pictures were stored in what folder—and so tedious when you're forced to examine the contents of numerous folders looking for the files you want. The Elements Organizer offers an array of powerful and versatile tools for organizing, sorting, and searching that make all that frustration a thing of the past.

The next set of exercises will demonstrate how a little time invested in applying tags and ratings to the photos you import can streamline the process of finding and sorting your images, regardless of how many files you have or where they're stored.

## Applying keyword tags and rating photos

Applying keywords to your photos and grouping those tags in categories can make it quick and easy to find exactly the images you're looking for. With a single click you can rate a photo from one to five stars, adding a simple way to narrow a search. In this exercise, you'll apply a rating to one of the images you imported into your CIB catalog, and then tag it with a keyword from the default set.

**1** If necessary, activate the find box beside the Lesson 02 tag in the Keyword Tags panel to isolate the images for this lesson. From the sorting menu to the right of the Thumbnail Size slider, choose Date (Newest First). Make sure that the menu options View > Details and View > Show File Names are activated.

**2** In the Media Browser, move the pointer slowly from left to right over the stars beneath one of the thumbnails showing a girl in a swimming pool. When you see four yellow stars, as in the illustration below, click to apply that rating.

**3** To find images based on the ratings you've assigned, use the stars and the adjacent menu located at the right end of the Find bar above the thumbnail display. For this example set the search criteria at 3 stars and higher. Only the image with the 4-star rating is displayed in the Media Browser.

**4** Click on the third star in the Find bar to deactivate the rating search.

**5** In the Keyword Tags panel, click the arrow beside the People category to expand that category so that you can see the two nested sub-categories: "Family" and "Friends."

**6** Drag the Family keyword tag to the thumbnail of the girl in a swimming pool.

**7** Collapse the People keyword tag category; then, Ctrl-click / Command-click to select all the other images featuring children.

**8** Click in the text box at the bottom of the Keywords Tags panel and type the letter **f**. As you type a list of the existing keywords starting with **f** appears; choose Family, and then click Apply. The tag is applied to all of the images selected in the Media Browser.

● **Note:** In the Media Browser, the keyword tag icon or icons that you see below the thumbnails will vary in appearance depending on the size at which the thumbnails are displayed. If the thumbnail size is very small, multiple color-coded tags may display as a single generic (beige) tag icon.

**9** Rest the pointer for a second or two over a tag icon beneath the thumbnail of any of your newly tagged photos; a tooltip message appears identifying the keyword tags that are attached to that image file.

**10** In the Keyword Tags panel, click the triangle to expand the People keyword tags category once more. Activate the Find box beside the Family sub-category. The Media Browser is updated to display only the group of images to which you assigned the Family tag.

**11** Click the Find box beside the Family tag again to clear the search. Once more the Media Browser displays all the Lesson 2 images.

## Creating new categories and sub-categories

It's easy to add or delete new keyword tag categories and sub-categories in the Keyword Tags panel to help you group and organize your keyword tags.

**1** At the top of the Keyword Tags panel, click the Create New Keyword Tag, Sub-category, Or Category button (✚) and choose New Category from the menu.

**2** In the Create Category dialog box, type **Sports** as the category name; then scroll the Category Icon menu and select an icon. Click OK.

**3** In the Keyword Tags panel, expand the People category if necessary; then click to select the Family sub-category. Click the Create New button (✚) and choose New Sub-Category from the menu.

**4** In the Create Sub-Category dialog box, type **Kids** as the new Sub-Category name. Ensure that Family is selected in the Parent Category or Sub-Category menu and click OK. Your new keyword tag category and sub-category have become part of this catalog.

## Applying and editing category assignments

You can assign keyword categories to (or remove them from) several files at once.

**1** In the Media Browser, click any of the photos featuring children; then hold down the Ctrl / Command key and click to add the rest to the selection.

**2** Click in the text box ar the bottom of the Keywords Tags panel and type the letter **k**; choose Kids and click Apply. The tag is applied to the selected images.

**3** Leaving the same images selected, drag the Sports keyword tag to one of the un-selected images of marathon runners. Selecting the thumbnail or deselecting the other thumbnails is not necessary; the keyword tag is applied to just this picture.

**4** Choose Edit > Deselect, and then Ctrl-click / Command-click to select the three un-tagged marathon photos. Drag your multiple selection onto the Sports tag in the Keyword Tags panel. The keyword tag Sports is applied to all three images at once.

▶ **Tip:** You can also show and hide the Properties panel by holding down the Alt / Option key on your keyboard, and then pressing Enter / Return.

**5** Select the image of the young girl swimming to which you applied a 4-star rating earlier in the lesson. Choose Window > Properties to open the Properties panel, and then click the Keyword Tags tab (🏷) to see which keyword tags are attached to this image.

**6** Remove the Family tag from the image by doing one of the following:

- In the Properties panel, right-click / Control-click the listing **Family, Kids**, and then choose Remove Family Sub-Category Keyword Tag.

- In the Media Browser, right-click / Control-click the thumbnail image and choose Remove Keyword Tag > Family from the context menu.

- Right-click / Control-click the tag icon beneath the thumbnail, and then choose Remove Family Sub-Category Keyword Tag from the context menu.

**7** Close the Properties panel by clicking the Close button—in the upper right corner of the panel on Windows, at the upper left on Mac OS—or by choosing Window > Properties again.

## Creating and applying new keyword tags

In the last exercise you created new keyword categories and sub-categories. This time you'll create, apply and edit a new keyword tag.

**1** In the Keyword Tags panel, click the Create New button (➕) and choose New Keyword Tag from the menu. The Create Keyword Tag dialog box appears.

**2**  In the Create Keyword Tag dialog box, choose Sports as the category, and then type **NY Marathon** for the tag Name. Click OK.

**3**  Drag the first of the images of runners, DSC_5740.jpg, to the new NY Marathon tag in the Keyword Tags panel.

The image becomes the default icon for the new tag because it's the first to have this keyword applied. You'll adjust the tag icon in the next steps, before applying the new keyword tag to additional photos.

**4**  In the Keyword Tags panel, select the NY Marathon keyword tag; then, click the Create New button (➕) above the list of keyword tags and choose Edit from the menu. You could also right-click / Control-click the NY Marathon keyword tag itself and choose Edit NY Marathon Keyword Tag from the context menu.

**5**  In the Edit Keyword Tag dialog box, click the Edit Icon button to open the Edit Keyword Tag Icon dialog box.

**6**  Drag the bounding box in the preview window as far to the right as possible. A thumbnail at the top of the dialog box shows you how your edit looks applied to the tag icon.

**7**  Click OK to close the dialog box; then click OK again to close the Edit Keyword Tag dialog box.

You'll update the keyword tag icon later to an image that works better as an icon for this tag.

**8**  Shift-click, or Ctrl-click / Command-click, to select the remaining three images showing marathon runners. Drag the NY Marathon keyword tag onto any of the selected photos. The NY Marathon tag is now attached to four images.

**9**  In the Keyword Tags panel, right-click / Control-click the NY Marathon tag and choose Edit NY Marathon Keyword Tag from the context menu. In the Edit Keyword Tag dialog box, click the Edit Icon button to open the Edit Keyword Tag Icon dialog box.

**10** In the Edit Keyword Tag Icon dialog box, click the arrow to the right of the Find button beneath the main preview image.

The Find arrows cycle through all photos with the same keyword tag. A small preview at the top of the dialog box shows how each image would look applied as a tag icon.

**11** Choose a new image for the tag icon; then, drag the bounding box on the main preview (and re-size it, if you wish) until you are satisfied with the way it looks in the small tag preview; then click OK to close the dialog box. Click OK again to close the Edit Keyword Tag dialog box.

## Converting keyword tags and categories

Changing the hierarchy of categories and keyword tags in the Keyword Tags panel is easy. Doing this will not remove the rearranged tags or categories from the images to which you've attached them.

**1**  Click the Find box next to the Kids sub-category. A binoculars icon (🔍) appears in the box to remind you that it is now activated. Only the photos you tagged with the Kids keyword are displayed in the Media Browser. Click the Show All button above the Media Browser so that all the images in the catalog are visible.

**2**  Right-click the Kids sub-category and choose Edit Kids Sub-Category from the context menu. The Edit Sub-Category dialog box appears.

**3**   From the Parent Category or Sub-Category menu, choose None (Convert To Category) and click OK.

Now Kids is no longer a sub-category under People, Family, but a category in its own right. Its new tag, featuring a stylized portrait icon, has been inherited from its former parent category, People.

**4**   Click the empty Find box beside the Kids category.
Notice that the set of images tagged with the Kids tag did not change. Move the pointer over the tag icons below any of the images featuring children; note the list of attached keywords. Click the Show All button above the Media Browser.

**5**   In the Keyword Tags panel, drag the Kids category onto the People category.

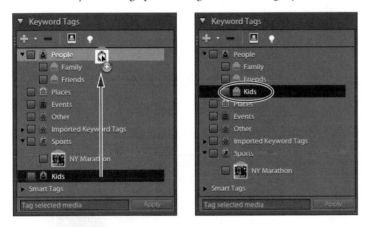

The Kids tag appears as a sub-category once more; this time listed under People. Because it's no longer a category, its tag reverts to the generic sub-category icon.

**6**   Activate the Find box beside the Kids category; then, move the pointer over the tag icons below any of the images displayed. Neither the selection of images tagged with the Kids keyword nor the list of attached keywords has changed. Click the Show All button.

**7**   Under the People category, right-click / Control-click the Family sub-category and choose Change Family Sub-Category To A Keyword Tag from the menu.

**8**   In the Media Browser, select the image DSC_9268.jpg—the photo of a girl wearing yellow swimming goggles—in preparation for the next exercise.

## Working with keyword tags in Full Screen mode

The Full Screen mode in Photoshop Elements has been improved to give you even more ways to work with keyword tags while reviewing and organizing your photos.

1  Click the View, Edit, Organize In Full Screen button (▦) above the Media Browser, or click the Display button (▦) at the upper right of the Organizer window and choose View, Edit, Organize In Full Screen from the menu.

2  Move the pointer over the full screen image to see the control bar at the bottom of the screen. If necessary, click the Pause button, and then click the Toggle Film Strip button or press Ctrl+F on your keyboard so that you can see a strip of thumbnails at the right of the screen as shown below.

3  Move the pointer to the left edge of the screen, as shown in the illustration below, to show the Quick Organize panel; then, click to deactivate the Auto Hide button at the top of the vertical title bar of the Quick Organize panel so that the panel remains open while you work.

4  Move the pointer over the keywords in the Keyword Tags pane of the Quick Organize panel; as you move over each keyword a tooltip message shows that you can click to either apply or remove any of these tags. All the existing tags in your catalog listed here in alphabetical order. Varying text sizes indicate the relative number of files tagged with each keyword. The keywords already attached to this image are highlighted.

**5** Click in the text box at the bottom of the Quick Organize panel and type **Lilly**; then click the Apply button (➕) to the right of the text box to attach the new keyword to this image.

**6** Repeat the process in step 5 to apply the keyword **Vacation** to this photo.

**7** In the film strip at the right of the screen, click the other photo of a girl swimming, then click the keyword Vacation in the Keyword Tags pane of the Quick Organize panel to apply that tag.

**8** Use the Previous Media and Next Media navigation arrow buttons in the control bar at the bottom of the screen—or the left and right arrow keys on your keyboard—to cycle through the other images in the film strip.

Click the keyword Vacation in the Quick Organize panel to apply that tag to each of the two photos of girls with skateboards and the four marathon images. Return the view to the original photo of Lilly with her yellow goggles.

**9** Click to activate the Quick Organize panel's Auto Hide button once more; then, move the pointer away; the panel closes after a second or so.

**10** Right-click / Control-click the image and choose Show Properties from the menu.

**11** At the top of the Properties panel, click the Keyword Tags tab (🏷) to see the keyword tags attached to this image. Right-click / Control-click the tag **Lilly** and choose Remove Lilly Keyword Tag. You'll explore a better way to tag people later in this chapter. Click the Close button in the header bar to close the Properties panel.

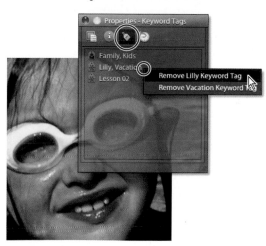

**12** Press the Esc key on your keyboard or click the Close button at the right of the control bar to exit Full Screen mode and return to thumbnail view.

## Using keyword tags to find pictures

The reason for creating, applying and sorting all these keyword tags is so that you can always find just the picture you want, just when you want it—easily and quickly. Once they share a keyword tag, a group of related photos can be retrieved with a single click; no matter how big your catalog, or across how many folders those images are scattered.

Before you go on to have fun with the People Recognition feature, let's become more familiar with using the Keyword Tags panel to sort and search your files.

1   Click the Show All button in the Find bar across the top of the Media browser. Drag the Thumbnail Size to the left so that you can see all the thumbnails in the Media Browser. The Media Browser is now displaying all of the files in your CIB catalog, including those you imported for Lesson 1.

2   In the Keyword Tags panel, activate the find box beside the Lesson 02 tag. The number of images in the Media Browser is reduced by twelve.

3   Leaving the Lesson 02 find box active, activate the new Vacation tag, in the keyword category Other; now only the eight images tagged with both keywords show in the Media Browser.

4   Click to activate the find box beside the Kids tag in the People category; only four images are returned by the narrowed search. The Find bar above the Media Browser shows that these images are tagged with all three keywords.

5   From the Options menu in the Find bar above the Media Browser, choose Show Close Match Results.

The thumbnail display is updated to show more photos: images that are tagged with *some*, but not all of the searched keywords. These close matches can be identified by a check mark icon in the upper left corner of their thumbnails.

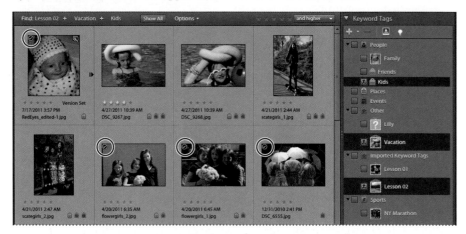

6   From the Options menu in the Find bar above the Media Browser, choose Hide Close Match Results. Click Show All to display all images. In the Keyword Tags panel, right-click / Control-click the tag **Lilly** and choose Delete Lilly Keyword Tag from the context menu. Click OK to confirm the deletion.

# Automatically finding faces for tagging

Undoubtedly, your growing photo library will include many photos of your family and friends. Photoshop Elements 10 makes it quick and easy to tag your photos of friends and family members with the People Recognition feature, taking most of the work out of sorting and organizing a large portion of your catalog.

People Recognition automatically finds the people in your photos and makes it easy for you to tag them. Once you begin using the feature it learns to recognize the faces you've already tagged and will automatically tag new photos with those faces.

## Using People Recognition

The first experience you'll have of People Recognition will probably be the "Who Is This?" prompt that appears as you move the pointer over a photo in the single-image view in the Elements Organizer. People Recognition displays these hints to help you identify and tag all the people in your photos. You can ignore the hints if you wish, but remember that the more people you identify, the smarter People Recognition gets at tagging faces for you automatically.

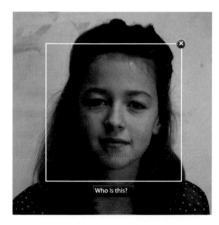

● **Note:** Once People Recognition begins to recognize a particular face, the "Who is this?" hint changes to read "Is this Emma?," giving you the opportunity to confirm or cancel automatic tagging.

The automatic "Who Is This" hints and the People Recognition feature itself can both be disabled. Before continuing, you need to make sure that both are activated. You can also import a few more images with faces for People Recognition to find.

1   In the Organizer, choose Edit > Preferences > Media-Analysis (Windows) / Adobe Elements 10 Organizer > Preferences (Mac OS). In the Media-Analysis pane of the Preferences dialog box, make sure that the option Analyze Photos For People Automatically is activated. Click OK to save your settings and close the Preferences dialog box.

2   In the View menu, make sure that Show People Recognition is activated.

3   Choose File > Get Photos And Videos > From Files And Folders. In the Get Photos And Videos From Files And Folders dialog box, locate and open your Lesson02 folder; then, click once to select the Faces folder.

4   Disable the options Automatically Fix Red Eyes and Automatically Suggest Photo Stacks. Click Get Media. In the Import Attached Keyword Tags dialog box, click Select All, and then click OK. Click OK to close any other alerts.

5   Above the Media Browser, click the Show All button to display all the images in your CIB catalog, and then choose Date (Newest First) for the sorting order.

## Tagging faces in the Media Browser

Photoshop Elements helps you with every step of the face tagging process.

1  In the Media Browser, double-click the photo, **faces_13.jpg**, to see it in the enlarged single image view. Move the pointer over the image; white boxes appear over any faces detected in the photo. People Recognition has found three of the four faces in this picture. Move the pointer over any of the boxes; the "Who is this?" prompt appears.

2  Starting with the girl at the left, click the "Who is this?" text in the black box, type the name **Lilly**, and then press Enter / return. Photoshop Elements creates a new keyword tag for Lilly. By default, the new tag appears in the People category in the Keyword Tags panel. Type **Kat** for the mother's name and tag the girl on the right **Pauline**. Be sure to press Enter / return for each tag.

3  Click the Add Missing Person button (🖼) below the lower right corner of the enlarged image. Drag the new face tagging box onto the face that was not detected; use the handles around the box to resize it so that it surrounds the face neatly. When you're done, click the green check mark to confirm the position of the box; then, type **Emma** in the text box and press Enter / return.

▶ **Tip:** Face tags are listed inside the People category by default, but you can move them if you choose; People Recognition will keep track of them.

● **Note:** Depending on your operating system, you may not see exactly the results from People Recognition that are referred to and illustrated in these exercises. The overall process, however, will be the same.

4  Click the left arrow key on your keyboard to move to the preceding photo. People Recognition already recognizes the girl on the right; click the green check mark to confirm the automatic tagging for **Lilly**. You haven't yet tagged a photo of the other girl; type **Sophie**, and then press Enter / return.

People Recognition will sometimes incorrectly identify a chance arrangement of light and shadow in an image as a face. For this image, this has happened twice.

5   Move the pointer over the tagging box above Lilly's head and click the X button at the upper right corner of the box to dismiss it; otherwise People Recognition will continue to register this as a person not yet named.

6   You may find it a little difficult at first to work with the other extraneous tagging box, as it overlaps the boxes for both of the girls. Click in the "Who is this?" text to keep the box active while you move the pointer to the X button to dismiss it.

7   Click the left arrow key on your keyboard to move to the preceding photo. This time, all five of the faces in the photo have been detected. Click in the "Who is this?" text box for the girl at the right of the frame. You haven't yet tagged enough faces for People Recognition to identify this girl, but you're offered a choice of possible tags from those available in the People category. Click the name **Sophie**, and then, if necessary, press Enter / return.

8   Use the same technique to tag **Lilly**—the girl at the far left—and **Pauline**, beside her. Type **Tom** for the father's name. Photoshop Elements doesn't yet know the older girl well enough to offer the correct choice. Type the name **Emma**, and then press Enter / return. Dismiss the extra tagging box at the top of the stairs.

● **Note:** When you type a name that matches a tag you created earlier, Photoshop Elements applies the existing keyword, rather than creating a new tag.

9   Double-click the image to return the Media Browser to Thumbnail view.

## Tagging faces in batches

When you want to do some serious face tagging, rather than work through your catalog one image at a time, you can let People Recognition bulk-process your files.

1   Reduce the size of the thumbnails so that you san see as many of the images in the Media Browser as possible. Ctrl-click / Command-click to select all of the photos of this family that have not yet been face-tagged—there are 27 in all.

2   Click the Start People Recognition button (🔲) at the top of the Keyword Tags panel. The People Recognition – Confirm Groups Of People dialog box opens.

In Confirm Groups Of People mode, People Recognition collates groups of faces that match known names, and then offers you the option to exclude any faces that don't belong. Click the X button at the top right of a face thumbnail to dismiss it.

**3** For our example images, there are no images to be excluded from groups to be tagged **Lilly** and **Pauline**. Click Save to confirm these groups; then, click Save again to confirm the next sets to be tagged **Emma** and **Sophie**. Continue the process, dismissing the thumbnails of any faces of which you are unsure, until the People Recognition – Label People Dialog box appears.

**4** In the People Recognition - Label People dialog box, tag as many of the faces as you can. Be sure to press Enter / return whenever you type. When you're done, click Save; then repeat the process for a new set of faces. Be patient—People Recognition is getting smarter with every click!

People Recognition will alternate between the Confirm Groups and Label People modes, until eventually, you'll be presented with a set of dimmed images like those in the illustration below. These may be faces obscured by shadows, hands, hats, or sunglasses—or sometimes just chance arrangements of color, light, and shadow with characteristics that have triggered the face recognition algorithms.

**5** Click the thumbnail of any face you recognize, and then click Save. If you click to include a face, you'll be returned to the Label People dialog box to tag it. Images you ignore will no longer be seen as faces by People Recognition.

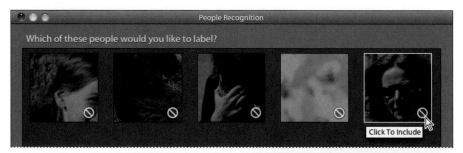

**6** Photoshop Elements will notify you when the tagging session is completed; click OK to dismiss the message and return to the Media Browser.

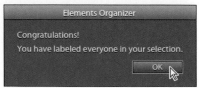

**7** In the keywords panel, activate the Find box beside the each of your new tags in turn, making sure to clear each search before starting the next. Try activating different combinations of Find boxes at the same time.

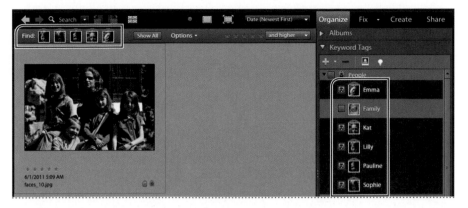

▶ **Tip:** The details of each search are shown in the Find bar above the thumbnail display. What you see in the Find bar may differ from the illustration, depending on your operating system.

**8** To deactivate all of the keyword tag Find boxes and clear the search, click the Show All button above the thumbnails pane.

## Sharing keyword tags with Facebook

If you have a Photoshop.com account, you can share your photos directly from Photoshop Elements to Facebook, complete with any tags you've applied in the Elements Organizer. Photoshop Elements can even download your friends list from Facebook, making it even easier to tag your photos.

**1** Make sure that you're signed in to your Photoshop.com account (see "Creating an Adobe ID" on page 22 in Lesson 1).

**2** Select the photos you wish to share selected in the Media Browser, click the Share tab at the top of the Task Pane, and then click Share To Facebook. If you are asked to confirm the action, click Yes.

**3** Photoshop Elements asks for your permission to access your Facebook account. Make sure that the option Download Facebook Friend List is activated, and then click Authorize.

**4** Facebook will also require your authorization. When the Facebook Request For Permission page opens in your default browser, click Allow; then, close the browser page and return to the Organizer.

**5** Click Complete Authorization. Photoshop Elements opens the Share To Facebook dialog box, where you can set up the details for your upload. Choose whether to upload photos to an existing Facebook album, or create and enter details for a new one. Specify who you wish to share your album to, and select an option for photo upload quality. You can add a photo to the selection to be uploaded, or exclude a picture, using the plus and minus buttons at the lower left of the preview pane. Make sure you activate the option Upload People Tags In These Photos, and then click Upload.

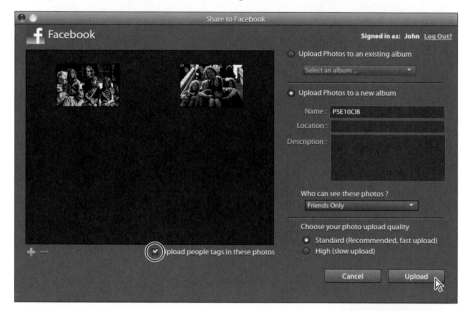

Photoshop Elements will download names from your Facebook friends list while your photos are being up-loaded. The next time you're tagging photos in Photoshop Elements, you'll notice that the names of your Facebook friends are offered as tagging suggestions.

You'll be notified when the upload is complete and given the option to return to the Elements Organizer or visit your Facebook page to view your newly shared photos.

**6** When you're done, click the Organise tab at the top of the Task pane to return to the Media Browser.

Congratulations, you've finished the lesson! You've imported files into the Elements Organizer using a variety of new techniques and learned several different ways to view and access the images in your catalog. You've also created, edited, and applied keyword tags to individual photographs so that they'll be easy to find in future. Before you move on, take a few moments to review the concepts and techniques presented in this lesson by working through the following questions and answers.

# Review questions

1 How do you open the Elements Organizer component of Adobe Photoshop Elements?

2 Name three ways to import photos from your computer hard disk into your catalog.

3 What is a "watched folder"? (Windows users only.)

4 Summarize the characteristics of the Media Browser and Date views in the Organizer.

# Review answers

1 Click the Organize button in the Welcome Screen when you start Photoshop Elements. Alternatively, if the Editor window is already open, click the Organizer button located at the top right of the Editor workspace.

2 This lesson demonstrated three different ways to import photos into Photoshop Elements:

- Drag-and-drop photographs from a Windows Explorer / Finder window into the Media Browser pane in the Organizer window.

- In the Organizer, choose File > Get Photos And Videos > From Files And Folders, and then navigate to the folder containing your photos. You can import a whole folder, specify whether to include subfolders, or select just those images you want to add to your catalog.

- In the Organizer, choose File > Get Photos And Videos > By Searching, and then select the folder on the hard disk that you wish Photoshop Elements to search. This method will locate all images in that folder and its subfolders and offer you the opportunity to select which images to import.

3 If you designate a folder on your computer as watched, Photoshop Elements is automatically alerted when new photos are saved or added to that folder. By default, the My Pictures folder is watched, but you change that, or add any number of watched folders. When new images appear in a watched folder, you can either have Photoshop Elements import them to the Organizer automatically, or ask you what to do.

4 In the default Media Browser view in the Organizer you can browse thumbnail images of your photos. You can choose to see them sorted by chronological order, by folder location, or by import batch. The Date view is organized in the form of a calendar where you can quickly find photos taken on a particular day, month, or year.

# 3 ADVANCED ORGANIZING

## Lesson Overview

As your collection grows to hundreds or even thousands of images, keeping track of your photos can be a daunting task. Photoshop Elements 10 delivers sophisticated organizing tools that not only get the job done, but actually make the work quite enjoyable.

In this lesson you'll learn a few new methods of importing images and some of the more advanced techniques for organizing, sorting, and searching your growing photo collection:

- Using advanced Photo Downloader options
- Acquiring still frames from video
- Importing pictures from a PDF document
- Using Version Sets and Stacks to organize photos
- Grouping photos in Albums and Smart Albums
- Viewing and managing files in the Folder Location view
- Finding photos by similarity, metadata, and text search
- Hiding unwanted files from view

 You'll probably need between one and two hours to complete this lesson.

Discover some advanced import options that will make organizing your photos even easier. Have Photoshop Elements apply tags and group images automatically during import so your files will already be organized by the time they arrive in your catalog! Simplify navigating your catalog with Stacks, Version Sets and Albums and learn about a range of powerful search features to help you find exactly the right files.

# Getting started

In this lesson you'll be working mainly in the Organizer workspace, though you will switch to the Editor in order to capture frames from a video and import images from a PDF document.

1   Start Photoshop Elements.

2   In the Welcome screen, click the Organize button at the left, and then wait while the Elements Organizer opens.

# Advanced import options

In Lesson 2 you imported images into the Organizer using a variety of methods, and learned how to apply keyword tags manually as a way of organizing photos once they are in your catalog. In the following exercise you'll explore some advanced import options that will make organizing your photos even easier. You can set up your import so that Photoshop Elements will automatically apply tags and create groups during the import process, so that your images will already be organized by the time they arrive in your catalog! You'll also learn about importing photos from some different sources: capturing still frames from a movie and extracting the images embedded in a PDF document.

## Photo Downloader options

If you have a digital camera or memory card at hand with your own photos on it, you can step through this first exercise using those images. To get the best results from this exercise, you should have several batches of pictures taken at different times on the same day. Alternatively, you can simply follow the process and refer to the illustrations in the book, without actually performing the exercise yourself, and then return to this exercise when you are prepared.

1   Connect your digital camera or card reader to your computer, following the manufacturer's instructions. If you're working on Mac OS, skip to step 3.

2   On Windows, the Auto Play dialog box may appear. You could choose the option Organize And Edit Using Adobe Elements Organizer 10, but for the purposes of this lesson, simply click Cancel to dismiss the dialog box. If the Photo Downloader dialog box appears automatically, you can skip to step 4; otherwise, continue to step 3.

**3**  Choose File > Get Photos And Videos > From Camera Or Card Reader.

**4**  If the Photo Downloader dialog box opens in the Advanced mode, click the Standard Dialog button located at the lower left corner of the dialog box.

**5**  From the Get Photos From menu at the top of the Photo Downloader dialog box, choose the name of the connected camera or card reader.

**6**  Under Import Settings, accept the default destination folder listed beside Location, or click Browse / Choose to specify a different destination. By default, the image files are saved to your My Pictures folder.

**7**  Without making any other changes to the settings, click the Advanced Dialog button in the lower left corner of the dialog box.

In advanced mode, the Photo Downloader Dialog displays thumbnail previews of all the photos on your camera's memory card, and also offers options for processing, tagging, and grouping your images during the import process.

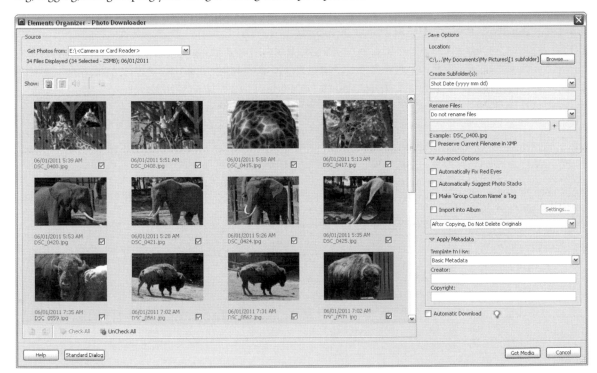

In the next steps you'll set up the automatic creation of subfolders for the files copied from your camera and apply keyword tags to the images as they are imported.

8   Under Save Options, choose Custom Groups (Advanced) from the Create Subfolder(s) menu. Your selection is reflected in the Location pathname.

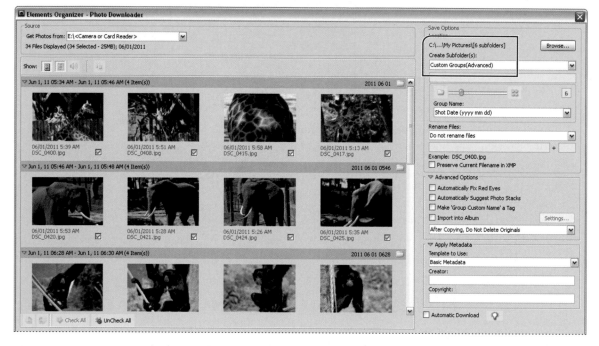

The images have been automatically divided into groups, based on capture time and date. A slider below the Create Subfolder(s) menu enables you to adjust the granularity of the subdivision and the box to the right of the slider shows the resulting number of groups. In our example, the automatic grouping based on capture time has done a good of job separating our subjects, producing six groups.

9   Experiment by moving the slider to the left to generate fewer groups (subfolders) or to the right to generate more. Scroll down the list of thumbnails to review the effect of the slider on the grouping of your photos. Note that the number of groups created is displayed in the box to the right of the slider.

▶ **Tip:** To increase or decrease the number of groups, you can also press Ctrl / Command together with Shift+M or Shift+L respectively on your keyboard.

**10** Next you'll apply custom names to the subfolders for your grouped photos. From the Group Name menu, choose Shot Date (yyyy mm dd) + Custom Name.

**11** On the right end of the separator bar above the thumbnails of the first group, click the Custom Name field and type a descriptive name in the text box.

**12** Repeat step 11 for the other groups in the list, giving each a distinct name. In our example, we used the animal names **Giraffe**, **Elephant**, **Monkey**, and so on.

**13** Under Advanced Options, activate the option Make 'Group Custom Name' A Tag by clicking the check box. This will automatically create keyword tags corresponding to the group custom names and apply them to your photos as they are imported into the Organizer. If any of the options Automatically Fix Red Eyes, Automatically Suggest Photo Stacks, and Import Into Album are currently activated, disable them now by clicking their checkboxes.

**14** Click Get Media. The photos are copied to your hard disk, organized in subfolders named for your custom import groups. If the Files Successfully Copied dialog box appears, click Yes. Click OK to dismiss any other message.

The Getting Media dialog box appears briefly while the photos are being imported into your catalog. The imported images appear in the Media Browser, automatically tagged during the import process with keywords drawn from the custom group names. The new tags are nested inside the keyword category Other.

▶ **Tip:** The more you take advantage of these advanced options when importing your photos, the less time and effort you'll need to spend sorting and organizing images, and looking for the photos you want.

## Acquiring still frames from a video

● **Note:** On Mac OS, WMV video files can be imported, but are not supported for playback.

You can capture frames from digital videos in any of the file formats supported by Photoshop Elements. These include: ASF, AVI, MLV, MOV, MPG, MPEG, and WMV. To capture and import frames from video, you'll need to open the Editor.

1 If you still have any images selected in the Organizer from the previous exercise, choose Edit > Deselect.

2 Click the arrow on the Fix tab at the top of the Task Pane and choose Full Photo Edit from the menu. In the Editor, choose File > Import > Frame From Video.

3 In the Frame From Video dialog box, click the Browse button. Navigate to your Lesson03 folder, select the file **Penguin.AVI**, and click Open.

4 To start video playback, click the Play button (▶). Click the Pause button (❚❚) after 3 or 4 seconds, and then use the arrow keys on your keyboard to move forward or back one frame at a time until you find a frame that you'd like to capture.

5 Click the Grab Frame button below the playback controls, or press your spacebar, when the frame you want is visible on the screen.

6 Continue to move forward and backward in the video to capture two or three additional frames. When you have all the frames you want, click Done.

Each captured video frame opens in its own image window in the Editor. Thumbnails for the open files appear in the Project bin below the Edit pane.

▶ **Tip:** If you can't find the My CIB Work folder, refer to "Creating a work folder" on page 3.

7 Choose File > Close All. For the first file, click Yes / Save to save before closing. In the Save As dialog box, navigate to your My CIB Work folder; then, click the New Folder button and name the new folder Penguin. Accept the default file name and choose JPEG from the Format menu. For the purposes of this exercise, make sure that the option Include In The Elements Organizer is disabled; then, click Save. Click OK to accept the default JPEG image quality. Save the other images to the same folder, with the same settings.

8 Use the task bar in Windows or the Dock in Mac OS to return to the Organizer.

# Removing video distortion

Sometimes still frames captured from a video show distortion resulting from the fact that a video picture consists of two interlaced half-images, which can momentarily appear to be misaligned.

The odd-numbered, horizontal scanlines in the image, also called *odd fields*, constitute one half of the picture, and the even-numbered scanlines—*even fields*—the other. Since the two halves of the picture were recorded at slightly different times, the captured still image might show a 'zigzag' distortion that is particularly noticeable where it interrupts vertical detail.

In Photoshop Elements you can remedy this problem with the De-Interlace filter, which will remove either the odd or even fields in an image captured from video, and then replace the discarded lines by either duplicating, or interpolating from the remaining lines, depending on the options you specify.

If you wish to correct a video capture showing this kind of distortion, you'll probably find it most convenient to work on the image in the Editor's Quick Edit mode, where you can set up synchronized before and after views at high magnification. Choose **Filter** > **Video** > **De-Interlace**; then, position the De-Interlace dialog box so that you can see both the before and after views.

The combination of de-interlacing settings that will produce the best results will vary from image to image, so you'll need to experiment a little. Eliminate the odd and even fields in turn and, for each alternative, try both the duplication and interpolation options for replacing the deleted fields. You can Undo after each trial until you are satisfied with the result.

## Importing from a PDF document

Photoshop Elements enables you to import either whole pages from a PDF document or to select and extract just the images you want.

1 Use the task bar in Windows or the Dock in Mac OS return to the Editor; then, choose File > Open.

2 In the Open dialog box, navigate to your Lesson03 folder, select the file NY.pdf, and then click Open. If you can't see the file NY.pdf in the Open dialog box, click the Files Of Type / Enable menu at the bottom of the dialog box and choose either All Formats / All Readable Documents or Photoshop PDF.

3 Use the radio buttons in the Select pane to set the Import PDF dialog box to import Images. Select Large from the Thumbnail Size menu below the preview.

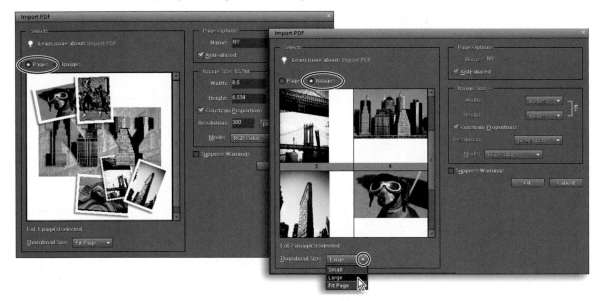

● **Note:** If you choose to import entire pages from a PDF file with more than one page, you can use the same method to multiple-select the pages. Pages are rasterized (converted to bit-mapped graphics) according to your choice of image size, resolution, and color mode. The imported result will be an image similar to that acquired by scanning a printed document.

4 Click to select an image you wish to import; then, scroll the preview pane and Ctrl-click / Command-click to add two or three more to the selection. Click OK.

Each image imported from the PDF file opens in its own document window in the Editor. Thumbnails for the open files appear in the Project bin below the Edit pane.

5 Choose File > Close All. For each file, click Yes / Save to save before closing. Save the images into your My CIB Work folder, accepting the default file names. Choose JPEG from the Format menu and make sure that the option Include In The Elements Organizer is activated; then click Save. Click OK to accept the default JPEG image quality.

6 Choose File > Exit / Adobe Photoshop Elements Editor > Quit to close the Editor and return to the Organizer, where thumbnails of the images you extracted from the PDF file now appear in the in the Media Browser.

# Organizing photos

Organizing your files and folders efficiently can be challenging. It's easy to forget what pictures are stored in which folder—and being forced to open and examine the content of numerous folders to find files can be both time consuming and extremely frustrating.

The Organizer can make the whole process much simpler and more enjoyable. The next set of exercises will show you how investing a little time in organizing your catalog can streamline the process of sorting through your image files, regardless of where they are stored.

## Working with version sets

A version set groups a photo in its original state with any edited copies, so that you can find all the versions of the image stacked behind a single thumbnail in the Media Browser, rather than scattered amongst the rest of the items in your catalog.

Photoshop Elements automatically creates a version set whenever you modify a photo in the Elements Organizer. When you edit an photo from your catalog in the Editor, however, you'll need to choose File > Save As, and then activate the option Save In Version Set With Original.

Grouping your work in this way not only makes it much easier for you to find the version you want, but also enables you to keep your original un-edited photo intact, easy to find and ready for a different treatment whenever you want to re-use it.

1   Check the name of the active catalog at the lower left of the Organizer window. If your CIB catalog is not loaded, choose File > Catalog, select the CIB Catalog from the list in the Catalog Manager dialog box, and then click Open.

2   Choose File > Get Photos And Videos > From Files And Folders. In the Get Photos And Videos From Files And Folders dialog box, navigate to your Lesson03 folder and select the folder Zoo. Activate the option Get Photos From Subfolders. Make sure that the options Automatically Fix Red Eyes and Automatically Suggest Photo Stacks option are disabled; then, click Get Media.

3   In the Import Attached Keyword Tags dialog box, click Select All to enable all eight tags, and then click OK. Click OK to close any other alert dialog box.

> **Tip:** You can also check the name of the currently active catalog by holding the pointer over the Organizer Icon at the upper left of the Organizer workspace.

Thumbnails of the thirty four images you've just added to your CIB catalog appear in the Media Browser.

4 If you don't see filenames displayed with the thumbnails in the Media Browser, activate the options Details and Show File Names in the View menu.

5 In the Keyword Tags panel, click the triangle beside the Imported Keyword Tags category, if necessary, to see the eight newly imported tags nested inside.

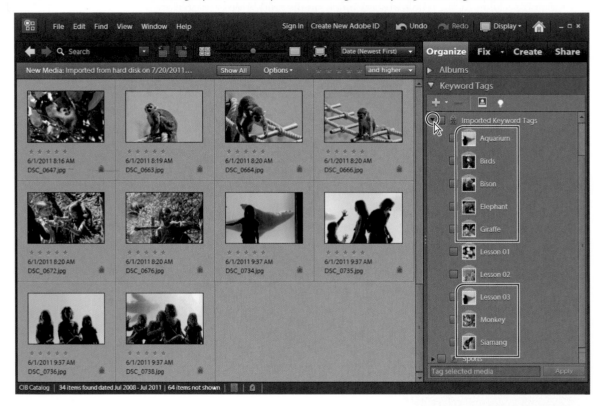

▶ **Tip:** Remember: if you edit an image in the Editor you need to choose File > Save As, and then activate the option Save In Version Set With Original.

6 Select the image DSC_0420.jpg, and then choose Edit > Auto Smart Fix. The Auto Smart Fix command corrects the overall color balance and improves shadow and highlight detail. The edited copy of the image is automatically grouped in a version set with the original, with the edited version topmost, and the filename has been extended to indicate that the photo has been edited. A version set can be identified in the Media Browser by the badge displayed in the upper right corner of the thumbnail and a label at the lower right.

**7** Click the expand button to the right of the thumbnail image to see the original and edited images in the version set displayed side by side.

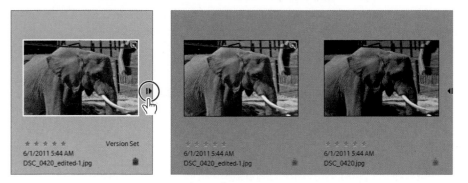

▶ **Tip:** If you edit a photo that's already in a version set, the edited copy is placed at the top of the existing version set. To specify a different photo as the topmost, select it in the expanded view of the version set, and then choose Edit > Version Set > Set As Top Item.

**8** To see only the topmost photo in the version set, click the collapse button to the right of the thumbnail image on the right, or right-click / Control-click any image in the set and choose Version Set > Collapse Items In Version Set from the context menu. Note the other commands available from the same context menu; these commands can also be found in the Edit > Version Set menu.

## About stacks

You can create a stack to group a set of related photos in the Media Browser, making them easier to manage. Stack a series, or multiple images of the same subject, to help reduce clutter in the Media Browser. For instance, you might create a stack for several photos of your family taken in the same pose, keeping the candidates together until you have a chance to pick the best shot—or for photos taken at a sports event using your camera's burst mode or auto-bracket feature. When you take photos this way you end up with many variations of what is essentially the same photo, but you only want the best version to appear in the Media Browser.

**1** In the Keyword Tags panel, activate the Find box beside the new Elephant tag in the Imported Keyword Tags category.

**2** Ctrl-click / Command-click to select the four photos; then, choose Edit > Stack > Stack Selected Photos. The images are stacked, with the photo you edited earlier on top, now marked with both the version set and stack badges and a Photo Stack label. Expand and collapse the stack by clicking the expand or collapse arrows at the right side of the stack frame.

**3** Expand the stack, and then right-click / Control-click the image at the right: DSC_0425.jpg. From the context menu, choose Stack > Set As Top Photo.

**4** Collapse the stack; the topmost image no longer displays both the version set and stack badges.

## Tips for working with stacks

▶ **Tip:** To access stack commands, right-click / Control-click any image in a stack and choose from the Stack sub-menu. Alternatively, select a photo in the stack and choose from the Edit > Stack menu.

You should keep these points in mind when you're working with stacks:

- To specify a new image as the topmost, expand the stack, right-click / Control-click the desired photo, and then choose Stack > Set As Top Photo.

- Combining two or more stacks merges them to form one new stack, with the most recent photo on top of the stack. The original groupings are not preserved.

- Many actions applied to a collapsed stack, such as editing, printing, and e-mailing, are applied to the topmost item only. To apply an action to multiple images in a stack, either expand the stack and group-select the images, or un-stack them first.

- If you edit a photo that you've already included in a stack, the photo and its edited copy will be grouped as a version set nested inside the stack.

- If you apply a keyword tag to a collapsed stack, the keyword tag is applied to all items in the stack. When you run a search on the keyword tag, the top photo in the stack appears in the search results marked with the stack icon. If you want to apply a keyword tag to only one photo in a stack, expand the stack first and apply the keyword tag to just that photo.

## Stacking photos automatically

You can automate the process of grouping related photos in your catalog by having Photoshop Elements suggest stacks, based on visual similarities between images.

**1** In the Find bar above the Media Browser, click the Show All button. In the Keyword Tags panel, activate the Find boxes beside the two imported keyword tags Birds and Bison.

**2** Choose Edit > Select All to select all twelve images. Choose Edit > Stack > Automatically Suggest Photo Stacks.

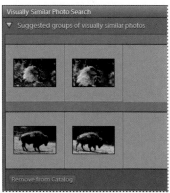

▶ **Tip:** Experiment with as many of your own photos as possible, so that you'll get a feel for the kind of images that perform best with this feature.

In the Visually Similar Photo Search dialog box, Photoshop has suggested a pair of very similar photos from each group as potential stacks. Before you go ahead and stack these groups, lets look at the options for tweaking the automatic stacking process manually.

**3** Click the small triangle to expand the Unique Photos pane at the bottom of the Visually Similar Photo Search dialog box. You can see that there is another bison photo that is very similar to those suggested for stacking. Drag the thumbnail from the Unique photos pane to add it to the group.

▶ **Tip:** You can simply reverse this process to remove a photo from a group suggested for stacking.

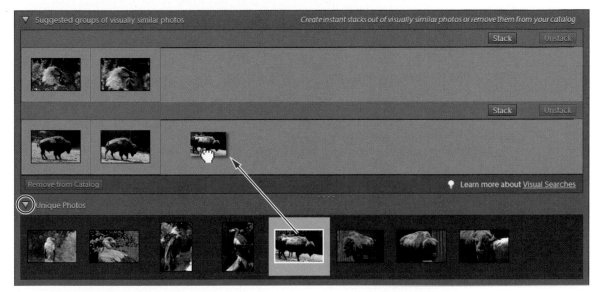

**4** Click the Stack button at the right of the divider bar above each of the groups. The images in each group are stacked behind the first image in the row, which now displays the stacked photos badge.

**5** Click the Unstack button to undo stacking for the two photos of the bird's head, and then click Done to dismiss the Visually Similar Photo Search dialog box.

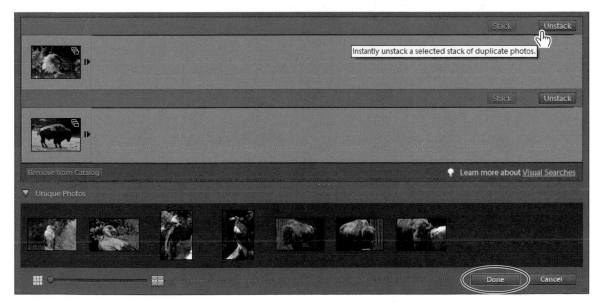

# Creating albums

Another way of grouping your photos is to organize them into albums. You might create a new album to group shots from a special occasion such as a wedding or a vacation, or to assemble the images that you intend to use in a project such as a presentation to a client or a slideshow.

An album is like a *virtual* folder where you can assemble a group of images that may be drawn from any number of *actual* folders on your hard disk.

The principal difference between grouping photos in an album and grouping them with a shared keyword tag is that in an album you can rearrange the order of the photos as you wish. In the Media Browser, each photo in an album displays a number in the upper left corner, representing its place in the order. You can drag photos to rearrange their order within the album, which will effect the order in which they appear in a slideshow or their placement in a project layout.

A photo can be added to more than one album—the same image might be the first in a New York album and the last in a National Monuments album. You can also group albums; for example, you might group your New York and San Francisco albums inside your Vacations album. Your San Francisco album may also be included in a Road Trips album while the New York album is not.

1  Click the Show All button above the Media Browser to clear the current search, and then click to activate the Find box beside the imported Lesson 03 tag in the Keyword Tags panel to isolate the images for this lesson.

2  If the Albums panel is collapsed, click the triangle in the panel's header bar to expand it.

3  To create a new album, click the Create New Album Or Album Category button (➕) at the upper left of the Albums panel and choose New Album from the menu.

4  In the Album Details pane, type **Day At The Zoo** as the name for the new album, leaving the Album Category set at None (Top Level). For the purposes of this exercise, disable the Backup/Sync option. Click Done.

5  Click the Create New Album Or Album Category button (➕) at the upper left of the Albums panel again, but this time, choose New Album Category from the menu. In the Create Album Category dialog box, type **Vacation 2011** as the name for the new album category. Leave the Parent Album Category set at None (Top Level). Click OK.

**6**  In the Albums panel, drag the album Day At The Zoo onto the entry for your new Vacation 2011 album category.

**7**  Right-click / Control-click the icon of the Day At The Zoo album and choose Edit Day At The Zoo Album from the menu.

**8**  Ctrl-click / Command-click to select about half of the Lesson 3 photos in the Media Browser; then, drag the group into the album Content box. Click Done.

▶ **Tip:** In the Album Details pane, you could rename the album or use the Album Category menu to move it out of its parent category and back to the top level.

**9**  Click Show All in the Find bar above the thumbnails pane. To isolate the contents of your new album, click the Day At The Zoo album entry in the Albums panel, or drag the album icon onto the Find bar. Notice the counter in the top left corner of each photo, denoting its order in the album.

● **Note:** You can't view more than one album at a time.

**▶ Tip:** If you don't
see the album badges
below the thumbnails
in the Media Browser,
use the slider above the
Find bar to increase the
size of the thumbnails.
Hold the pointer over
the album badge to see
which album or albums
a photo belongs to.

10 Leaving the Day At The Zoo album search (or *filter*)
active, activate the Find box beside the Lesson 03
tag. If you don't see all of the Lesson 3 images in the
Media Browser, choose Show Close Match Results
from the Options menu in the Find bar. If the thumbnails are set to display at a large enough size, photos
that are included in your new album can be differenti-
ated from the rest of the Lesson 3 images by the green
album badges below their thumbnails.

## Adding more photos to an album

As you add images to your catalog, you may have new photos that you'd like to
add to existing albums—an easy way to sort and organize a fresh import.

1 Keeping the combined filter (Day At The Zoo album + Lesson 03 keyword)
active, choose Hide Best Match Results from the Options menu in the Find
bar. Choose Edit > Select All; then, drag the selection onto the Day At The Zoo
album entry in the Albums panel. (Alternatively, you could drag the album icon
from the Albums panel onto any of the selected photos in the Media Browser.)

2 Choose Show Best Match Results from the Options menu in the Find bar. All of
the Lesson 3 images are now visible in the Media Browser, and all are marked
with an album badge to indicate that they're included in the Day At The Zoo
album. Disable the Find box for the Lesson 03 keyword tag.

**3** To remove a photo from the album, right-click / Control-click its thumbnail in the album view, and then choose Remove From Album > Day At The Zoo from the context menu. Choose Edit > Undo Remove Item(s) From Album.

**4** To change the order of the images in your album, select one or more photos in the Media Browser, and then simply drag the selection to the new position. The photos in the album are reordered when you release the mouse button.

**5** To delete the album, right-click / Control-click its entry in the Albums panel, and choose Delete Day At The Zoo Album from the context menu. For this exercise, click Cancel in the Confirm Album Deletion dialog box.

**6** Click Show All above the Media Browser.

● **Note:** Deleting an album will not remove the photos it contains from your catalog or your hard disk. Albums store only references to the actual image files.

## Working with smart albums

For a smart album you don't select and add photos manually, as you do for an ordinary album—you only need to specify search criteria. Once you set the criteria for a smart album, any photo in your catalog—and any new photo imported—matching the specified attributes will automatically appear in that album. In other words, a Smart Album is like an ongoing search that keeps itself up-to-date.

**1** To create a new smart album, click the Create New Album Or Album Category button (✚) in the Albums panel and choose New Smart Album from the menu.

● **Note:** You cannot change the order of the photos in a smart album, or add photos by dragging them onto the album's icon; a smart album can contain only images that match its criteria.

**2** In the New Smart Album dialog box, type **Best Animal Shots** as the album name.

**3** Under Search Criteria, activate the option All Of The Following Search Criteria [And]. From the first search criteria menu, choose Keyword Tags, and from the associated value menu, choose the keyword Lesson 03. Click the Add Additional Criteria button (+) to the right of the first criteria. Set the second search criteria to Rating > Is Higher Than > 2 Stars, and then click OK.

Your new Best Animal Shots album appears in the Albums panel; the blue album icon indicates that this is a smart album. As yet, there are no images in your catalog that match both the criteria, so the Media Browser is empty.

**4** Click Show All in the Find bar; then, activate the Find box for the Lesson 03 keyword tag to isolate the photos for this lesson.

**5** In the Media Browser, apply 3-, 4-, or 5-star ratings to the best five or six images by clicking the appropriate star below each thumbnail.

**6** Click the smart album Best Animal Shots in the Albums panel; the album now contains the photos that you rated in step 5.

**7** Make sure your smart album is selected in the Albums panel; then click Options in the Find bar and choose Modify Search Criteria from the menu.

**8** In the Find By Details (Metadata) dialog box, use the criteria menus to change the first rule to Catalog Date > Is Within The Last > 6 > Months.

If you clicked Search now, your changes to the criteria would affect the results of the current search—effectively functioning as a one-off filter–but would not be saved to the existing smart album.

**9** Activate the option Save This Search Criteria As Smart Album, and then type **Best - Last 6 Months** as the name for the new smart album. Click Search.

● **Note:** The content of a smart album may change over time, even without adding photos to, or removing them from your catalog. For example, a smart album may be set up to filter for photos captured within the last six months; photos matching that criteria today may not fall within the date range tomorrow.

The new smart album, containing all the photos that you've rated since you began working through the lessons in this book, is added to the Albums panel.

**10** Right-click / Control-click the smart album Best - Last 6 Months and choose Delete Best - Last 6 Months Smart Album from the context menu. Click OK to confirm the deletion. If it's visible, click the Show All button in the Find bar.

# Viewing and finding photos

Photoshop Elements offers a variety of options for sorting and viewing the media in your catalog, and a range of tools to help you quickly find just the files you need. In the Organizer you can search your catalog by media type, filename, date, folder location, star rating, album, keyword tag, text, or a range of other criteria, and then refine, sort and view the search results by album or in chronological order.

* **The Find bar**  You can drag a photo, keyword tag, creation, or album onto the Find bar across the top of the Media Browser to locate similar photos and media files. The Find bar also offers options for sorting the search results.

* **The Find menu**  Use the Find menu commands to search your catalog by date, caption, file name, history, media type, metadata, or by visual similarity. The Find menu also provides options for finding photos and media files that have unknown dates, are un-tagged, or are not included in any album.

* **Keyword Tags, Albums and Star Ratings**  View only those files with a selected keyword tag, or combination of tags, by clicking the Find boxes in the Keyword Tags panel, or files in a particular album by clicking in the Albums panel. Use the Star Ratings filter in the Find bar to see just those photos and media files with a specified rating, or to narrow a search based on any other criteria.

* **Text Search box**  Type in the text box above the Find bar to locate media with matching text—whether it's in the filename, caption, metadata, or album name. The Text Search box also includes a dynamic list of all your existing keywords.

- **The Timeline**  Choose Window > Timeline to display the timeline above the Media Browser. Use the Timeline as a search tool in its own right, or in combination with any of the other tools and views to help you refine a search or navigate the results. You might search for photos with a particular keyword tag, and then use the Timeline to limit the search to a specific folder or date range.

  In Thumbnail view, click a month or set a date range in the Timeline to find photos and media files by capture date. The Timeline shows you a breakdown of your catalog by import date in the Import Batch view and an overview of the folder by folder distribution of your media files in Folder Location view. The height of the bars in the timeline indicates the relative number of files in each group. The Timeline becomes particularly useful when your catalog contains a large number of files captured over a period of several years and spread over many folders on your hard disk.

## Viewing and managing files by folder location

In the Folder Location view you can rename, move, and delete files and folders, add files to your catalog, create instant albums and—on Windows—add folders to, or remove them from, the Watched Folder list.

1  If necessary, click the Show All button; then, use the Keyword Tags panel to isolate the Lesson 3 images. Select any photo in the Media Browser, and then click the Display button (⬛) above the Task Pane and choose Folder Location.

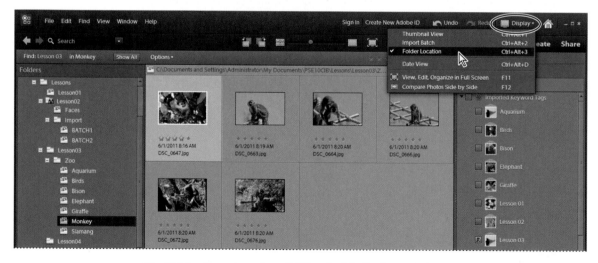

The Folder Location view divides the Media Browser into two parts. On the left, the Folders panel displays the hierarchy of folders on your hard disk. Folders containing *managed* files (files that you've already imported to the current catalog) are indicated by a Managed folder icon (▣). Watched folders (on Windows only) have a Watched folder icon (▣). The viewing pane on the right displays thumbnail images of the contents of any managed folder selected in the Folders panel.

**2**   Press Ctrl+A / Command+A to select all the photos in the Media Browser; then, drag the selection to the Zoo folder in the Folders panel. In the Folders panel, the folder from which you just moved the photos has lost its Managed folder icon (🖼), while the Zoo folder has acquired one. You may need to make the Folders panel wider to see the complete folder names.

**3**   Right-click / Control-click the folder from which you moved the photos and choose Delete Folder from the context menu. Click Yes to confirm the deletion.

**4**   Right-click / Control-click the Zoo folder and choose Reveal In Explorer / Reveal In Finder from the context menu. A Windows Explorer / Finder window opens to display the contents of the Zoo folder. You can see that the files you moved in the Folders panel have actually been moved on your hard disk, and the folder you deleted no longer exists. Switch back to the Elements Organizer.

**5**   Right-click / Control-click the Zoo folder and choose New Folder from the context menu; a new sub-folder is created inside the Zoo folder. Type a name for the new folder—if you remember it, you can use the name of the folder you deleted in step 3.

**6**   Click the Zoo folder. Drag the thumbnails for the photos in the Zoo folder from the Media Browser into the new sub-folder. The Zoo folder has lost its Managed folder icon (🖼), while the new sub-folder has acquired one.

**7**   In the Folders panel, select the Monkey folder (inside the Zoo folder); then, click the Create Instant Album button at the right of the header above the thumb-nails. Dismiss any alerts. The new Monkey album appears in the Albums panel.

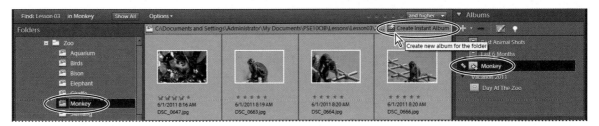

**8**   With the album Monkey selected in the in the Albums panel and click the Edit button (🖉) at the top of the panel. In the Album Details pane, disable the Backup/Sync option, and then click Done.

## Importing files in the Folder Location view

In the preceding exercise you discovered that you can move files and folders, rename, delete, or create a folder, and create an instant album—all without leaving the Folder Location view. The great advantage of organizing your folders and image files from within the Folder Location view, rather than in Windows Explorer or the Mac OS Finder, is that Photoshop Elements can easily keep track of all the files and folders included in your catalog—so you won't need to deal with missing file alerts.

In this exercise, you'll stay in the Folder Location view to add new files to your catalog, and then tag them.

▶ **Tip:** If you don't see the Penguin folder, you need to work through the exercise "Acquiring still frames from a video" on page 64.

1  In the Folders panel, scroll down if necessary, to find your My CIB Work folder. Click the plus sign (Windows) or arrow (Mac OS) beside the folder entry to expand it so that you can see the Penguin subfolder inside.

2  Drag the Penguin folder into the Zoo folder.

3  Right-click / Control-click the Penguin folder in its new location and choose Import To Elements Organizer from the context menu. Your video frames are imported to the CIB catalog. Click OK to dismiss any alerts.

4  Select all your penguin images, and then drag the Lesson 03 tag from the Keyword Tags panel to any of the selected thumbnails. Keep the photos selected.

5  In the Keyword Tags panel, click the Create New button (➕) and choose New Keyword Tag from the menu.

6  In the Create Keyword Tag dialog box, choose Imported Keyword Tags as the category, and then type **Penguin** for the tag Name. Click OK.

7  Drag the selection of penguin pictures from the viewing pane onto the new tag in the Keyword Tags panel.

8  Click the Display button (▣) above the Task Pane and choose Thumbnail View from the menu. Click the Show All button in the Find bar.

## Viewing video files

In Photoshop Elements 10, you can play video files without ever leaving the Organizer. Simply double-click the video file in the Media Browser to open the new integrated playback window, where you can even apply keyword tags.
You can now also play videos in the Full Screen mode.

# Finding photos using details and metadata

Searching your catalog by metadata detail is useful when you want to narrow a search by applying multiple criteria. Some of the metadata that may be attached to an image file is generated automatically by your camera; some is added when you spend time organizing your catalog. Searchable metadata includes file attributes, keyword tags, ratings, albums, version sets, captions, notes, capture date, and a range of camera, lens, and exposure details—to mention just a few!

1  Choose Find > By Details (Metadata).

If you've completed the smart albums exercises, you're already familiar with setting up a multiple-criteria search. In fact, any metadata search you define can be saved as a new smart album by simply activating that option below the search rules.

To add a new criteria to your search, click the plus (+) button beside an existing rule; then, use the menus to specify a category and values. To remove a criteria, click the minus sign (-) beside the rule. Activate the appropriate option to find files that either match *any* of the criteria (rule *or* rule), or *all* of them (rule *and* rule).

2  Under Search Criteria, click the first menu and scroll down the list, noting the many categories available. Choose a criteria category and experiment with defining the rule by choosing values from the other menu or menus. Click the plus icon (+) to the right of your first rule and define several more criteria.

3  Click Cancel to dismiss the Find > By Details (Metadata) dialog box.

# Using a text search to find photos

You can quickly find the photos you want using a text-based search. Type a word in the Text Search box just above the left end of the Find bar, and the Organizer will display images that match the text across a wide range of criteria. Matches can include items such as author, captions, dates, filenames, keyword tags, metadata, notes, album names, album groups, and camera information; Photoshop Elements will look for the search term in *any* text that is associated with the file.

You can use a text search as a convenient shortcut—for example, type the name of a tag, rather than navigating to the Keyword Tags panel. The text search feature has been enhanced to make it even easier and quicker to use; the search box has been augmented with a dynamic list of existing tags. As soon as you type a letter, the search box displays a list of tags starting with that letter; as you type more text the list changes to offer tags that match whatever you type. Click the item you want in the list and the Media Browser displays only the images tagged with that keyword.

Text search also supports the operators **and**, **or**, and **not**, if they are preceded and followed by a space. For example, you could type **vacation and kids** to find only images with both words in their metadata, not just either one. Some words can be processed by Photoshop Elements as special instructions, not as specific search criteria. For example, you may want to search for a file tagged Birthday, but only among your video files. You can use the Media **Type** and **Video** keywords. So, you would type **Type: Video Tag: Birthday**. For a list of supported operators and special tags, please refer to Photoshop Elements Help.

## Hiding files

You've already learned how you can simplify the process of working with your growing catalog by creating stacks and version sets to help reduce clutter and repetition in the Media Browser.

Stacking related shots and grouping edited versions with their originals effectively reduces the number of images on view; you can choose the most interesting image in a stack or version set as the topmost and keep the other images tucked out of sight until you choose to work with them. However, in many cases it may be more effective to hide those images from view entirely.

Once you've settled on the best of a stack of similar photos, or of several edits in a version set, you can hide the other images from view so that they will no longer appear in search results to distract you when making selections, or need to be taken into consideration when applying commands.

Hiding a photo does not delete it from its folder on your hard disk, remove it from your catalog, or even from an album—you can un-hide it at any time if you start a new project where it might be useful or if you find that you could make use of a differently edited version.

1   In the Keyword Tags panel, activate the Find box beside the Penguin tag.

2   Ctrl-click / Command-click to select all your penguin video stills; then, choose Edit > Auto Smart Fix Selected Photos. Auto Smart Fix is applied to all of the images and each is automatically grouped in a separate version set with the edited version topmost.

3   With all of the new version sets selected, choose Edit > Version Set > Convert Version Set To Individual Items. There are now twice as many penguin images displayed in the Media Browser—the originals together with their edited copies.

4   Activate the option Show All Files in the Edit > Visibility menu.

5   Ctrl-click / Command-click to select all of the original, un-edited penguin photos, and then add any one of the edited versions to the selection. Choose Edit > Visibility > Mark As Hidden. The Hidden File icon appears in the lower left corner of all of the selected thumbnails.

6   Ctrl-click / Command-click to de-select the un-edited originals, leaving only the single edited version selected in the Media Browser. Choose Edit > Visibility > Mark As Visible. The selected photo loses its Hidden File icon.

7   Choose Edit > Visibility > Hide Hidden Files. The un-edited penguin pictures are removed from the Media Browser view.

8   Click the Show All button in the Find bar.

9   Choose Edit > Visibility > Show Only Hidden Files. Select all the hidden images and choose Edit > Delete Selected Items From Catalog. In the Confirm Deletion From Catalog dialog box, activate the option Also Delete Selected Items From The Hard Disk, and then click OK. Choose Edit > Visibility > Hide Hidden Files.

# Finding photos by visual similarity

In Lesson 2, we looked at the People Recognition feature and discovered how help-ful it can be in quickly organizing your catalog. In this section we'll look at another tool that harnesses the power of the same automatic image analysis software.

Photoshop Elements 10 introduces an improved visual search feature, with even more ways of finding similar photos to help manage your growing photo library.

**1** Click Show All, if it's visible, and then activate the Lesson 03 tag to isolate the images for this lesson. Drag the image DSC_0609.jpg to the Find bar.

● **Note:** The search results you see on screen may vary from those illustrated here, depending on your operating system.

The search returns images displayed in the Media Browser in descending order of visual similarity to the photo you dragged to the Find bar. A marker displaying the calculated percentage of visual similarity for each image appears in the bottom left corner of its thumbnail, and a slider appears at the Find bar for tweaking the search results. The optimum position for the slider will vary for each image searched.

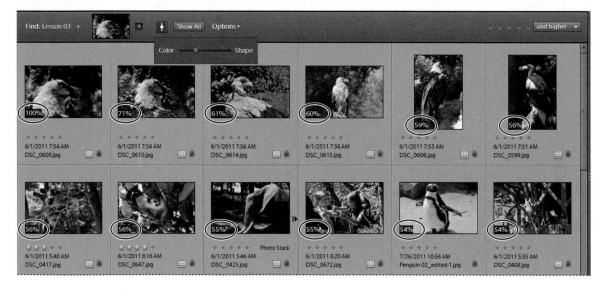

**2** Experiment with the slider. A move to the left weights the analysis towards similarities in color, texture, and pattern; moving the slider to the right returns images that share more in terms of shape, proportion, and composition.

**3** Right-click / Control-click the thumbnail in the Find bar and choose Remove From Search. Click another image in the Media browser to make it the object of a new search. Experiment with the Color–Shape slider, then repeat the process for several more images.

In some cases it may be helpful to add a second reference photo to your visual search. You can either drag a second image to the find bar, or click the plus sign (+) to the right

of the first reference photo in the Find bar and select a second image from the Media Browser. The search will look for a combination of visual attributes.

If you prefer, you can launch a visual similarity search with a menu command. Instead of dragging an image to the Find bar, select it in the Media Browser and choose Find > By Visual Searches > Search For Visually Similar Photos And Videos.

**4** Click the Show All button to clear this search; then isolate the Lesson 3 images.

## Finding objects in photos

In Photoshop Elements 10, you can search your photo library for a specific object.

**1** In the Media Browser, select the image DSC_0472.jpg, a photo of a Siamang.

**2** Choose Find > By Visual Searches > Search For Objects Within Photos.

**3** In the enlarged view, drag the bounding box to the ape's head. Use the handles at the corners of the bounding box to fit it neatly around the shape, and then click Search Object.

Once again, the results are ranked by similarity to the reference object. As for all visual searches, you can refine the results by tweaking the Color–Shape slider.

# Finding and removing duplicate photos

The last kind of visual search finds and groups duplicated or very similar images, and enables you to either stack them or delete them from your catalog.

**1** Click the Show All button to clear this search; then isolate the Lesson 3 images.

**2** Choose Find > By Visual Searches > Search For Duplicate Photos. Because you initiated the search without first making a selection of images Photoshop Elements searches for duplicates amongst all the photos currently displayed in the Media Browser.

▶ **Tip:** The Duplicate Photos search can be particularly helpful when you're dealing with photos captured with your camera's auto-bracketing or multi-burst modes.

**3** Work through the list of suggested groups of similar photos. For each group, either click the Stack button at the right of the group header to create a stack, remove selected photos from your catalog by clicking the button at the lower left, or do nothing. Don't forget that you can drag photos in and out of the Unique Photos pane to customize the groups. When you're done, click Done.

Congratulations—you've reached the end of Lesson 3! In this lesson, you've explored advanced options for importing photos from your camera and learned how to acquire images from a video or a PDF file. You've created version sets, stacks, and albums, and discovered more techniques for finding and managing your files.

Before you move on, take a moment to review what you've learned, and test your command of the concepts and techniques presented in this lesson by working through the following questions and answers.

# Review questions

**1** How can you automatically create and apply keyword tags to images while importing them from a digital camera or card reader?

**2** What does the Photoshop Elements De-Interlace filter do?

**3** What does the Auto Smart Fix command do?

**4** What are Version Sets and Stacks?

**5** What is the main difference between grouping files using shared keyword tags and grouping them in an album?

# Review answers

**1** In the Advanced Photo Downloader dialog box, choose Custom Groups (Advanced) from the Create Subfolder(s) menu. Next, choose an option including Custom Name from the Group Name menu, and then enter a Group Name in the Custom Name field on the separator bar above each group of thumbnails. Finally, activate the option Make 'Group Custom Name' A Tag before clicking Get Photos.

**2** The Photoshop Elements De-Interlace filter can improve the appearance of a still frame acquired from a video by removing the artifacts caused by the fact that a video picture consists of two interlaced half-pictures taken at slightly different times. The De-Interlace filter removes either the odd or even fields in a still image from video and replaces the discarded lines by duplication or interpolation from the remaining lines.

**3** The Auto Smart Fix command corrects the overall color balance and improves shadow and highlight detail, if necessary. The Auto Smart Fix command automatically groups the edited copy of the photo with the original in a version set.

**4** A version set groups an original photo and its edited versions. Stacks are used to group a set of similar photos, such as multiple shots of the same subject or photos taken using your camera's burst mode or auto-bracket feature. A version set can be nested inside a stack: if you edit a photo that's already in a stack, the photo and its edited copy are put in a version set that is nested inside the original stack.

**5** The main difference between grouping files in an album, rather than with a shared keyword tag, is that in an album you can rearrange the order of the files.

# 4 CREATING PROJECTS

## Lesson Overview

Photoshop Elements makes it simple to create stylish, professional-looking projects to showcase your photos. Choose from the preset themes and layouts—or create your own designs from scratch—as you put together a range of creations from greeting cards and Photo Books to animated slide shows and online albums.

Use your own images in personalized CD or DVD jackets and labels, calendars, collages, and digital flip-books. Combine images, text, animation and even music and narration, to produce unique multi-media creations.

Whether you're designing your own coffee table book, sharing your photos online, or creating personalized gifts for family and friends, Photoshop Elements will help unleash your creativity.

This lesson will familiarize you with the Create mode by stepping you through some basic techniques and simple projects:

- Using artwork from the Content library
- Creating a personalized greeting card
- Working with layers, layer styles, and effects
- Telling a story with a stylish Photo Book
- Fitting text to a project

 You'll probably need around two hours to complete this lesson.

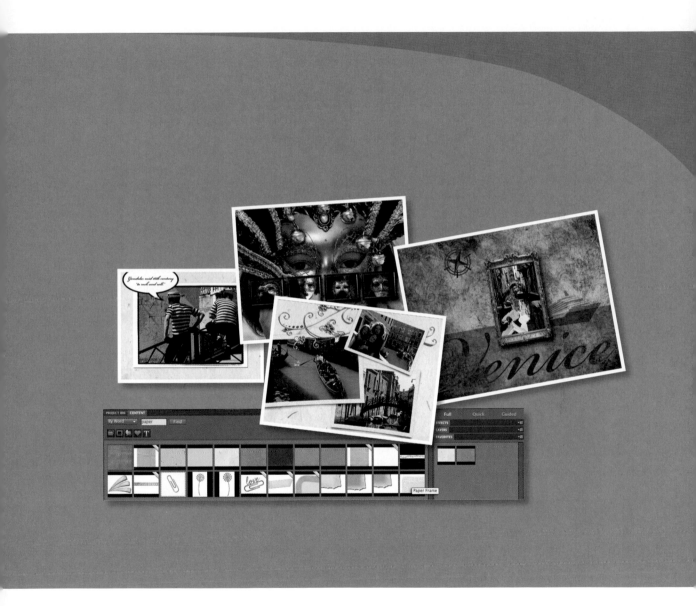

Photoshop elements offers a huge library of design themes, layout templates, and clip graphics that make it easy to produce eye-catching projects using your own photos. Show loved ones how much you care with stylish personalized greeting cards; preserve and share your precious memories in a sophisticated Photo Book or combine pictures and mementos to tell an evocative story in an artistic Photo Collage.

# Getting started

● **Note:** Before you start working on this lesson, make sure that you've installed the software on your computer from the application CD (see the Photoshop Elements 10 documentation) and that you have correctly copied the Lessons folder from the CD in the back of this book onto your computer's hard disk (see "Copying the Classroom in a Book files" on page 2). You should also have created a working catalog (see "Creating a new catalog" on page 8).

You can start by importing the sample images for this lesson to the CIB Catalog that you created at the beginning of Lesson 1.

1   Start Photoshop Elements and click Organize in the Welcome Screen. If the Backup/Synchronization dialog box appears, click Remind Me Later. You'll learn about this feature in Lesson 5.

2   Check the name of the active catalog in the lower left corner of the Organizer window. If your CIB Catalog is already loaded, you can skip step to step 3. If another catalog is currently loaded, choose File > Catalog, select your CIB Catalog in the Catalogs list, and then click Open.

3   Choose File > Get Photos And Video > From Files And Folders. In the Get Photos And Videos From Files And Folders dialog box, locate and select your Lesson04 folder. Disable the option Get Photos From Subfolders and all of the automatic processing options; then, click Get Media.

4   In the Import Attached Keyword Tags dialog box, select the Lesson 04 keyword, and then click OK. Click OK to close any other alert dialog box.

Thumbnails of the images you've just imported appear in the Media Browser and the Lesson 04 tag has been listed in the category Imported Keyword Tags. If you've already completed Lessons 1, 2, and 3, the Imported Keyword Tags category has become a little too cluttered to be useful. You can take this opportunity to do some housekeeping before the lesson begins.

5   If necessary, collapse the Albums panel so that you can see as much of the content of the Keyword Tags panel as possible. In the Keyword Tags panel, collapse all but the Imported Keyword Tags category. Control-click / Command-click to select all the imported keywords other than the four numbered Lesson tags; then, drag the selected tags to the category Other.

## Exploring the artwork library

▶ **Tip:** By upgrading your basic Elements Membership to Plus, you can access an even wider range of templates, themes, and artwork, and fresh content will be delivered directly to your computer regularly.

Photoshop Elements makes it quick and easy to create distinctive photo projects by providing an extensive collection of themes, backgrounds, frames, text styles, clip-art shapes and graphics in the Content library. Although this artwork is also available in the Create mode, we'll start by exploring the Content panel.

1   In the Organizer, choose Edit > Deselect to make sure you have no images selected in the Media Browser. Click the arrow on the Fix tab above the Task Pane and choose Full Photo Edit from the menu.

2   In Full Edit mode, choose Window > Reset Panels or click the Reset Panels button (⬛) at the top of the workspace. By default, the Effects, Content, and Layers panels are open in the Panel Bin. Choose Window > Favorites to open the Favorites panel as well.

**3** Drag the Content panel by its name tab out of the Panels Bin, onto the header of the Project Bin. When you see a blue highlight around the Project Bin, release the mouse button. Enlarge the Content panel by dragging the top border of its header bar upwards. In the Panels Bin, collapse the Layers and Effects panels by double-clicking their headers. The Favorites panel expands to fill the Panels Bin.

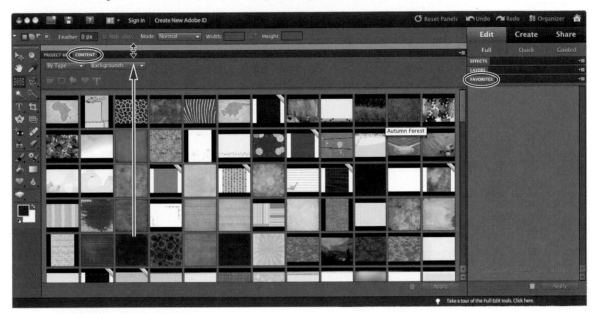

What you see displayed in the Content panel depends on the options set with the sorting menus and filter buttons above the sample swatches.

**4** In the Content panel, By Type is selected in the sorting menu at the upper left of the panel. With this setting, the contents of the library are sorted by functional category. The second sorting menu, to the right, lists the categories Backgrounds, Frames, Graphics, Shapes, Text, and Show All. Choose each option in turn and scroll down the Content panel see the artwork available.

● **Note:** Swatches that are marked with a gold band are accessible to Plus members only.

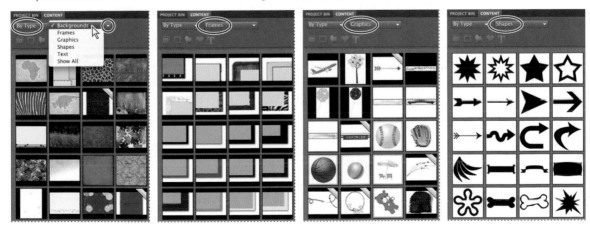

▶ **Tip:** To see the name of an artwork item displayed in a tooltip, hold the pointer over the swatch for a moment. Use the same method to see the names of the content filter buttons.

**5** Choose By Word from the sorting menu; then, type **paper** in the search box and click Find. Make sure that all of the filter buttons below the sorting menu are activated, as shown in the illustration below. Drag the fifth swatch—the background "Handmade Paper 03"—into the Favorites panel and release the mouse button when you see a blue line highlighting the panel. Add the background "Handmade Paper 04" and the frame "Paper Frame" to the Favorites panel. You'll use these items later in this lesson.

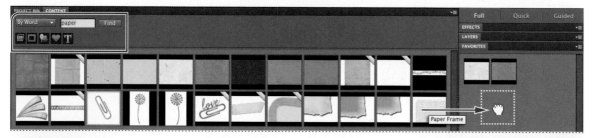

**6** Swipe over the word "paper" in the search box and type **travel**. Click to disable the Backgrounds, Frames, Shapes, and Text Effects filters below the sorting menu, leaving only the Graphics filter active. Click Find. Drag the items "Compass 02" and "Cruise Ship" into the Favorites panel.

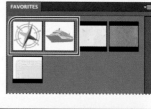

**7** Activate the Backgrounds and Frames filters once more. From the sorting menu, choose By Color; then choose Black from the colors menu. Add the background "Black Folded Paper" and also the frame "Basic Black 40px" to your collection in the Favorites panel.

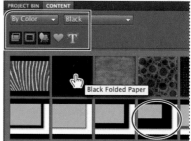

**8** From the sorting menu, choose By Style and select Vintage from the styles menu. Collect the background "Blue Swirly" and the frames "Gold Frame 1," "Gold Frame Ornate," "Gold Frame Round 2," and "Old Black & Gold Frame." Disable the Backgrounds and Frames filters, leaving only the Graphics filter active. Choose Decorative from the styles menu; then, add "Brass Leaves" and "Silver Flower Spray" to your favorites.

As you've seen, the Content library includes a great many backgrounds, frames, graphics, shapes and text styles. At first, the number of choices may seem a little overwhelming, but a little practice with the sorting and filtering controls will make it quick and easy to locate the artwork items you need. The search and filter functions in the Content panel are not available on the Artwork tab in Create mode, so it can save you time to do a little advance planning and assemble the items you want for a project while you're in Full Edit mode, using the Content and Favorites panels in tandem as you've just done.

You can also use the Favorites panel to store Filters and Layer Styles from the Effects panel. To complete this exercise, you can add a few effects that you'll use to liven up and refine your photo projects.

9  Expand the Effects panel by clicking its name tab. Activate the Layer Styles filter at the top of the panel and choose Bevels from the categories menu. Drag the Simple Sharp Inner bevel style swatch to the Favorites panel. Change the Layer Styles category to Drop Shadows and add both the "High" and "Low" drop shadow swatches.

10  Click the Reset Panels button (⟳) at the top of the workspace; then, click the Organizer button (⊞) at the top right to return to the Organizer.

# Creating a greeting card

Personalized greeting cards based on your own photos make a great way to show friends and family how much you care—a really attractive card can spend months on a loved one's mantelpiece and may even be framed and displayed with pride.

You can include one or more images on each page of a greeting card and either print it on your home printer, order prints online, or save it to your hard disk, and then send it via e-mail. Once you've begun your greeting card, the Create tab offers controls for navigating between pages, and easy access to layout templates, artwork, and effects to help you to create sophisticated designs quickly and easily.

## Choosing a size and theme

For this project you'll use two photos to create a folded invitation card.

1  In the Organizer, click Show All in the Find bar above the Media Browser. In the Keyword Tags panel, expand the Imported Keyword Tags category, and click the find box beside the Lesson 04 tag to isolate the images for this lesson.

2  In the Media Browser, select the images card_1.jpg and card_2.jpg.

3  Click the Create tab above the Task Pane. On the Create tab, click the Greeting Card button. The Greeting Card window opens.

▶ **Tip:** If you don't see file names displayed below the thumbnail images in the Media Browser, ensure that the Details check box in the bar above the browser pane is activated and choose View > Show File Names.

**4** At the left, the Sizes pane lists size options for various online services; choose the third listing under Shutterfly: 7.00 x 5.00 inches (Folded, Landscape). From the Themes pane, choose Colorful. You can use a theme "as is", or as a design template that you can customize. The preview shows that this theme will make a good starting-point for our design, with a front page layout occupied by a single image. Make sure Autofill With Selected Images is activated; then, click OK.

● **Note:** Although the Sizes pane lists options compatible with various online services, any greeting card can also be printed from your home printer. The choice of online services depends on your location and your operating system.

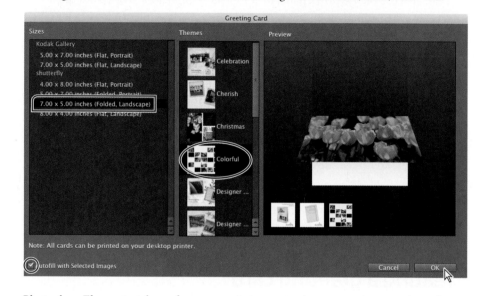

Photoshop Elements takes a few moments to create the appropriate number of pages, place the selected images in the template, and generate a preview. The card design appears in the Edit window and the Create tab presents the Pages panel, where you can click the thumbnails to navigate between the pages in your layout. A thumbnail for your as-yet-untitled photo project appears in the Project Bin.

## Positioning photos and replacing frames

You can start to customise your project by tweaking the layout for both pages.

**1** Right-click / Control-click the cover page photo in the Edit window and choose Position Photo In Frame from the context menu. A control bar appears at the upper left of the image, with a scaling slider and buttons to re-orient the image or replace it with another.

**2** Drag the scaling slider to the left, reducing the size of the photo until it is just a little wider than the page. Keep an eye on the Width (W) and Height (H) values in the tool options bar above the Edit window; we reduced the photo to 72.7%. Use the arrow keys on your keyboard, or simply drag the image to position it as shown in the illustration at the right. When you're satisfied with the size and position of the photo, click the green check mark at the right of the control bar to commit the changes you've made.

**3** In the Pages panel on the Create tab, select the Inside layout. Click inside either of the empty image place-holders to select it, taking care not to click too close to the instruction text. Shift-click the other empty frame to add it to the selection; then, press Backspace / Delete on your keyboard. Click Yes to confirm the deletion, and then delete both text frames in the lower part of the layout.

**4** Right-click / Control-click the occupied image frame and choose Fit Frame To Photo from the context menu. Drag the handle at the lower right of the bounding box to scale the photo to about 120%. You don't need to use the Shift key; the proportions are constrained by default. Drag the photo a little to the right to centre it horizontally on the page. When you're satisfied with the result, click the green check mark at the lower right of the image to commit the changes.

**5** Click Artwork at the top of the Create tab. The thumbnail menus present a subset of the artwork from the Content library, with choices most likely to be appropriate for the theme you selected. Collapse the Backgrounds category, and then scroll down in the frames menu to locate the "Groovy" frame.

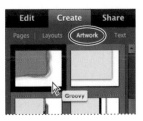

**6** With the photo still selected in the Inside layout, either drag the "Groovy" frame swatch from the Artwork panel and drop it directly onto the image, or simply double-click the swatch in the Artwork menu.

## Replacing the background image

Each photo project theme consists of a different preset combination of background artwork, image frame, graphics, layer effects and text styles. In some cases you may be happy with the un-edited result once your image has been placed in the layout but in other instances you may wish to treat the theme as a starting point or template and go on to customize the design.

All the design elements can be moved, replaced, or deleted. Images (with or without frames) can also be duplicated, which is one way to add more photos to the layout if you wish.

**1** Click the Switch To Advanced Mode button at the left below the Edit pane.

There are two major changes in the workspace: the Layers panel has opened below the Create tab, and the Artwork menu now contains all of the backgrounds, frames, and graphics from the Content library, rather than a limited set. Note, however, that the sort and filter functions you used in the Content panel in Full Edit mode are not available on the Artwork tab.

**2** Hide the Project Bin by double-clicking its header. Drag the upper edge of the Layers panel's header bar upwards as far as it will go. You can see that at this point this page is made up of four layers. Items on higher layers appear in front of the contents of lower layers.

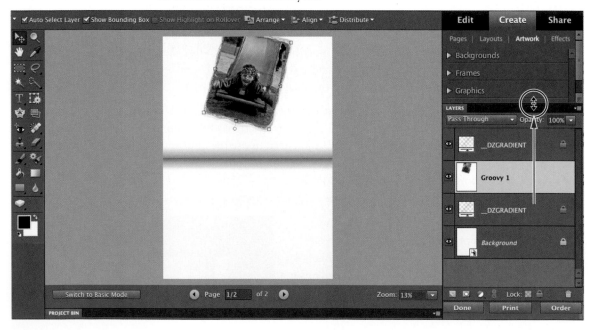

The Layers panel displays a separate layer for each element in the layout.

Starting from the bottom, the Background layer contains background art from the Content library, marked with a Smart Object icon in the lower right corner. You can ignore the locked _DZGRADIENT layers—these non-printing layers contain the shading between facing pages for on screen viewing. Above the Background in the stacking order is the layer with the currently selected framed photo.

3 Click to activate the Artwork tab. Scroll down a little in the Backgrounds menu to Locate the background "Balloons." Either double-click the Balloons background swatch, or drag it onto the background in the Edit window, keeping an eye on what happens in the Layers panel, as well as the preview.

Photoshop elements automatically replaces the old background with your new choice, despite the fact that the background layer was not selected. Background artwork can be scaled, rotated, and moved—but for the purposes of this exercise we'll accept the default placement.

## Adding graphics from the Content library

You can use clip-art items from the Content library to create atmosphere, to add dimension, movement, or humour to a design, or to suggest associations that will link your images with other elements in the layout in a way that tells a story.

1 Scroll through the Graphics category on the Artwork tab to locate the red balloon (Balloon 07). Drag the swatch onto the lower half of the Inside layout.

2 Drag the graphic to position it on the page, and use the bounding box handles to scale it as shown in the illustration. When you're satisfied with the placement of the item, click the Commit button (✓) to commit the changes.

> **Note:** A Smart Object is resolution independent; it can be scaled or rotated repeatedly without any degradation of the image. For each transformation, the image data is re-drawn from a source file that remains in its original state.

> **Tip:** When the Move tool is active, you can use the arrow keys on your keyboard to move the project elements in small steps instead of dragging them.

## Adding text to a layout

With the Type tools accessible in the Advanced Mode, you can place editable type anywhere in your layout in several different ways. Photoshop Elements includes several variants of the Type tool. We'll start with the default variant.

1 In the toolbox, select the Horizontal Type tool (**T**).

2 Set up the tool options bar as shown in the illustration below. Choose Comic Sans MS from the Font Family menu and Bold from the Font Style menu. In the Font Size text box, type **30** pt and then press Enter / Return on your keyboard. Choose Center Text (■) from the paragraph alignment options. Click the color swatch to open the color picker.

3 Move the pointer over the preview in the edit window and sample the light blue of the balloon at the lower right. Click OK.

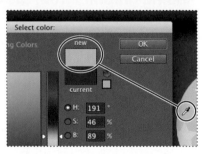

► **Tip:** Don't press the Enter or Return keys on the main part of your keyboard to accept text changes. When you have active text in your file, these keys add a line break in the text. Click the Commit button in the tool options bar to accept the text or press the Enter key in the numeric keypad section of your keyboard.

4 Click to place the type insertion cursor a little above the center of the red balloon. Type **Saturday**, press Enter / Return on your keyboard, and then type **May 15th 2pm**. Press Enter / Return again; then, type **at City Park**. Click the Commit button (✔) in the tool options bar to commit the text.

5 Select the Move tool (▶⊕) in the toolbox; then, center the text on the red balloon.

6 Select the Type tool again and click the color swatch in the tool options bar. Sample the yellow of the balloon at the upper left. Change the font size to 44 pt. Click between the framed image and the central fold of the card layout and type **Don't miss the fun!**. Click the green Commit button in the tool options bar to commit the text; then, use the Move tool to adjust its placement as necessary.

In the Layers panel the design now has two more layers: one for each text message. Most of the space on the text layers is transparent, so that only the text itself interrupts your view of the layers below.

Whenever you use the Type tool, Photoshop Elements automatically creates a new text layer in your image or layout. The type you enter remains active on the text layer, just like type in a word processing document—you can return to edit its content, scale it, reposition it, or change its color at any time.

## Warping text

It's easy to stretch and skew text into unusual shapes using the Photoshop Elements Warp Text effects; the hard part is to avoid *over*using them!

**1**   Make sure the Type tool is active, and then click anywhere on the text "Don't miss the fun!" in the Edit window. It's not necessary to highlight the text because warp effects are automatically applied to the entire text layer.

**2**   In the tool options bar, click the Create Warped Text button ( ) to open the Warp Text dialog box. Choose the Arc effect from the Style menu, making sure the Horizontal variant is activated.

**3**   The Warp Text dialog offers several controls for changing the way the effect is applied. Set the Bend value to **–50**%, reversing the direction of the Arc curve. Set the Horizontal Distortion to **+50**%, and then click OK to close the Warp Text dialog box. In the Layers panel, the text layer thumbnail now displays a Warped Text icon.

**4**   The text layer is still editable. To check this out, first click the text layer; then, swipe to select the D with the Type tool and type a lower-case **d** over it.

**5**   With the Type tool, click anywhere on the text in the red balloon, and then, click the Create Warped Text button in the tool options bar. This time, choose the Bulge effect from the warp Style menu. Make sure the Horizontal variant is activated, and then set the Bend value to +60% and click OK.

**6** Select the Move tool and hold it just outside any of the bounding box handles. Drag with the curved double-arrow cursor to rotate the bulged text slightly in a clockwise direction. Confirm the change. If necessary, use the arrow keys on your keyboard to center the text on the balloon.

## Using layers and layer styles to refine a project

Now that all the elements of this page design are in place, you can add a little polish to your project with a few quick touches from the Effects menu.

**1** In the Layers panel, make sure the layer "Saturday..." is selected.

**2** Choose Window > Favorites to open the Favorites panel. If the Favorites panel opens in an inconvenient position, drag it into the Panels Bin by its header bar or position it where it won't obstruct your view of the card or the Layers panel. In the Favorites panel, double-click the Low drop shadow swatch, and then the Simple Sharp Inner bevel swatch.

**3** In the Layers panel, right-click / Control-click the layer "Saturday..." and choose Copy Layer Style from the context menu. Right-click / Control-click the layer "don't miss the fun!" and choose Paste Layer Style.

**4** Finally, select the layer "Balloon 07" in the Layers panel; then double-click the High drop shadow swatch n the Favorites panel. Repeat this process for the layer Groovy 1.

▶ **Tip:** In the Layers panel, there are now four layers marked with the *fx* icon, indicating that these layers have styles applied. A layer style can be edited by double-clicking the *fx* icon and adjusting the controls in the Style Settings dialog box.

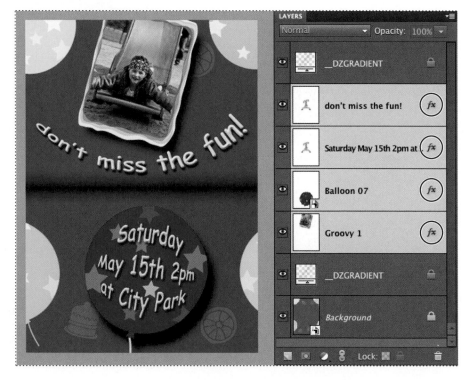

## Fitting text to an image

Photoshop Elements 10 introduces three new variants of the Text tool: the Text On Selection tool, the Text On Shape tool, and the Text On Custom Path tool.

These new tools all enable you to shape your text creatively so that it fits with image elements in your photo. In this exercise, you'll use the Text On Selection tool to fit a playful message to the photo on the front page of the card layout.

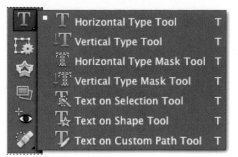

1  With the Horizontal Type tool, click in the yellow text, and then click the Commit button in the tool options bar. This ensures that the Text tool is "loaded" with our bright yellow. Choose Select > Deselect Layers. In the tool options bar, change the font size to 30 pt.

2  In the Layers panel, right-click / Control-click the layer "don't miss the fun!" and choose Copy Layer Style from the context menu. In the Pages preview on the Create tab, click the Front page thumbnail.

Like all images placed in a photo project layout, our front page photo is contained in a frame; the frame and photo are grouped together on a layer that takes the name of the frame preset. In this particular case, the frame preset is effectively an *invisible* frame, named "No Frame." Before you can work in this image with a selection tool, you'll need to partially ungroup the photo and its invisible container.

3  In the Layers panel, right-click / Control-click the layer "No Frame 1" and choose Simplify Layer from the context menu.

4  Right-click / Control-click the Text tool in the toolbar and choose Text On Selection from the tool variants menu. Over the Edit window, the pointer changes to a selection cursor. Click and drag inside the red panel on the near side of the slide.

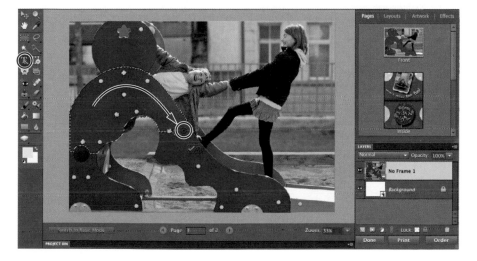

▶ **Tip:** If you make a mistake, hold down the Alt / Option key as you paint to subtract from the selection, or click the Cancel button at the lower right of the selection and start again.

**5**  When you're happy with your selection, drag the Offset slider in the tool options bar all the way to the left to contract the selection a little, then click the green Commit button in the Edit window.

**6**  Move the pointer over the upper edge of the selection; the pointer changes to a text insertion cursor. Click the edge of the selection at a point about half-way down the slide, and then type **Please come to Lilly's party!**. Click the green Commit button in the tool options bar to commit the text.

**7**  Select the Move tool and drag the text, together with its selection path, slightly downwards and to the left, so that it sits within the red panel rather than along its top edge. Activate the Text On Selection tool again and click between the "t" and the "o" in the word "to," where you can see a small square on the text path marking your original insertion point.

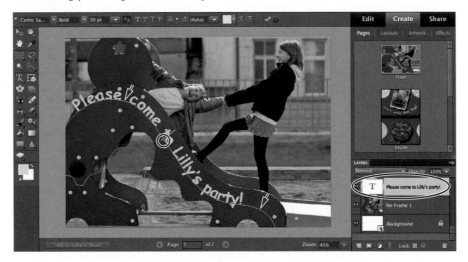

**8**  Hold down the Control / Command key, while holding the pointer over the text insertion point; the text cursor changes to show two black arrows. Drag the text backwards and forwards a little along the text path, taking care to keep the pointer above the path. When you're happy with your placement, click the Commit button in the tool options bar.

**9** In the Layers panel, right-click / Control-click the text layer and choose Paste Layer Style from the context menu. In the menu bar, choose Layer > Deselect Layers. Congratulations; you've completed your first photo project!

**10** Choose File > Save. Name the file **Invitation** and save it to your PSE10CIB > Lessons > My CIB Work folder in Photo Project Format. Activate the option Include In The Elements Organizer, and then click Save. Choose File > Close, click the Reset Panels button (  ), and then return to the Organizer.

▶ **Tip:** If you can't find the My CIB Work folder, refer to "Creating a work folder" on page 3.

## Text on a path and text on a shape

Refer to Photoshop Elements Help for detailed instructions on using the other two new Text Tool variants, the Text On Custom Path tool and the Text On Shape tool, and then enjoy experimenting with fun, creative ways to add atmosphere, movement, and humour to your images, projects, and presentations.

# About type

A font is a collection of characters—letters, numerals, punctuation marks, and symbols—in a particular typeface, which share design characteristics such as size, weight, and style. A typeface family is a collection of similar fonts designed to be used together. One example is the Myriad typeface family, which is a collection of fonts in a number of styles including Regular, Bold, Italic, Condensed and other variations. Other typeface families might consist of different font style variations.

---

Font family
## Myriad Pro
Font style
## Regular, **Bold**, *Italic*, Condensed

## Times New Roman

Regular, **Bold**, *Italic*

---

Traditionally, font sizes are measured in points, but can also be specified in millimeters or inches, as with large lettering on signs, for example. The most common formats for computer fonts are Type 1 PostScript, TrueType, and OpenType.

Each font conveys a feeling or mood. Some are playful or amusing, some are serious and businesslike, while others might convey an impression of elegance and sophistication. To get a feel for which typeface best suits your project, it's a good idea to try out several fonts. One way to find out more about type is to go to www.adobe.com/type. Adobe Type offers more than 2,200 fonts from the world's leading type designers, which you can browse by categories such as style, use, theme, classification, and designer. This will make it easy to find the perfect font for any assignment. You can even type in your sample copy and compare different fonts.

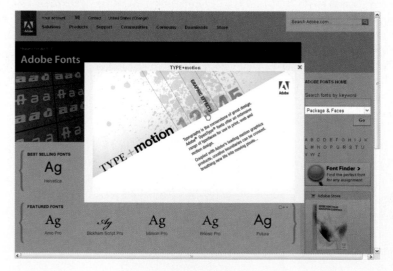

# Producing a Photo Book

A Photo Book is a multi-page digital project that offers an attractive way to present and share your memories and makes the perfect personalized gift for a loved one.

You can either have your completed Photo Book commercially printed and bound by ordering through an online service—great for a sophisticated gift—or print it yourself on your home printer. However, unless you have high-quality, double-sided paper in a large enough size you may have to make some design compromises and possibly scale your layout in the printer dialog box to fit standard paper sizes.

1   Check that you still have the images for this lesson isolated in the Organizer. If you do, you can skip this step; if not, click Show All (if it's visible) in the Find bar above the Media Browser. In the Keyword Tags panel, activate the find box beside the Lesson 04 tag.

2   Above the Media Browser and the Find bar, set the sorting order to Date (Oldest First). In the Media Browser, select the image photobook_01.jpg; then Shift-click the image photobook_26.jpg to select all the images for this exercise.

▶ **Tip:** If you don't see file names displayed below the thumbnail images in the Media Browser, ensure that the Details check box in the bar above the browser pane is activated and choose View > Show File Names.

3   Click the Create tab above the Task pane; then, click the Photo Book button. The Photo Book window opens.

4   At the left, the Sizes pane lists size options for various online printing services. Under Print Locally, choose 11.00 x 8.50 inches. From the Themes menu, choose the Colorful template. At the bottom of the dialog box, set the number of pages for the photo book to 8. For the purposes of this exercise, disable the option Autofill With Selected Images; then, click OK.

**Note:** Although the Sizes pane lists options compatible with various online services, any of the photo book formats can also be printed from your home printer.

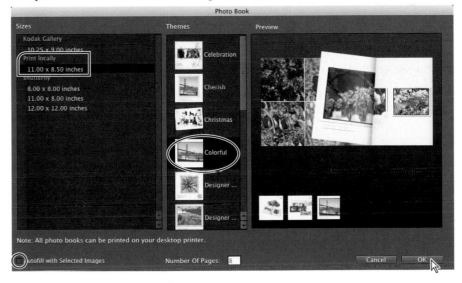

You'll see a progress bar while Photoshop Elements creates pages and generates previews, and then the title page of the photo book appears in the Edit window.

The Pages panel on the Create tab displays thumbnail previews for the title page and four two-page spreads.

5  Thumbnails of the photos you selected in the Media Browser are displayed in the Project Bin. To see more of the images in the Project Bin, drag the top edge of the header bar upwards to increase the depth of the panel, or use the scroll bar.

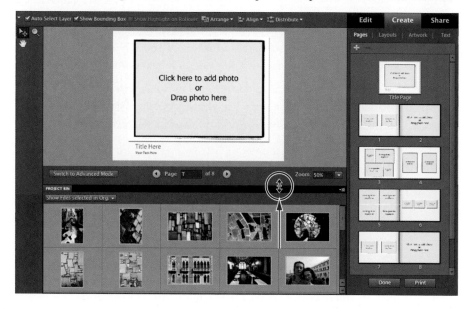

## Changing page layouts

When Photoshop Elements generates Photo Book pages automatically, it applies a different layout to each page randomly, varying the number, size, and positioning of photos so that every spread has a unique design. You can see this reflected in the previews in the Pages panel.

You could, of course, accept the automatic layout as is, but for the purposes of this project, we'll customise the design page by page. To save time in this exercise, we've prepared a tweaked layout designed to fit the lesson images, leaving it up to you to finalize the page layout for the final spread.

▶ **Tip:** On Windows, you may see an alert warning that some text layers in the file might need to be updated. In the alert dialog box, activate the option Don't Show Again, and then click Update.

1  At the bottom of the Create tab, click Done, and then click Don't Save to discard the default layout. Choose File > Open. Navigate to and open your Lesson04 folder; then, select the file Venice_Book.pse and click Open. On Windows, select the nested file Venice_Book.pse and click Open.

2  In the Pages panel, click to select the last two-page spread, pages 7 and 8.

3  Click Layouts at the top of the Create tab. In the first category, Different Layouts, locate the page design "4 Up Photobook Landscape" and drag it onto the left page of the Page 7/8 spread in the Edit window.

**4** Scroll down the Layouts menu to the One Photo category. Locate the Photobook Landscape template at the left on the bottom row in this category, and drag the layout swatch to the right page of the spread in the Edit window.

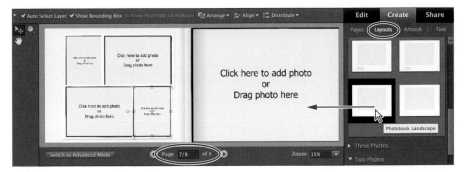

**5** Inspect the completed base layout in the Pages panel. Including the cover page, the design now includes placeholders for all 26 of the lesson photos. Three of the place-holder frames may be hard to spot as they occupy whole pages (pages 2, 4, and 5) and have smaller frames arranged on top of them.

**6** Click to select the Title Page at the top of the Pages preview.

## Rearranging the order of images in a project

When you create a photo book—or any other photo project—and have Photoshop Elements place your photos automatically, the images are arranged in the layout template in the order in which they appear in the Project Bin.

For a multiple-page project such as a photo book, you can save a lot of time and effort by arranging your photos before you begin. An easy way to do this is to shuffle your images in the Project Bin in the Editor.

**1** Right-click / Control-click any of the thumbnails in the Project Bin and choose Show Filenames from the context menu.

**2** Drag the image photobook_05.jpg to a new position to the left of the image photobook_02.jpg, so that it becomes the second image in the Project Bin.

▶ **Tip:** If you don't see thumbnails of the lesson images in the Project Bin, choose Show Files Selected In Organizer from the menu just below the Project Bin's name tab.

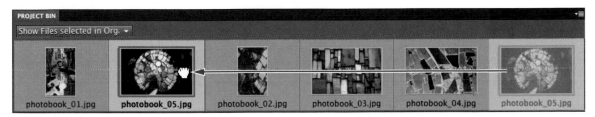

It's that easy! You can move multiple selections of images in the same way. If you find you can't drag a thumbnail to a new position, you probably have all of the images in the Project Bin selected.

**3** Right-click / Control-click the image photobook_05.jpg and choose Auto Fill With Project Bin Photos. Wait while Photoshop Elements places the images and regenerates previews.

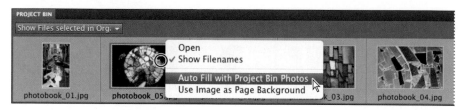

**4** Hide the Project Bin by double-clicking its header bar.

## Working with backgrounds

You can change the background, like any other element in a preset theme template, as easily as you changed the page layout. You can move, rotate, scale, or even delete the preset background, just as you can with a frame or clip-art graphic.

Unlike a framed photo however, you can't simply select and drag the background image—being the basis for the file, the locked Background layer is a special case. The Background graphic is also a Smart Object, which means that for some operations, it will first need to be "simplified"—unlocked and converted to bit-mapped data—before it can be edited as can other layers.

**1** In the Pages panel, click the first two-page spread, pages 1 and 2. Click the Switch To Advanced Mode button, at the left below the Edit window. Choose Window > Favorites to open the Favorites panel. If the Favorites panel opens in an inconvenient position, drag it into the Panels Bin by its header bar or position it where it won't obstruct your view of the layout or the Layers panel.

**2** In the Favorites panel, double-click the swatch for the background Black Folded Paper. Watch as the Background layer in the Layers panel is updated.

The background image has been scaled to fit the width of the two-page spread, though the full-page image on page 2 is obscuring the right half.

We could make more of the sparse, subtle textural detail in this background by reducing it so that it covers only the area where it is needed. To move, scale, or rotate the background, you first need to "free" the Content library image on the Background layer, much as you need to temporarily ungroup a photo from its frame before you can move the image independently within the frame.

3   Right-click / Control-click the full-page image on the right page of the spread and choose Clear Frame from the context menu. You now have a clear view of the line where the inside edges of the facing pages meet.

4   Right-click / Control-click the background on the left page and choose Move Background. The Background layer becomes active in the Layers panel and a bounding box surrounds the graphic, though most if it is out of view; the image is larger than the two-page spread. Test this by dragging the background downwards. Click the Cancel button at the lower right of the bounding box.

5   In order to scale or rotate the background manually, you could drag the image until one of the control handles was visible, but in this case it will be more convenient to use the controls in the tool options bar. Type **50**% in the Width (W) text box; with the Constrain Proportions option activated, the Height (H) value is updated automatically. The background image is scaled by 50% from its center.

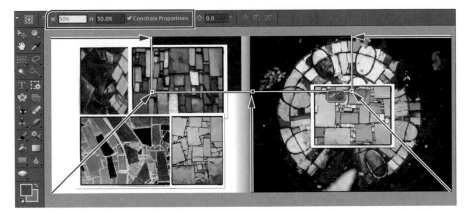

6   Drag the reduced background artwork and position it flush with the left edge of page 1. Move the image up and down until you're pleased with the placement of the detail, and then click the Commit button (✓) to commit the changes.

7   Without the background covering the entire spread, there is a thin margin of white showing around the large photo on the right page. Click the image; then, click once on any of the bounding box handles. Rather than drag the handles to scale the image and its containing frame, type **101**% in either the W ot H text box in the tool options bar and Commit the change.

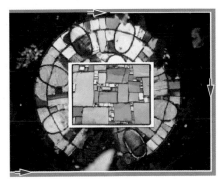

**8** Drag the Basic Black 40px frame swatch from the Favorites panel onto each of the five frames photos in the layout.

**9** In the Pages panel, click the third spread in the photo book: pages 5 and 6. Alternatively, navigate to the Page 5/6 spread using the blue right-arrow button below the Edit window preview.

## Working with photos and frames

The design theme you chose as a first step in creating your photo book places every photo in a default frame, but each theme's design differs. You already substituted frames with artwork from the Content library; in this exercise you'll learn how to manipulate a photo and its frame as a group, and how to modify a photo's position and orientation independently of its frame.

**1** You can start by replacing all seven frames in the spread. Drag the Old Black & Gold Frame swatch from the Favorites panel onto each of the four small images on the left page, and the Paper Frame swatch onto the three photos on the right.

**2** Double-click the Handmade Paper 04 swatch to replace the background; then, right-click / Control-click the full-page image on the left and choose Clear Frame from the context menu.

▶ **Tip:** When the Move tool is active, you can use the arrow keys on your keyboard to move a selected project element in small steps instead of dragging them with the mouse.

**3** To move a framed photo in the layout, simply drag it with the Move tool (🔼). Shift-click to select all four of the small images on the left page. Hold down the shift key to constrain the movement and drag the row of photos downwards to position them half-way between the girl's eyes and the mouth of her mask.

**4** Click the background to deselect the photos, and then re-select the one on the left. Hold down the Shift key as you drag the framed image about halfway to the left edge of the page. Move the photo on the right end of the row the same distance in the opposite direction. Select all four images; then, click Distribute in the tool options bar and choose Horizontal Centers from the menu.

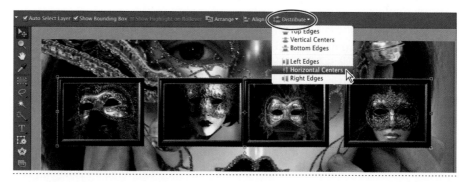

**5** Right-click / Control-click each of the three photos on the right page and choose Fit Frame To Photo from the context menu. The frames are re-sized so that their outside borders conform to the edge of the images. Click to select the image at the right, and then drag the handle at the lower right of the bounding box to enlarge the photo—together with its frame—until the right edge extends beyond the limits of the page. You don't need to use the Shift key; the proportions of the frame group are constrained by default. Click the Commit button.

**6** Drag or nudge the three tilted photos into a pleasing arrangement, scaling or rotating them as you wish. To rotate a framed photo manually, select the photo; then, move the pointer close to one of the corner handles, staying just outside the bounding box. When the curved double-arrow cursor appears, drag to rotate the image. Hold down the Shift key as you drag to constrain the rotation to 15° increments. Always click the Commit button (✔) to commit the changes.

▶ **Tip:** If your photos do not automatically fill their frames, right-click / Control-click each photo and choose Fit Frame To Photo, and then resize the frame and photo together using the handles on the bounding box. Alternatively, double-click the photo and resize it within its frame by using the slider, as discussed in "Adjusting a photo inside a frame" below.

**7** In the Pages panel, click the last spread in the photo book: pages 7 and 8.

## Adjusting a photo inside a frame

A photo frame and the image it surrounds occupy the same layer—even though the frame appears to be overlaid on the photo. In fact, by default the layer entry in the Layers panel even takes its name from the frame.

**1** You can start by replacing the background and the four smaller frames in the spread. Double-click the Handmade Paper 03 swatch to replace the background; then, drag the Basic Black 40px frame swatch from the Favorites panel onto each of the four images on the left page. You can keep the default frame for the large photo on the right page. Select both of the text frames below the lower left corner of the large image and press Backspace / Delete on your keyboard.

When you move, or scale or rotate a framed photo using the bounding box handles, the photo and frame are transformed together. To move or transform an image independently within its frame, you first need to right-click / Control-click the image and choose Position Photo In Frame from the context menu—or alternatively, isolate the image from its frame group by double-clicking the photo inside the frame with the Move tool (⊕).

Whichever of these actions you take to isolate the image, a control bar appears above the photo, with a scaling slider and buttons to re-orient the image or replace it with another.

2   Right-click / Control-click the image on the right page and choose Position Photo In Frame from the context menu. Hold down the Shift key to constrain the movement as you drag the image to the left within its frame, so that the gondolier on the right is no longer cut off by the border. Commit the change.

3   Use the Zoom tool to focus on the group of four photos on the left page. For each of these photos except the image at the lower right, right-click / Control-click the image and choose Position Photo In Frame. Use the scaling slider to show as much of each image as possible, without resizing the frames. Drag each photo within its frame to reveal the most interesting crop. Commit the changes. We'll deal with the image at the lower right in the next step.

4   You can rotate the last of the four photos within its frame to straighten the blue and white gondola poles. Right-click / Control-click the image and choose Position Photo In Frame. To rotate the photo inside its frame, move the pointer close to any bounding box handle; when the pointer becomes a curved double-arrow cursor, drag the handle in either direction. Scale and position the photo within its frame as you did with its three neighbors; then, commit the changes.

**5** Move the large photo on the right downwards to center it on the page. Double-click the Hand tool to see the entire spread.

**6** In the Pages panel, click the second spread in the photo book: pages 3 and 4.

## Refining your Photo Book layout using layers and effects

In this exercise you'll begin to polish your Photo Book design while you refresh some of the skills you've picked up in the course this lesson.

You'll start by customizing pages 3 and 4—the last un-treated spread—then, add some sophistication to the layout using a little layer magic.

**1** Double-click the Handmade Paper 03 swatch to replace the background; then, drag the Paper Frame swatch from the Favorites panel onto each of the three images on the left page. Drag the Gold Frame Ornate swatch from the Favorites panel onto the photo of an antique interior on the right page, and the Gold Frame Round 2 swatch onto the photo of the couple. Right-click / Control-click the large image on the right and choose Clear Frame from the context menu.

**2** Right-click / Control-click each of the three photos on the left page and choose Fit Frame To Photo from the context menu. Drag or nudge the three tilted photos to position them, and scale or rotate them as you wish. If you want to change the stacking order of a photo, right-click / Control-click the image and choose Bring To Front, Bring Forward, Send Backwards, or Send To Back from the context menu. Scale, move or rotate each photo within its frame as needed, referring to the previous exercises if you need to refresh your memory.

**3** For each of the two gold-framed photos, first make sure you are happy with scaling and placement; then, select the framed image, right-click / Control-click its layer in the Layers panel, and choose Simplify Layer. Without this step, it would not be possible to apply layer styles to these particular framing groups.

**4** Drag the High drop shadow swatch from the Favorites panel onto each of the simplified images. Double-click the *fx* icon on each of the simplified layers in the Layers panel to open the Style Settings dialog box where you can tweak the drop shadow effect. In both cases, reduce the Distance setting to 55px, and then click OK.

**5** Click to select the full-page image on the right of the spread. At the top of the Layers panel, use the slider to reduce the selected layer's opacity to 40%. Don't forget that this image can also be scaled, moved, or rotated within its image container frame, even though the frame graphic has been removed.

**6** Revisit the Page 5/6 spread and apply the High drop shadow effect to the four small photos on the left page, first simplifying the respective layers in the Layers panel, as you did in step 3, and then editing the effect as you did in step 4.

## Re-ordering the pages in a Photo Book

If you feel that a particular spread would look better placed at a different point in your photo book, it's very easy to change the page order.

**1** You can start by revisiting the Page 1/2 spread. Move, tilt and scale the upper right photo of the group on page 1 to break up the regular arrangement a little. Rotate and position the smaller image on page 2 to cover the out-of-focus foliage at the bottom of the full-page image.

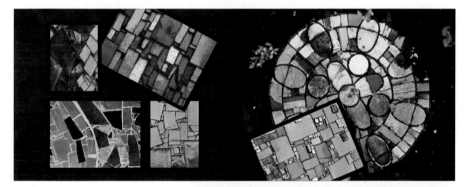

**2** In the Pages panel, drag the Page 1/2 spread downwards. Release the mouse button when you see an insertion line appear between the Page 3/4 and Page 5/6 spreads.

The Pages panel previews are regenerated and the pages are re-numbered. If the layout preview is slow refreshing, click each spread in the Pages panel in turn.

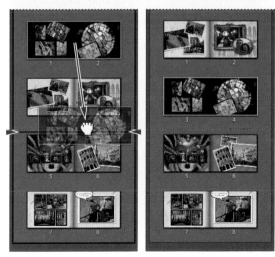

## Adding graphics to a project

The Photo Book is almost complete. Before adding text, you can liven up the design with a judicious use of graphics from the content library. You can start by creating some atmosphere on the title page: the front cover of your photo book.

1   Use the blue navigation buttons below the Edit pane, or click in the Pages preview, to move to the title page.

2   The preset text frames included in many of the page layout templates are very useful for simple titles, captioning, and notes, but you'll create your own text layers in the next exercise. Select both of the text frames below the lower left corner of the framed image and press Backspace / Delete on your keyboard; then, confirm the deletions.

3   Select the framed photo, and then click any of the bounding box handles. In the tool options bar, type **30**% in the Width (W) text box; with Constrain Proportions activated, the Height (H) value is updated automatically. Click the Commit button. While the framed photo is still selected, double-click the Gold Frame Ornate swatch in the Favorites panel. Right-click / Control-click the image and choose Fit Frame To Photo.

4   In the Favorites panel, double-click the Blue Swirly swatch to replace the background. In the Layers panel, right-click / Control click the Background layer and choose Duplicate Layer from the context menu. Click OK to accept the default name for the duplicate layer. At the top of the Layers panel, set the layer blending mode to Multiply, and the opacity to 50%.

5   In the Edit window, hold down the Shift key to constrain the movement as you drag the new layer downwards until it covers only the lower third of the page.

**6** Drag the swatch for the graphic Cruise Ship from the Favorites panel to the right side of the page. Drag the bounding box handles to scale the graphic up to around 200%. Choose Image > Rotate > Flip Layer Horizontal, and then drag the ship to position as shown in the illustration below. To move the graphic behind the framed photo, right-click / Control-click the cruise ship and choose Send Backward from the context menu.

**7** Drag the graphic Compass 02 from the Favorites panel to the upper left of the page, placing it as shown. At the top of the Layers panel, change the blending mode for the new layer to Difference, and set the layer's opacity to 70%. Change the opacity for the Cruise Ship layer to the same value.

## Placing text in a layout

In this exercise you'll create a title for the front page, and add a text message on the last page of the photo book.

**1** Select the Horizontal Type tool; then, choose Bickham Script Pro from the font menu in the tool options bar across the top of the Edit pane. Set the font style to Regular and type **460** pt in the font size text box. Ensure that the Anti-aliased button beside the font size text box is activated so that the edges of the letters are smoothed, and then choose Center Text from the text alignment menu. Click the small white triangle beside the text color swatch in the tool options bar—not the swatch itself—and sample Light Green Cyan for the text color.

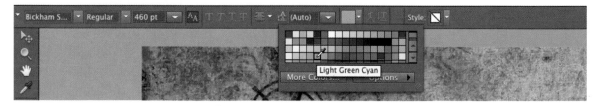

**2** Click below the photo and Type **Venice**, then commit the text. In the Layers panel, change the blending mode for the text layer to Difference and the layer opacity to 90%; then drag the text layer downwards to position it below (behind) the framed photo. Center the title horizontally. Select the compass and the photo together and drag them to the right to center the frame above the "n" in Venice. De-select the compass and move the frame up to the height of the dot on the "i."

**3** Finally, right-click / Control-click the text layer in the Layers panel and choose Simplify Layer from the context menu; then, apply the High drop shadow effect. In the Layers panel, double-click the *fx* icon on the text layer and reduce the drop shadow's Distance setting to 55px (*see the illustration on the next page*).

**4** In the Pages panel, click the last spread in the layout, and then click Artwork at the top of the Create tab. Scroll down the artwork menu to locate the graphic "Speech Bubble 03." Drag the bubble onto page 8; then, choose Image > Rotate > Flip Layer Horizontal. Use the handles on the bounding box to scale the shape and position it as shown in the illustration at the right.

**5** With the speech bubble graphic still selected, switch to the Type tool again. Keep the same font, but change the font size to 36 pt and the font style to Semibold. Click the white arrow beside the Leading text box—to the left of the text color swatch—and change the setting from Auto to 30 pt. Click in the center of the speech bubble and type **Gondola: mid 16th century**. Press Enter / Return, and then type **"to rock and roll."** (include the quote marks and period). Click the Confirm button and drag the text to adjust its position.

**6** Just two more flourishes and you're done! Use the navigation buttons below the Edit window preview, or the Pages panel, to move to the Page 1/2 spread. Drag the graphic Silver Flower Spray onto the left page. Rotate the artwork 90° counter-clockwise, and scale it to almost the width of the page. Move the flower spray so that it extends off the top edge of the page. In the Layers panel, move the layer Silver Flower Spray down in the order, so that it lies below (behind) at least one of the paper-framed photos, and above (in front of) at least one other.

7   Drag the Brass Leaves graphic onto the right page of the Page 5/6 spread *twice*. Scale and rotate each copy so that plenty of the leaves lie in areas not occupied by framed photos, particularly at the right side of the page. In the Layers panel, move both Brass Leaves layers below (behind) all of the Paper Frame layers. Change the blending mode for both Brass Leaves layers to Screen.

8   The Photo Book is complete; choose File > Save. By default photo projects are saved in Photo Project Format, a multi-page document format that preserves text and layers so that they can be edited later. You could also choose to save the project as a PDF file that can be shared as an e-mail attachment.

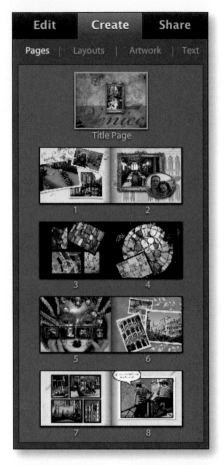

9   Choose File > Export Photobook. In the Export Photobook dialog box, choose
    PDF from the Format menu. Click Browse to specify your My CIB Work folder
    as the Save To Location; then, click OK. Choose File > Close.

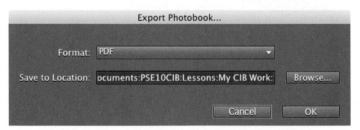

Congratulations! You've completed the lesson. You've learned about using the preset Theme and Layout templates, explored the Content library, and become familiar
with a variety of methods for locating the content you need. You've also learned
how to manipulate backgrounds, frames, and text, and the basics of working with
layers and applying layer styles. Before you move on to the next lesson, take a
moment to refresh your new skills by reading through the review on the next page.

# Review questions

1  How do you begin a new project such as a greeting card or Photo Book?

2  How do you scale and reposition a photo in a photo project?

3  How do you change the order of the pictures in a photo book?

4  How can you find the items you want amongst all the choices in the Content library?

5  What are layers, how do they work, and how do you work with them?


# Review answers

1  To create a project, select a project option on the Create tab in the Panel Bin by clicking one of the project buttons or choosing from the More Options menu. The Create tab presents page previews and navigation controls, and provides access to layout templates, backgrounds, frames, graphics and effects.

2  You can scale or rotate a framed photo by dragging the bounding box handles and move it by dragging. To scale, rotate, or move a photo within its frame you need to double-click the image to isolate it before using the same techniques, so that the changes affect the photo independently of its frame.

3  You can change the order of images in a photo book by dragging them to new positions in the Project Bin below the Edit pane.

4  You can sort and search the items in the Content library by using the menus and buttons at the top of the Content panel. You can sort the content by type, activity, mood, season, color, keywords and other attributes. Use the Favorites panel to assemble a collection of the items you're most likely to use, rather than looking through the entire library every time you want to add an artwork item to a project.

5  Layers are like transparent overlays on which you can paint or place photos, artwork, or text. Each element in a photo project occupies its own layer—the background is at the bottom and the other elements are overlaid in the order in which they are added to the project. Photos from the Project Bin are placed in the order of their capture date, so that the oldest is on the lowest layer. You can drag the thumbnails in the Project Bin to change that order. You work with layers in the Layers panel, where you can toggle their visibility, change their order and add layer styles and effects. The checkerboard grid areas in the layer thumbnails represent the transparent parts of the layers through which you can see the layers below.

# 5 PRINTING, SHARING, AND EXPORTING

## Lesson Overview

In previous lessons you've imported images from a range of sources, explored a variety of ways to organize and find your files, and created projects and presentations to showcase your photos.

In this lesson, you'll learn how you can output your images and creations to share them with family, friends, or the world at large:

- Printing at home and ordering prints online
- Fine-tuning the composition of an image in the print preview
- Sharing photos by e-mail and Photo Mail
- Backing up and synchronizing your files
- Synchronizing multiple computers
- Creating your own Online Album or Web Gallery
- Using an online sharing service
- Exporting images for use on the Web

 You'll probably need between one and two hours to complete this lesson.

Now that you've learned how to find your way around the Photoshop Elements workspace, how to organize and find the photos and other media in your growing collection, and how to create photo projects and digital presentations, you're ready to share your images and creations with the world as printed output, by e-mail, or online.

# Getting started

● **Note:** Before you start working on this lesson, make sure that you've installed the software on your computer from the application CD (see the Photoshop Elements 10 documentation) and that you have correctly copied the Lessons folder from the CD in the back of this book onto your computer's hard disk (see "Copying the Classroom in a Book files" on page 2). You should also have created a working catalog (see "Creating a new catalog" on page 8).

To start, you'll import the sample images for this lesson to the CIB Catalog that you created at the beginning of Lesson 1.

1   Start Photoshop Elements and click Organize in the Welcome Screen. If the Backup/Synchronization dialog box appears, click Remind Me Later. You'll learn about this feature later in this lesson.

2   Check the name of the active catalog in the lower left corner of the Organizer window. If your CIB Catalog is already loaded, you can skip step to step 3. If another catalog is currently loaded, choose File > Catalog, select your CIB Catalog in the Catalogs list, and then click Open.

3   Choose File > Get Photos And Video > From Files And Folders. In the Get Photos And Videos From Files And Folders dialog box, locate and select your Lesson05 folder. Activate the option Get Photos From Subfolders and disable the automatic processing options; then, click Get Media.

4   In the Import Attached Keyword Tags dialog box, click Select All, and then click OK. Click OK to close any other alert dialog box.

Thumbnails of the images you've just imported appear in the Media Browser.

# About printing

Whether you wish to use your home printer or order professional prints from an online service, Photoshop Elements offers a range of options for printing your photographs, as well as your Photo Projects such as photo books, greeting cards, and collages.

You can print your photos individually or in picture packages with one or more photos repeated at a variety of sizes on the same page, or preview a multiple selection of photos printed as thumbnail images arranged on a contact sheet.

## Printing a contact sheet

A contact sheet is a great way to print-preview a multiple selection of images by printing them at thumbnail size, arranged on a single page in a grid layout.

***To learn how to set up a contact sheet on Mac OS, skip ahead to page 126.***

### Printing a contact sheet on Windows

1   Click the Show All button in the Find bar above the Media Browser.

2   In the Keyword Tags panel, click to activate the Find box beside the keyword tag To Print (in the Imported Keyword Tags category), and then press Ctrl+A to select all the images tagged with the keyword To Print.

**3** Choose File > Print.

The Prints dialog box opens. The column on the left displays thumbnails of all the photos you selected for this print job. At center stage is the print preview.

▶ **Tip:** You can also open the Prints dialog box in contact sheet mode from the Create tab in the Task pane. Click Photo Prints, and then click the Print Contact Sheet button.

**4** Set up the options in the Prints dialog box as shown in the illustration below. Choose a printer from the Select Printer menu. For the purposes of this demonstration choose Letter from the Select Paper Size menu. From the Select Type Of Print menu, choose Contact Sheet, and then disable the Crop To Fit option.

▶ **Tip:** To remove a photo from the contact sheet, select its thumbnail in the image menu column and click the Remove button (▬) below the menu pane.

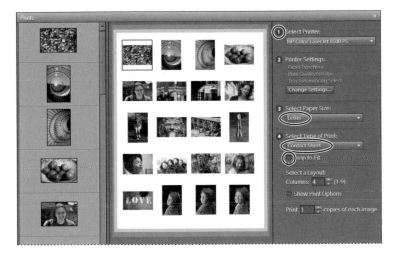

The contact sheet layout includes all the images in the thumbnail menu column at the left. With a four-column layout, all twenty photos fit neatly on a single page; the page count below the print preview indicates that you are viewing page 1 of 1.

**5**  Under Select A Layout, click the down arrow button beside the Columns number or type **3** in the text box: With only three columns the images are larger, but only nine photos will fit on a single page at this paper size; the page count below the print preview now indicates that you are viewing page 1 of 3. Use the Next Page and Previous page buttons on either side of the page count to navigate between the pages. Change the number of columns to nine, which is the maximum. You can see that a single letter page can accommodate many photos at this setting. Return the layout to four columns.

**6**  Click to select any photo in the print preview; then, use the slider below the print preview to zoom in. Drag the photo to reposition it within the frame of its image cell. Select another image, and then use the Rotate buttons to the left of the zoom slider to change the photo's orientation.

● **Note:** Some words in the text label may be truncated, depending on the page setup and column layout.

**7**  To print information extracted from the images' metadata below each photo on the contact sheet, first click to activate Show Print Options (just below the Columns setting), and then activate any or all of the Text Label options.

**8**  Click Print or Cancel and skip to "Printing a Picture Package" on the next page.

### Printing a contact sheet on Mac OS

On Mac OS, you need to initiate a contact sheet print from the Editor. For this demonstration, in which we'll use all the photos in a single folder; it will be quicker to open the Editor without first making a selection in the Organizer. If you want to print a contact sheet with photos drawn from multiple folders, you'll need to select the images in the Media Browser, and then switch to the Editor.

**1**  Press Shift+Command+A to deselect any images that are currently selected in the Media Browser. Click the small arrow on the Fix tab at the top of the Task Pane and choose Full Photo Edit from the menu.

▶ **Tip:** The alternative option in the Use menu under Source Images fills your contact sheet with whatever images are already open in the Editor. This is the setting you would use if you had made a selection of images in the Media Browser before switching to the Editor.

**2**  When the Editor opens choose File > Contact Sheet II. Set up the Contact Sheet dialog box as shown in the illustration at the right. Choose Folder from the Use menu under Source Images. Click Choose and locate your Lesson05 > Printing folder. Under Document, specify a size for your contact sheet. Under Thumbnails, specify the order in which the images will be placed. Activate Use Auto-Spacing; then, type **4** and **5** in the Columns and Rows text boxes respectively. Your Columns and Rows settings are reflected in the layout preview at the right. Disable Rotate For Best Fit, and activate Use Filename As Caption.

**3** Click OK, and then wait while Photoshop Elements places the image thumbnails.

In our example, all twenty images fit onto a single page. When the number of images selected for printing exceeds the capacity of a single page at the layout settings specified, Photoshop Elements will generate more pages to accommodate them.

**4** Select the contact sheet page(s) in the Project Bin. Choose File > Print if you wish to print the contact sheet. If not, choose File > Close; then, click Don't Save.

▶ **Tip:** You can also open the Contact Sheet dialog box from the Create tab in the Task pane. Click Photo Prints, and then click the Print Contact Sheet button. If you do this from the Organizer, you'll see a message asking if you'd like to open the Editor to initiate printing.

## Printing a Picture Package

A Picture Package layout lets you print a photo repeated at a choice of sizes on the same page, much as professional portrait studios do. You can choose from a variety of layout options and range of image sizes to customize your picture package print.

*To learn how to set up a picture package on Mac OS, skip ahead to page 129.*

### Printing a Picture Package on Windows

**1** Select two or more pictures in the Media Browser, and then choose File > Print.

**2** In the Prints dialog box, choose a printer from the Select Printer menu and a paper size from the Select Paper Size menu. Which layout options are available for your picture package depends on your choice of paper size; for the purposes of this exercise, choose Letter.

**3** Choose Picture Package from the Select Type Of Print menu. If a Printing Warning dialog box cautioning against enlarging pictures appears, click OK; for this exercise you'll print multiple images at smaller sizes.

**4** Choose a layout from the Select A Layout menu, and then activate the option Fill Page With First Photo. This will result in a page with a single photo repeated at a variety of sizes, according to the layout you have chosen. If you selected more than one photo in the Media browser, a separate Print Package page will be generated for each photo selected; you can see the print preview for each page by clicking the page navigation buttons below the preview pane.

▶ **Tip:** You can also open the Prints dialog box in picture package mode from the Create tab in the Task pane. Click Photo Prints, and then click the Print Picture Package button.

The layout options available for a Picture Package depend on the paper size specified in the Prints dialog box, the page setup, and the printer preferences. To change the paper size, choose from the Select Paper Size menu or click either the Page Setup button at the lower left of the Prints dialog box or the Change Settings button under Printer Settings. Depending on your printer, you may need to look for the paper size options in the Advanced preferences settings.

**5** Try a few of the options in the Select A Frame menu. For this demonstration, we chose Antique Rectangle 2. You can select only one style per picture package print; it will be applied to every picture in the layout.

**6** Toggle the Crop To Fit option and assess the result; the Crop To Fit option may fit the multiple images more closely to the layout to better fill the printable area, especially when your photo is of non-standard proportions.

● **Note:** The images in a Picture Package layout are automatically oriented to make the best use of the printable paper area for the layout you have chosen. You cannot manually rotate the image cells (or *print wells*) in a picture package layout; however, you can still zoom or rotate each image within its print well using the zoom slider and orientation buttons below the preview. Drag any image in the picture package to adjust its position within its print well.

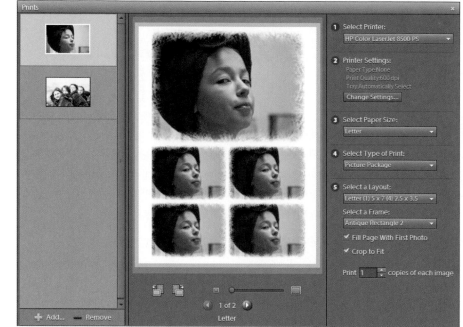

**7** Click the Add button (✚) below the photo menu at the left. In the Add Photos dialog box, you can add images to your print job by choosing from those photos currently visible in the Media Browser, from your entire catalog, or from the images included in a specific album or tagged with a particular keyword. Choose one or more photos from any of these sets, and then click Done; the selected images are added to the print job and now appear in the photo menu column in the Prints dialog box.

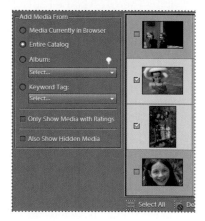

**8** Drag the thumbnail of one of your newly acquired photos from the thumbnails column onto any image cell in the print preview; the original image is replaced.

**9** Click Print or Cancel and skip to "Printing individual photos" in 136.

## Printing a Picture Package on Mac OS

1  If necessary, switch to the Organizer, leaving the Editor open. Select two or more photos in the Media Browser.

2  Click the small arrow on the Fix tab at the top of the Task Pane and choose Full Photo Edit from the menu.

3  When the Editor opens, double-click whichever image in the Project Bin that you'd like to print first. Choose File > Picture Package.

4  Under Document in the Picture Package dialog box, make a selection from the Page Size and Layout menus, and then click the Edit Layout button below the Layout preview box.

5  In the Picture Package Edit Layout dialog box, click to select an image in the layout preview, and then click the Delete Zone button in the Image Zones options at the left. Select another image in the preview and drag it to a new position on the page preview. Drag the handles on the image's bounding box to scale it or change its orientation.

> ▶ **Tip:** You can open the Picture Package dialog box from the Create tab in the Task pane. Click Photo Prints, and then click the Print Picture Package button. If you do this from the Organizer, you'll see a message asking if you'd like to open the Editor to initiate printing.

6  Option-click an image in the Edit Layout preview and try out some of the menu choices; then experiment with the other settings and buttons in the Image Zones options. Click Cancel, and then click No to avoid overwriting the default settings for the layout preset you selected.

7  Click OK in the Picture Package dialog box, and then wait while Photoshop Elements creates a new document and places the images for your Picture Package. If you wish to see the Picture Package printed choose File > Print; otherwise choose File > Close All, and then click Don't Save.

## Printing individual photos

The Photoshop Elements Prints dialog box presents all your printing options in one convenient place and also enables you to fine-tune the placement of each image within its own print well (its frame in the print preview). You can zoom or rotate an image with the controls beneath the preview and drag to reposition it, enabling you to get the image placed just right for printing without first editing it.

1 In the Organizer, Ctrl-click / Command-click to select eight or more images.

2 Choose File > Print. Alternatively, click the Create tab in the Task pane, click Photo Prints, and then click the Print With Local Printer button. On Mac OS, click Yes to continue to the Editor, where printing will be initiated.

3 In the Prints / Print dialog box, select a printer, paper size and print size from the menus at the right. On Windows, choose Individual Prints from the Select Type Of Print menu. If you see a print resolution alert, click OK to dismiss it.

● **Note:** On Mac OS, the options in the Print dialog box differ from those illustrated here. For more detailed information on printing on Mac OS, please refer to Photoshop Elements Help and search other online resources in Community Help.

4 Experiment with the controls below the Print preview. Click to select an image in the preview and zoom in and out inside the image cell using the zoom slider. Use the Rotate Left and Rotate Right buttons beside the zoom slider to change the orientation of the image within its print well frame. Drag the selected image to reposition it within the frame. Toggle the Crop To Fit option below the Select Print Size menu and observe the effect in the print preview.

**5** Select any image thumbnail in the menu column on the left side of the dialog box and click the Remove Selected Photo(s) button (➖).

**6** Click the Add Photos button (➕) below the thumbnails menu. In the Add Media dialog box, choose a source option under Add Media From; select from photos currently visible in the Media Browser, from your entire catalog, or from the images included in a specific album or tagged with a particular keyword. Choose one or more photos from any of these sets, and then click Add Selected Media. The selected images are added to the thumbnails column in the Print dialog box, and the Add Media dialog box remains open. Choose a different source option, select one or more photos; then, click Done to add the photos to your print job and dismiss the Add Media dialog box.

● **Note:** You can add images to the selection to be printed only if they are part of the currently active catalog.

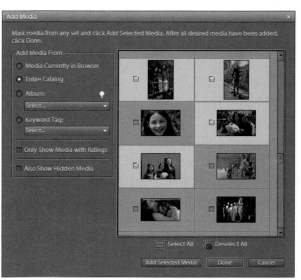

If you've selected more pictures than will fit on one page at the image dimensions you specified, Photoshop Elements automatically generates extra pages.

**7** Check the page count below the Print Preview. If your print job has more than one page, preview the other pages by clicking the arrow buttons at either side of the page count.

**8** Click the More Options button at the bottom of the dialog box and explore the settings available in the More Options dialog box. In the Printing Choices section, you can choose to print text details with your images, add image borders or a background color, and print crop marks to help you trim your images. The More Options dialog box also offers Custom Print Size and Color Management settings. Click Cancel to close the More Options dialog box.

**9** In the Prints / Print dialog box, click Print if you wish to see these images printed; otherwise, click Cancel to save your ink and paper for your own prints. On Mac OS, choose File > Close All.

# Ordering professionally printed photos online

● **Note:** You need an active Internet connection to order prints online.

If you want high quality prints of your photos and photo projects—for yourself or to share with others—you can order professional prints from an online service.

Photoshop Elements provides integrated links to online printing partners that you can conveniently access from anywhere in the workspace. In this exercise you'll learn how to order individual prints from the Organizer.

1   In the Organizer, select one or more photos in the Media Browser, and then do one of the following:

  • Choose File > Order Prints > Order Shutterfly Prints.

  • Click the Create tab at the top of the Task pane. On the Create tab, click the Photo Prints button, and then click Order Prints From Shutterfly.

2   In the Order Shutterfly Prints dialog box, do one of the following:

  • If you are already a Shutterfly member, click the "Already a member? Sign in." link, enter e-mail address and password and click Sign In.

  • If you are not already a Shutterfly member, create a new account by entering your name, e-mail address, and a password of at least six characters. If you accept the Shutterfly Terms and Conditions, click the check box below the personal details fields, and then click Join Now / Next.

Whether you choose to order prints from Shutterfly or Kodak, the experience is similar. Both services lead you through the ordering process in easy-to-follow steps.

**3** In the first step—Size/Qty for Shutterfly, Customize for Kodak—you can customize your order by specifying print sizes and quantities for the photos in your order. Click Remove under a thumbnail image in the list on the left side of the dialog box to remove that photo from your order.

Icons beside the thumbnails let you know whether your selected photos have a high enough resolution for high-quality prints at the sizes you've selected.

**4** When you're done reviewing your order, click Next.

**5** As you proceed with your order, you'll add the names and delivery addresses of recipients, review your order—making changes if necessary, provide your credit card details in the Payment / Billing dialog box, upload your images and confirm your order. For this exercise, click Cancel. A dialog box appears to ask if you want to stop using this service. Click OK.

# Sharing pictures

In this section we'll look at a variety of ways to share your pictures with friends, family, clients, or the world at large.

## Sharing photos in e-mail

Perhaps the most basic way to share a photo is by attaching it to an e-mail. The Organizer's e-mail function makes it easy—automatically optimizing your images specifically for sending via e-mail.

**Note:** The first time you access this feature you may be presented with the E-mail dialog box. Choose your e-mail client (such as Outlook Express or Adobe E-mail Service / Mail or Microsoft Entourage) from the menu, and then click Continue. You can review or change your settings later by choosing Sharing from the Preferences menu.

1  In the Media Browser, select a photo to attach to an e-mail. Click the Share tab at the top of the Task Pane; then click the E-mail Attachments button.

2  Drag another photo from the Media Browser to the Items pane to add to your selection for e-mailing.

3  Choose one of the smaller size options from the Maximum Photo Size menu and adjust the image quality using the Quality slider. The higher the quality setting, the larger the file size will be and therefore, the longer the download time. The estimated file size and download time for a 56 Kbps dial-up modem are displayed for your reference. When you're done, click Next.

4  Select the example text in the Message box and type a message of your own.

5  Click the Edit Recipients In Contact Book button (📷) above the Select Recipients box to create a new Contact Book entry. In the Contact Book dialog box, click New Contact.

6  In the New Contact dialog box, type in the personal details and e-mail address of the person to whom you wish to e-mail the pictures. Click OK to close the New Contact dialog box, and then click OK again to close the Contact Book dialog box.

7  Make sure that there is a check mark beside the new contact in the Select Recipients box, and then click Next. Photoshop Elements automatically launches your default e-mail application and opens an e-mail message with the images you selected already attached. You can edit the Subject line and the message as you wish. When you're done, either click Send if you want to go ahead and send this example e-mail, or close the message without saving or sending it.

8  Click the Organize tab above the Task Pane to switch back to the standard Elements Organizer workspace.

## Using Photo Mail

*Photo Mail is not supported on Mac OS; if you're working on Mac OS, you can skip ahead to "Creating an Online Album" on page 136.*

On Windows, another way to share your images by e-mail is to use the Photo Mail feature, which embeds photos in the body of an e-mail, within a customized layout.

1  In the Organizer, select one or more photos in the Media Browser, and then click the Photo Mail button in the Share panel.

2  Activate the Include Caption option beside Items, and then click Next.

3  In the Message text box, delete the default text and type a message of your own.

4  Select a recipient for your Photo Mail from the list in the Select Recipients pane. If your recipient list is still empty, click the Edit Recipients In Contact Book button (■) and create a new entry in the Contact Book dialog box.

5  Click Next. In the Stationery & Layouts Wizard dialog box, click each category in the list at the left in turn to see the range of designs available. Choose a stationery style appropriate to your selected photos; then, click Next Step.

6  Customize the layout by choosing a Photo Size and Layout option. Choose a font; then click the color swatch beside the font menu and choose a text color. To edit the message or caption, first click the text to make it active. Click Next.

▶ **Tip:** If this is the first time you've accessed an e-mail feature in Photoshop Elements, you'll be presented with the E-mail dialog box. Choose your e-mail client, enter your name and e-mail address, and then click Continue. You can change these settings on the Sharing tab in the Elements Organizer Preferences.

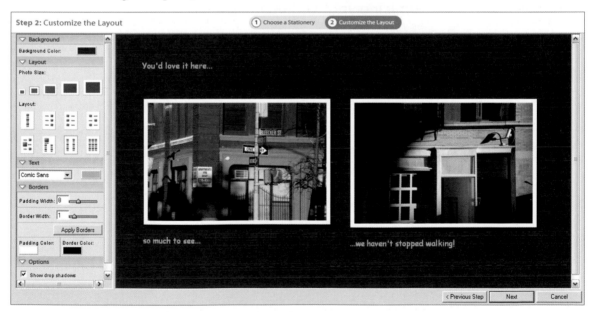

Photoshop Elements opens your default e-mail application, creates an e-mail, and embeds your layout in the body of the message.

7  Switch back to the Elements Organizer.

## Creating an Online Album

● **Note:** You can only share your album to Photoshop.com if you are a U.S. resident and have already signed up to Photoshop.com. For information on the other album sharing options, refer to Help.

▶ **Tip:** If you find that you can't activate the Photoshop.com option, make sure that you are signed in with your Adobe ID. If the option is still unavailable, activate the Backup/Sync Is On option on the Backup/ Synchronization tab of the Elements Organizer preferences.

A great way to share and showcase your photos is by creating an Online Album. You can choose from a variety of interactive layout templates that are optimized for viewing photos on the Web. Photoshop Elements guides you through the process of adding and arranging photos, applying templates, and sharing your files.

1   Click the Show All button in the Find bar. From the sorting menu above the Find bar, choose Date (oldest First). In the Keyword Tags panel, click to activate the Find box beside the keyword tag Wedding, and then Shift-click to select the first ten wedding images in the Media Browser.

2   Click the Share tab at the top of the Task pane; then click the Online Album button. The Share panel presents you with a choice of options. Activate the option Create New Album; from the Share To options, select Photoshop.com.

3   Click Next; the selected photos are added to the new album and their thumbnails are displayed in the Content pane on the Share tab.

4   In the Album Name text box under Album Details, type **Annie & Jim's Big Day**.

## Customizing your Online Album

1   In the Media Browser, select half of the photos that have not yet been added to the album; then, click the Add Items Selected In Media browser button (➕) below the Content pane. The selected photos now appear in the Content pane.

2   Drag the remaining images directly from the Media Browser into the Content pane. All sixteen photos should now be included in the album.

3   To rearrange the order in which the photos will appear in your album, select two or more thumbnails in the Content pane and drag them to a new position. Move more photos singly. If you're not happy with the order of the photos once you've finished creating your album, you can always return to rearrange them later—even once the album is shared online.

4   Click the Sharing tab at the top of the Content pane. A progress bar appears while Photoshop Elements builds a default album preview. A filmstrip menu across the top of the preview shows thumbnails for available album templates. Hold the pointer over a thumbnail to see a brief description.

**5** Double-click the Classic template in the filmstrip menu. The preview is updated to reflect your choice. A semi-transparent Slideshow Settings panel floats in front of the preview; it becomes opaque when you move the pointer over it.

▶ **Tip:** Click the check-box beside the name of any contact in the list at the right to send an automatically gener-ated e-mail invitation to view your album. Type a message to be added to your e-mail invitation in the Message text box. To add more contacts to the list, click the Edit Recipients In Contact Book button (📷), and then create new entries in the Contact Book dialog box.

**6** In the Sharing pane at the right, activate the option Share To Photoshop.com. Activate Display In My Gallery to share the album publicly; leave the option disabled if you wish the album to be accessible only to invited friends.

**7** Scroll the templates menu to the right. Locate and double-click the Photo Book template. To hide the Slideshow Settings panel, click the Show/Hide Slideshow Settings button (▣) above the templates menu.

● **Note:** The View Online button in the Sharing pane will not become active until online sharing has been initiated and the upload is complete.

▶ **Tip:** Provided you have a Photoshop.com account, it's easy to convert any existing album into an Online Album. Either click the Share button (■) to the right of the album's name in the Albums panel, or click the Share tab, and then the Online Album button. Select the album you wish to share in the Online Album sharing options. Make sure the options Share Existing Album and Share To Photoshop.com are activated; then click Next to set up a template and sharing options.

**8** Click Done; then click the Organize tab. In the Albums palette, the new album is marked with an Online Album badge (■). You may see an icon with a pair of green arrows to the left of the Online Album badge; this indicates that Photoshop Elements has not yet completed uploading the album. Wait a minute or so until the green arrows disappear, and then right-click / Control-click the new shared album and choose View Annie & Jim's Big Day Album Online. Your default web browser opens to show the album in your Photoshop.com gallery.

**9** Switch back to the Elements Organizer. Click Show All, and then click the entry for your new album in the Albums panel. In the Media browser, a number in the upper left corner of each photo indicates its place in the album. Below each thumbnail, the Album badge (■) shows that the photo is part of an album. You may also see a Backup/Synchronization Complete icon (■) indicting that the image has been successfully uploaded.

**10** (Optional) Click the Stop Sharing button (■) to the right of the album name to stop sharing it to Photoshop.com. Click the Share button (■) to edit the album or send more e-mail invitations before reactivating sharing.

## Using an online sharing service

From within Photoshop Elements, you can use Adobe Photoshop Services to upload your images and creations directly from the Organizer to social networking and photo sharing web sites. You can also use these services to download photos.

First, select the photos you wish to share in the Media Browser; then, click the Share tab above the Task Pane.

At the bottom of the Share tab, you'll find buttons for sharing to Flickr, Facebook, and SmugMug.

Click the More Options button to access the CEIVA Photo Frame and Kodak Easyshare Gallery services.

Depending on whether you already have an account with the service you wish to use, you may first need to sign up. If you're sharing to Flickr or Facebook, you'll be asked to authorize Photoshop Elements to connect to your account.

Although the procedure for logging in and sharing may differ slightly for each of these services, the process is essentially similar, and you'll be guided step by step.

*Note: With Adobe Photoshop Elements 10, you can now also upload videos directly from the Elements Organizer to YouTube.*

# Backing up and synchronizing media files

If you've signed up for Elements Membership, you can choose to synchronize the files in your Photoshop Elements catalog with your Photoshop.com account, making your photos and videos available to you anywhere through Photoshop.com and Photoshop Express. You can manage your media from any web browser: add, delete, edit, or re-organize items at home or on the road. Any changes you make online will be synchronized back to Photoshop Elements on your desktop. Don't worry; the Synchronization feature will not overwrite anything on your base computer—Photoshop Elements creates a Version Set on your computer, so you'll still have the original file. If you delete something online, a copy is kept on your computer unless you confirm that you want it deleted from your catalog.

● **Note:** This feature is available only to Photoshop Elements users in the U.S. who have signed up for Elements Membership and a Photoshop.com account.

In previous versions of Photoshop Elements only Albums could be backed up and synchronized in this way, but in Photoshop Elements 10 you can choose to back up your entire catalog, making it easier to protect your precious files. Another exciting feature in Photoshop Elements 10 is Multi Machine Sync. If you have separate installations of Photoshop Elements on more than one computer—perhaps on desktop computers at home and at the office, as well as the laptop you use when you travel—you can now synchronize them all to your Photoshop.com account. Any changes you make in your catalog on one computer, such as adding, deleting, editing or reorganizing images, will be replicated on your other computers.

In Photoshop Elements 10 it's easier than ever to manage and monitor backup and synchronization—simply click the Backup/Synchronization Agent icon (🔲), either at the bottom of the Organizer workspace or in the Windows System Tray (XP), in the Notification Area (Vista), or at the right of the menu bar on Mac OS.

## Setting backup and synchronization options

It's a good idea to become familiar with the Backup/Synchronization preferences in the Elements Organizer, where you can find out everything there is to know about the current Backup and Synchronization status of your catalog:

1 In the Organizer, click the Backup/Synchronization Agent icon (🔲) at the bottom of the Organizer workspace and choose Open Backup/Synchronization Preferences. In the Backup/Synchronization Preferences dialog box, click the triangle beside Advanced Backup/Sync Options.

**Tip:** You'll also find a status bar indicating online space usage, together with a link to manage your backup and synchronization preferences, in the Welcome screen.

2  Examine the Backup/Synchronization settings, from the top down:

- Backup and Synchronization is activated. The status bar shows how much of your online storage space is being used and how much free space you have.

- New albums are set to backup and synchronize by default, and by default you will be asked for confirmation before files deleted online are deleted from your computer. Conflicts between the data in your catalog and your backed-up data online will not be resolved without a decision on your part, and there is currently no restriction on backup for large files.

- All media file types supported for import are enabled for synchronization. By default, creations built in Photoshop Elements will not be backed up.

**Tip:** In the Backup/ Synchronization Prefer- ences dialog box, you'll also find a button for upgrading your basic Elements Membership to Plus Membership, which increases your online storage space at Photoshop.com.

- In the table below the advanced options, you can see that synchronization is not enabled for media that is not included in any album, and that only the album you created in this lesson is enabled for backup and synchronization. The Online Album icon ( ) indicates that this album is currently being shared; the dimmed check-mark in the Sync column reflects the fact that synchronization cannot be disabled for an album while it is being shared.

Above the synchronization table is a setting for specifying a downloads folder, and below it, a button to enable backup and synchronization for your entire catalog.

3  Click OK to close the Backup/Synchronization Preferences dialog box.

## Checking backup and synchronization status

The Backup/Synchronization Agent ( ) at the bottom of the Organizer workspace makes it easy to check on backup and synchronization status for your files without needing to open the preferences dialog box. It also offers additional commands that can be accessed without interrupting your workflow:

**Tip:** You can also find the Backup/ Synchronization Agent in the System Tray on Windows XP, in the Notification Area on Windows Vista, and in the Mac OS Menu Bar. Here you'll find some commands that can't be accessed from the agent in the Organizer: Backup/Sync Only When Idle, and Stop Backup/ Synchronization. To access these commands, right-click the System Tray / Notification Area agent on Windows, or click the Menu Bar agent on Mac OS.

- View Backed Up/Synchronized Files command filters the Media Browser display to show only the photos for which synchronization is up-to-date.

- View Backup/Synchronization Status opens a dialog box that shows whether your catalog is currently in sync with your online account. If backup and synchronization is in progress, the Elements Backup/Synchronization Status dialog box shows a status bar tracking the real-time transfer of data from your desktop catalog to your storage space at Photoshop.com.

## Synchronizing separate computers

To synchronize your Photoshop Elements catalog across multiple computers, you first need to connect the machines to be synchronized to the same Photoshop.com account by signing in from Photoshop Elements on each machine. It's not necessary that you do this at the same time.

On each computer, turn on Backup/Sync and enable it for your entire catalog. By the time one or two synchronization cycles have run, all your computers should have identical catalogs, with exactly the same Albums, keyword tags, image captions, and so on. Don't attempt to aid the process; for example, by deliberately recreating a new album on your laptop to match the one you created on your desktop computer. In fact, Photoshop Elements would see these as two different files and you would end up with multiple copies on each machine. Simply make your changes on whichever computer you're working on and Photoshop Elements will update the other copies of your catalog.

The exception to this rule is that Photoshop Elements will not synchronize Stacks and Version Sets across multiple computers. The images inside your Stacks will be synchronised, but you'll need to recreate the stacking on each machine. For Version Sets, only the top-most version—your edited version—will be synchronized.

If you wish to make sure that the changes you're making on one computer are synchronized to your other machines before you need to work with them, click the Backup/Synchronization Agent and choose View Backup/Synchronization Status. In the Elements Backup/Synchronization Status dialog box, click Sync Now; then, do the same when you get to the next machine.

# Exporting copies of your photos for the Web

As a final exercise in this lesson you'll convert a file to JPEG format and optimize it for use on the Web. The JPEG file format reduces the file size and can be displayed by web browsers such as Internet Explorer. If your file contains multiple layers, the conversion to the JPEG file format will flatten them into one layer.

For this operation you'll use the Save For Web feature, which enables you to tweak the export settings while comparing the original image file with the proposed web-ready version of the image.

1   In the Media Browser, select a photo you want to export for use on the Web.

2   Click the small arrow on the Fix tab at the top of the Task Pane and choose any of the three Edit modes—the Save For Web command is available from anywhere in the Editor.

3   In the Editor, choose File > Save For Web.

**4** In the Save For Web dialog box, choose Fit On Screen from the Zoom menu in the lower left corner of the dialog box.

▶ **Tip:** While you're previewing photos in the Save For Web dialog box, you can magnify an image with the Zoom tool (🔍) in the toolbox at the upper left of the dialog box. Alt-click / Option-click the image with the Zoom tool to zoom out. While you're zoomed in, you can drag either of the images with the Hand tool (✋); the images move in unison so that you see the same part of the photo in both views.

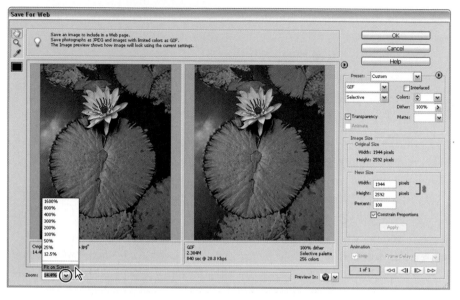

**5** Notice the file-size information under each view of the image. The view on the left displays the file size of the original document.

**6** On the right side of the dialog box, select JPEG Medium from the Preset menu. Notice the change in file size for the JPEG image on the right.

▶ **Tip:** To further reduce the file size, choose the JPEG Low setting. Tweak the Quality setting to specify levels between these preset options.

**7** Under New Size, select Constrain Proportions and type **300** in the Width field. The Height is adjusted automatically to retain the image's original proportions. Click the Apply button. Once again, notice the change in the file size displayed beneath the JPEG view of the image. If necessary, choose Fit On Screen from the Zoom menu.

▶ **Tip:** If you can't find the My CIB Work folder, refer to "Creating a work folder" on page 3.

**8** Click OK. Navigate to the My CIB Work folder in the Save Optimized As dialog box, add **_Work** to the end of the file name, and then click Save.

The JPEG format reduces the file size by using JPEG compression, which discards some of the data. The amount of data lost, and the resulting image quality, will vary depending on the image you're working with and the settings you choose.

**9** In the Editor, choose File > Close, without saving changes.

Congratulations! You've completed this lesson and should now have a working understanding of the basics of printing and sharing your photos from Photoshop Elements. You've learned how to set up single or multiple images for printing at home, how to order professional prints online and how to share photos in e-mail or upload them to an online sharing service. You've created on Online Album and exported photos for use on the Web. Before you move on to the next lesson, take a few moments to work through the following review.

# Review questions

1  What is Photo Mail? (Windows)

2  What is a Picture Package?

3  How can you fine-tune the composition of a photo for printing?

4  What are the advantages of backing up and synchronizing your catalog to your Photoshop.com account?

5  Is the Save For Web command available only in Full Edit mode?

# Review answers

1  The Photo Mail feature embeds selected photos in the body of an e-mail within a colorful custom layout. You can tweak the layout and image size, choose backgrounds, frames, and effects, and add text messages and captions. You can send Photo Mail through Outlook Express, Outlook, or Adobe E-mail Service.

2  A Picture Package lets you print a photo repeated at a choice of sizes on the same page. You can choose from a variety of layout options with a range of image sizes to customize your picture package print.

3  You can now fine-tune the placement of each image within its own print well frame in the print preview, enabling you to get the image placed just right for printing without first editing it. Zoom or rotate an image with the controls beneath the print preview and drag to reposition it in the frame.

4  Backing up and synchronizing your catalog to your Photoshop.com account means that you can manage your media from any web browser—and any changes made to your catalog online will be synchronized back to Photoshop Elements on your desktop. Furthermore, with Multi Machine Sync you can now even synchronize your files across separate computers. Any changes you make to your catalog on one computer, such as adding, deleting, editing or reorganizing images or albums, will be replicated on your other machines. The capability to backup and synchronize your entire catalog now makes it even easier to manage and protect your precious files.

5  The Save For Web command is available in all three Edit modes: Full Edit, Quick Edit and Guided Edit.

# 6 EASY EDITING

## Lesson Overview

Photoshop Elements offers a suite of easy-to-use tools and a choice of three editing modes that make it easy to achieve impressive results, whatever your level of experience. The Guided Edit mode helps digital imaging novices to learn as they work, Quick Edit presents an array of one-touch controls for correcting some of the most common image problems, and Full Edit mode delivers all the power and sophistication experienced users expect from a Photoshop application.

This lesson takes you on a test drive of the three editing modes, and then introduces you to a range of quick and easy techniques to help you get more from your photos in just a few clicks:

- Making quick and easy edits in the Organizer
- Batch-processing photos
- Using automatic options to improve images
- Working in Guided Edit mode
- Making Quick Edit adjustments
- Using adjustment previews to modify settings
- Applying editing presets with the Smart Brush
- Correcting an image using Smart Fix
- Using the image canvas to create a border

 You'll probably need about one and a half hours to complete this lesson.

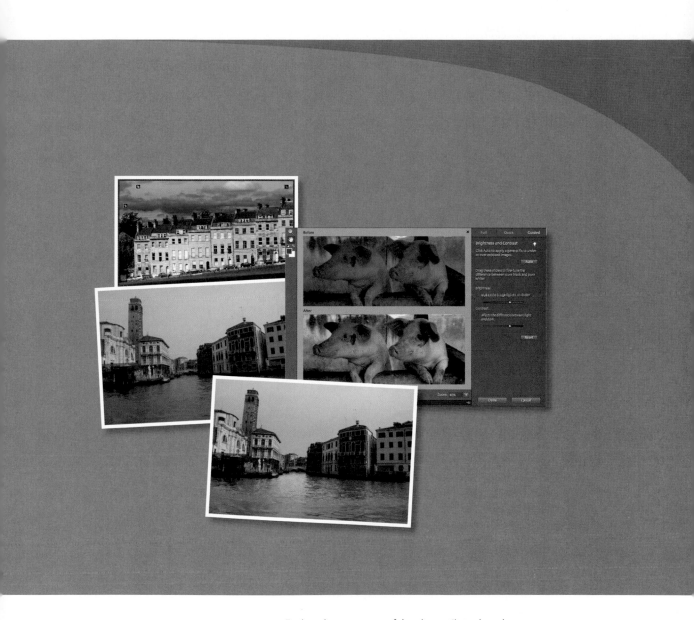

Explore the many powerful and versatile tools and options that make it easy to get more from your photos in Photoshop Elements—even if you're a beginner. Start with a few of the easy-to-use, one-step image correction features, and then experiment with a few more advanced techniques, such as layering preset adjustments with the Smart Brush.

**Note:** Before you start working on this lesson, make sure that you've installed the software on your computer from the application CD (see the Photoshop Elements 10 documentation) and that you have correctly copied the Lessons folder from the CD in the back of this book onto your computer's hard disk (see "Copying the Classroom in a Book files" on page 2). You should also have created a working catalog (see "Creating a new catalog" on page 8).

# Getting started

You can start by importing the sample images for this lesson to the CIB Catalog that you created at the beginning of Lesson 1.

1 Start Photoshop Elements and click Organize in the Welcome Screen. When the Organizer opens, make sure that your CIB Catalog is loaded (if you need to refresh your memory, refer to step 2 in the Getting Started section in Lesson 5).

2 Choose File > Get Photos And Video > From Files And Folders. In the Get Photos And Videos From Files And Folders dialog box, locate and select your Lesson06 folder. Activate the option Get Photos From Subfolders and disable the automatic processing options; then, click Get Media.

3 In the Import Attached Keyword Tags dialog box, select the Lesson 06 tag, and then click OK. Click OK to close any other alert dialog box.

# Editing photos in the Organizer

Some of the easiest and most convenient ways to quickly fix many of the most common image problems are at your fingertips, without even leaving the Organizer.

1 In the Media Browser, select the image DSC_2076.jpg. Click the Fix tab at the top of the Task pane; then, click the Auto Smart Fix button. The edited file is grouped with the original in a Version Set. In the Media Browser, the edited version appears as the top image in the collapsed (or closed) Version Set. Click the arrow at the right of the image frame to expand the Version Set.

**Tip:** The most recent edited version always appears at the left in an expanded version set and becomes the top image when the Version Set is collapsed.

2 In the expanded Version Set, select the original photo, DSC_2076.jpg, in its un-edited state. On the Fix tab, click the Auto Color button. Repeat the process for the Auto Levels button, and then again for the Auto Contrast button.

3 Double-click the original image to see it in the single image view. Use the left arrow key on your keyboard to compare the un-edited photo with the results of your single-click adjustments. Double-click the enlarged image to return to the thumbnail view. Select all four edited versions; then, right-click / Control-click any of the selected thumbnails and choose Delete Selected Items From Catalog.

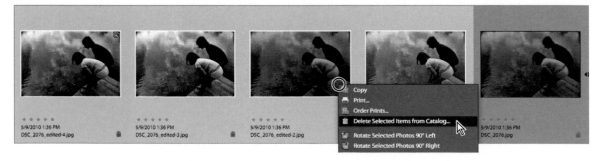

**4**  In the Confirm Deletion From Catalog dialog box, click to activate the option Also Delete Selected Item(s) From The Hard Disk; then, click OK. Click the Organize tab above the Task pane.

## Editing in Full Screen mode

Full Screen mode in the Organizer provides access to the same automatic editing commands you'll find on the Fix tab. The controls in the Full Screen mode Quick Edit panel enable you to make substantial improvements to an image with just a click or two and assess the results at a conveniently high zoom level.

**1**  In the Media Browser, select the image DSC_3583.jpg. Click the View, Edit, Organize In Full Screen button (▣) above the Find bar.

**2**  Hold the Ctrl / Command key and press the Plus key (+) on your keyboard to zoom in. Click anywhere in the photo and drag to reposition the view. Double-click the image to fit the photo to the screen.

**3**  Move the pointer to the upper left edge of the screen to show the Quick Edit panel; then, click to deactivate the Auto Hide button at the top of the panel's title bar, so that the Quick Edit panel remains open while you work.

**4**  In the Quick Edit panel, hold the pointer over each button in turn to see a tooltip describing the effect it will have on the photo. Click the Auto Levels button, and then click the Auto Red Eye Fix button. Click OK to accept the creation of a new Version Set.

**5**  Click to re-activate the Quick Edit panel's Auto Hide button, and then move the pointer away; the Quick Edit panel closes after a second or so.

You've improved this photo dramatically with just two clicks, without leaving the Organizer.

▶ **Tip:** You can use the Quick Edit panel to correct image problems even while reviewing your photos as a full-screen slideshow.

**6**  Press the Esc key, or click the Close button (x) in the control bar to exit Full Screen mode. In the Media Browser, expand the new Version Set; then, right-click / Command-click the edited version of the image and choose Delete From Catalog from the menu. In the Confirm Deletion From Catalog dialog box, activate the option Also Delete Selected Item(s) From The Hard Disk; then, click OK. You'll be using a different technique to fix this photo later in the lesson.

# Getting to know the Edit modes

For some photos, applying one-click fixes in the Organizer will be enough, but when you want more control—and access to the full power of Photoshop Elements editing, adjustment and correction tools—you'll work in the Editor. In the rest of this lesson you'll improve images in each of the three Editor modes: Full Edit, Quick Edit, and Guided Edit. Before you continue with the exercises, you can take a few minutes to familiarize yourself with switching between the three working modes, and to get an overview of the different editing workspaces.

## Full Edit mode

1   Select two or three images in the Media Browser; then, click the small arrow on the Fix tab at the top of the Task Pane and choose Full Photo Edit from the menu.

2   In Full Edit mode, choose Window > Reset Panels or click the Reset Panels button ( ) at the top of the workspace. By default, the Effects, Content, and Layers panels are open in the Panel Bin.

The Full Edit mode is Photoshop Elements' most powerful and versatile image editing environment, with commands for correcting exposure and color and tools for making precise selections and fixing image imperfections. The Full Edit tool bar even includes painting and text editing tools. You can arrange the flexible Full Edit workspace to suit the way you prefer to work by floating, hiding, and showing panels.

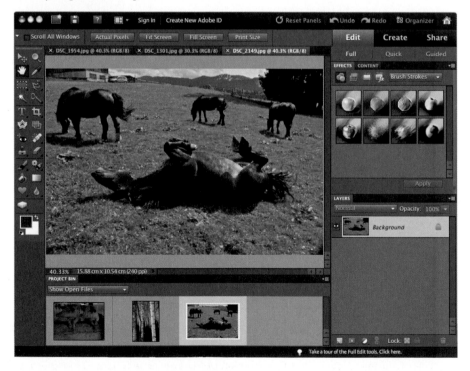

The Project Bin below the Edit pane displays thumbnails of the photos you opened for editing. In the Project Bin menu, you can also choose to display files currently selected in the Organizer, or show the contents of any of your albums.

**3** Click a thumbnail in the Project Bin to select an image. Double-click a thumbnail to bring that image to the front. At the top of the Edit pane, the name tab of the foremost image is highlighted. Click another name tab to bring that photo to the front.

**4** Drag any panel out of the Panel Bin by its header bar, to float the panel wherever you like in the workspace. Click the Close button (x) in the header bar of the floating panel to close it.

**5** Choose the name of the panel you just closed from the Window menu. Check-marks are displayed beside the names of panels that are currently open. Drag the re-opened floating panel back into the Panel Bin. You can dock the panel as part of a tabbed panel group by dragging it to the header of another panel, or drop it between the frames of other panels. Whichever way you choose, release the mouse button when a blue line appears to highlight the targeted position.

**6** Experiment with dragging the Toolbox and Project Bin to float over the Edit pane, and then re-docking them. When you're done exploring, click the Reset Panels button (⟳), and then click the Quick Edit tab at the top of the Panel Bin.

## Quick Edit mode

Each Edit mode offers a different set of tools, controls and views. In Quick Edit mode, the Panel Bin is occupied by the Quick Fix panel, with separate panes for Smart Fix, Lighting, Color, Balance, and Sharpness controls.

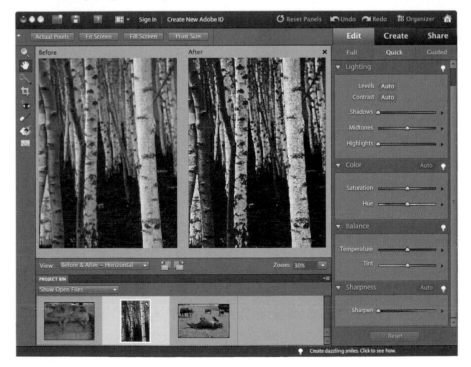

**Note:** In this lesson you will not be working with floating image windows. If your images open in floating windows, choose Images > Consolidate All To Tabs from the Window menu.

▶ **Tip:** You can review the techniques for working with panels in "Using panels and the Panel Bin" on page 20.

▶ **Tip:** In Quick Edit mode you cannot add, remove or float panels. To clear extra screen space, collapse the Project Bin by double-clicking its header bar and hide the Toolbox by un-checking Tools in the Window menu.

1  Choose a Before & After view option from the View menu below the Edit pane.

2  Collapse and expand any of the control panes in the Quick Fix panel by clicking the triangle at the left of the header of that pane.

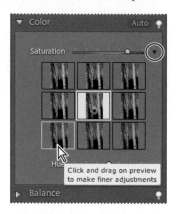

3  Click the small black arrow to the right of any control slider. A grid of preview thumbnails is displayed, showing the full range of variation possible with that control. A white frame highlights the current setting. Move the pointer slowly over each preview thumbnail in the grid to see that level of adjustment applied temporarily to your image in the After view.

4  Click the Reset button at the bottom of the Quick Fix panel to discard any changes you've made. Click the Reset Panels button (⟳), and then click the Guided Edit tab at the top of the Panel Bin.

## Guided Edit mode

▶ **Tip:** If you're new to digital imaging, the Guided Edit mode enables you to learn as you work, making it a great starting point for fixing and modifying your photos.

In Guided Edit mode the Panel Bin displays the Guided Edit panel, with grouped listings for a wide range of common—and not-so-common—image editing tasks.

1  Click any listing to find simple step-by-step instructions and any tools or controls that you'll need for that task. Try several of the guided procedures.

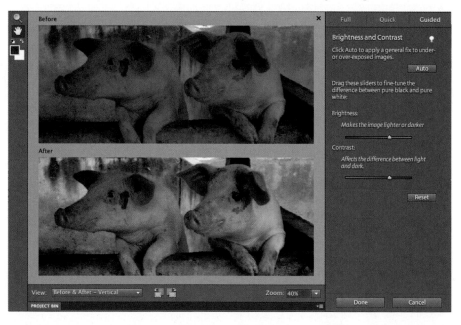

▶ **Tip:** In Guided Edit mode you can't add, remove or float panels or image windows as you would in Full Edit mode. To clear extra screen space, you can collapse the Project Bin by double-clicking its header bar.

2  When you're done experimenting, choose File > Close All. Click Don't Save to discard any changes you made, keeping the images intact for the next exercise.

# Making easy color and lighting adjustments

Many of the photographs used for the lessons in this book were chosen to illustrate common image faults that people face every day as they try to make the most of their photographs. Artificial light, unusual conditions, and incorrect camera settings can all result in tonal imbalances and unwelcome color casts in an image. You can make adjustments using the simple controls in Quick Edit mode, let the Guided Edit mode step you through a wide range of editing tasks, perform sophisticated edits selectively in Full Edit mode—or even have Photoshop Elements batch-process your photos, applying your choice of automatic corrections.

## Fixing files automatically in batches

In this exercise, you'll batch process all the image files used in this lesson. You'll save the auto-adjusted files as copies so that at the end of each project you can compare these automatic results to the edits you've made using other techniques.

1    Make sure you're in Full Edit mode; then choose File > Process Multiple Files. Under Quick Fix, at the upper right of the Process Multiple Files dialog box, click the checkboxes to activate all four of the auto-fix options: Auto Levels, Auto Contrast, Auto Color, and Sharpen.

2    At the left of the dialog box, choose Folder from the Process Files From menu. Under Source, click the Browse button; then, locate and select the Lesson06 folder as the source folder for the images to be processed. Click OK / Choose. Under Destination, use the same method to set the My CIB Work folder as the destination for the processed copies.

> **Tip:** If you can't find the My CIB Work folder, refer to "Creating a work folder" on page 3.

3    Under File Naming, activate the Rename Files option. Choose Document Name from the menu on the left, and then type _Autofix in the second field. This will add the appendix "_Autofix" to the existing document names as the processed copies are saved.

4    Review the settings in the dialog box. Make sure that the options Resize Images and Convert Files are disabled, and then click OK.

> **Note:** For Windows users; ignore any alert warning that files could not be processed. This is caused by a hidden system file and has no effect on the success of your project.

Photoshop Elements goes to work, automatically opening and closing image windows. All you need to do is sit back and wait for the process to finish. The newly copied files are automatically tagged with the same keywords as the source files.

## Adding the auto-corrected files to your catalog

When you modify an image in the Editor, the Include In Organizer option in the Save and Save As dialog boxes is activated by default. However, when you batch-edit files with the Process Multiple Files command, this option isn't part of the process—you must add the edited copies to the Organizer manually.

1  Switch to the Organizer; then, choose File > Get Photos And Videos > From Files And Folders. In the Get Photos From Files And Folders dialog box, locate and open your My CIB Work folder, and then Ctrl-click / Command-click or marquee-select all the files with the suffix "_Autofix."

2  Activate Automatically Fix Red Eyes and disable any other automatic processing option that is currently active; then, click Get Media. If the Auto Red Eye Fix Complete dialog box appears, click OK to accept the creation of a Version Set.

3  In the Import Attached Keyword Tags dialog box, click Select All, and then click OK. Click OK to dismiss any other dialog box.

The files are imported to your CIB Catalog and the Organizer displays thumbnails of the newly added images in the Media Browser.

# Correcting a photo in Quick Edit mode

In the Quick Edit mode, Photoshop Elements conveniently groups easy-to-use slider controls for many basic image correction operations and presents them in the Quick Fix panel.

Previously you applied a combination of automatic fixes using the Process Multiple Files command. In this exercise, you'll use some of the same automatic fix options one at a time, enabling you to see how each step affects an image and giving you the opportunity to fine-tune the default settings.

1  You should be in the Organizer from the last exercise; isolate the lesson images by activating the Find box beside the Lesson 06 tag in the Keyword Tags panel.

2  Select the original photo of the perfume bottles, DSC_2474.jpg, making sure not to confuse the original file with the autofix copy; then, click the small arrow on the Fix tab at the top of the Task Pane and choose Quick Photo Edit. Wait while the image opens in the Editor.

## Using Smart Fix

In the Quick Edit workspace, the Quick Fix panel at the right contains five adjustment panes—Smart Fix, Lighting, Color, Balance, and Sharpness.

Smart Fix is actually a combination of several adjustments applied at once; it corrects overall color balance and improves shadow and highlight detail. As with the other tools in Quick Edit mode, you can click the Auto button to apply the correction automatically, use the slider control to fine-tune the adjustment manually, or combine these methods, as you'll do in this exercise.

1  Choose Before & After - Horizontal from the View menu below the Edit pane. In the Quick Fix panel, click the Auto button in the Smart Fix pane. Notice the immediate effect on the image in the After view.

**2** Now, move the Smart Fix Amount slider to change the color balance and the highlight and shadow settings for your image. Experiment to find the setting you prefer. We set the Smart Fix Amount to a value of 70.

**3** Click the Commit button (✓) in the header of the Smart Fix pane to commit the changes.

## Applying more automatic fixes

Four more automatic Quick Fix adjustments are available in the Lighting, Color, and Sharpness panes. (There is no Auto Balance adjustment.)

**1** In the Lighting pane, click both the Auto Levels and Auto Contrast buttons. You may or may not see a significant shift in the tonal balance of this image, depending on the adjustment you made with the Smart Fix edit.

**2** Click the Auto Color and Auto Sharpness buttons, noting the effects of each of these adjustments in the After view.

**3** In the Quick Fix Color pane, click the small black arrow to the right of the Saturation slider.

A grid of nine preview thumbnails shows the full range of variation possible with the Saturation slider. A white frame highlights the central preview thumbnail, which represents the current saturation setting.

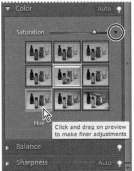

**4** Move the pointer slowly over each preview thumbnail in the grid to see that level of saturation applied temporarily to your image in the After view.

▶ **Tip:** Click a thumbnail to apply the respective level of adjustment; drag left or right to fine-tune the adjustment. The Quick Fix previews not only provide a intuitive editing interface but also make a great way to learn about the effects of the various adjustment controls as you work with them.

**5** Experiment with the slider controls and Quick Fix preview grids in each pane of the Quick Fix panel. When you're satisfied with an adjustment, click the Commit button (✓) in the title bar of that pane to accept the changes. If you wish to undo your modifications and start again with the original version of the image, click the Reset button at the bottom of the Quick Fix panel.

**6** When you've achieved the results you want, choose File > Save As. In the Save As dialog box, activate the option Include In The Organizer and disable Save In Version Set With Original. Save the file to your My CIB Work folder, in JPEG format. Type **DSC_2474_Quick** as the file name; then, click Save. In the JPEG Options dialog box, choose High from the Quality menu, and then click OK. Choose File > Close.

# Fixing color and lighting in Guided Edit mode

● **Note:** As you try more advanced tasks in Photoshop Elements 10, you may find that you need more information to solve any problems you encounter. For help with some common problems you might have while working through the lessons in this book, see the section "Why won't Photoshop Elements do what I tell it to do?" in Lesson 7.

If you're a newcomer to digital image editing, the Guided Edit mode is a great place to start. By letting Photoshop Elements step you through the process of improving your photos you'll not only achieve impressive results quickly, but also learn a lot about image problems and solutions as you work. Even experienced users will enjoy the ease of working in Guided Edit mode—and may just pick up some new tricks.

For this exercise, you'll work once again with the image of the old perfume bottles, which has an obvious color cast as a result of inadequate artificial lighting.

**1** If you're not already in the Organizer, switch to it now by clicking the Organizer button (⊞) at the top right of the Editor workspace. If necessary, use the Lesson 06 tag to isolate the Lesson 6 images in the Media Browser.

**2** Select the photo of the perfume bottles, DSC_2474.jpg, making sure not to confuse the original file with the edited copies. Click the small arrow on the Fix tab at the top of the Task Pane and choose Guided Photo Edit from the menu.

**3** From the View menu at the left of the bar below the Edit pane, choose the Before & After - Horizontal view. If necessary, click the triangle to expand the Color And Lighting pane in the Guided Edit panel. Click Remove A Color Cast.

**4** Read the instructions under Correct Color Cast. Then, using the Color Cast Eyedropper tool, click the bright area in the lower left corner of the Before image to remove the color cast. Notice the change in the After image.

▶ **Tip:** If you're not satisfied with the result, click the Reset button in the Correct Color Cast pane, and then click a different point in the Before image with the Color Cast Eyedropper.

**5** When you're satisfied with what you see in the After image, click Done.

As is often the case with poorly exposed photos, this photo has more than just one problem. Although the color cast has been removed, the image is still quite flat and dull; it would obviously benefit from some lighting adjustments.

**6** If necessary, expand the Color And Lighting pane in the Guided Edit panel so that you can see the options in that group, and then click Lighten Or Darken. In the Lighten Or Darken A Photo controls, click the Auto button. Notice the substantial improvement in the appearance of the image.

**7** Use the Lighten Shadows, Darken Highlights, and Midtone Contrast sliders to fine-tune the lighting for this image. We set a value of 50 for Lighten Shadows, left the Darken Highlights slider at 0, and set Midtone Contrast to a value of 70.

**Tip:** Your choice of settings may differ from those illustrated, depending on the results of your color correction step 4, and your preferences for the look of the final image.

**8** When you're satisfied with the results of your lighting adjustment, click Done.

**9** In the Guided Edit panel, click Sharpen Photo in the Basic Edits group. Click the Auto button near the top of the Sharpen Photo pane. Use the slider to fine-tune the sharpening to your liking, and then click Done.

**10** Choose File > Save As. Activate Include In The Elements Organizer and disable Save In Version Set With Original. Name the file **DSC_2474_Guided**, to be saved to your My CIB Work folder. Leaving the JPEG file format selected, click Save. In the JPEG Options dialog box, choose from the Quality menu, and then click OK. Choose File > Close, and then switch back to the Organizer.

**Tip:** To be able to recognize and avoid the image artifacts that can result from over-sharpening, sharpening is best applied at a magnification of 100%. Use the menu below the Edit pane to change the display to the After Only view, and then choose View > Actual Pixels.

With just a few clicks you've improved the appearance of the photo dramatically. You don't need to have prior experience using an image editor to get good results in Guided Edit mode.

Try the Guided Activities—Touch Up Scratches And Blemishes, Guide For Editing A Photo, and Fix Keystone Distortion—with some of your own photos. Each of these procedures will step you through several image editing tasks in the order recommended to achieve professional-looking results.

## Creative fun with Guided Edit

The Guided Edit panel offers far more than just correction and retouching tasks. The Photomerge pane includes procedures for combining multiple photos, and the Lens Effects, Photography Effects and Photo Play panes let you experiment with a range of striking and unusual creative treatments for your photos.

1   From the Lesson 6 images in the Media Browser, select the original image of the girls on unicycles, making sure not to confuse it with the _Autofix copy. Click the arrow on the Fix tab and Choose Guided Photo Edit from the menu.

2   Hide the Project Bin; then click the Fit Screen button above the Edit pane. In the Guided Edit panel, expand the Photo Play pane and click Out Of Bounds.

3   Follow the instructions in the Guided Edit panel. Start by clicking Add A Frame, and then let Guided Edit step you through the process of setting up the frame as you see in the illustration below. When you're happy with the frame, click the green Commit button (✓) at the lower right corner.

▶ **Tip:** Remember these pointers when you're using the Quick Selection tool during this guided edit:
• Use Ctrl / Command+[ to decrease the brush size, Ctrl / Command+] to increase it.
• Hold down the Alt / Option key to subtract from the selection.
• Difficult selections can be made much easier by making use of the Auto-Enhance and Refine Edge options in the tool options bar above the Edit pane.

4   Continue with the guided steps until you can replicate something similar to what you see in the illustration below; then, click Done. Don't be discouraged if you need a few attempts—with a little practice you'll get great results.

**5** Choose File > Save As. Activate the Include In The Elements Organizer option, disable Save In Version Set With Original, name the file, and save it to your My CIB Work folder. Close the file.

Experiment with the other guided edits in the Lens Effects, Photography Effects and Photo Play groups. Apply these effects as they come, use them as inspiration, or treat them as a starting point for further editing in the Full Edit mode. Photoshop Elements 10 introduces several new creative guided photo treatments.

In the Lens Effects category, Depth Of Field offers a choice of Simple or Custom modes, enabling you to create a depth of field effect by masking the image elements you wish to appear sharply focused, while applying a blur to the rest of the image.

The Orton Effect, in the Photography Effects group, combines an out-of-focus glow and intensified color to produce an evocative, dreamy effect in your photos.

In the Photo Play category, you'll find the Picture Stack treatment, which turns your image into a scattered stack of photos. As with all the Guided Edit effects, you can fine-tune the result using the tools and controls provided, together with tips and instructions, on the Guided Edit tab.

# Selective editing with the Smart Brush

Sometimes the best way to enhance a photo is to modify just part of the image, or to treat separate areas—such as background and foreground elements—differently, rather than applying an adjustment to the whole photo.

The quickest and easiest way to do this is to paint your adjustments directly onto the image with the Smart Brush tool.

The Smart Brush is both a selection tool and an image adjustment tool—as you paint, it creates a selection based on similarities in color and texture, through which your choice of editing preset is applied.

1   In the Organizer, make sure that the Lesson 6 images are isolated in the Media Browser. Double-click the image DSC_8492.jpg—a photo taken on a dull day in Venice—to see it in the single image view. Use the left and right arrow keys on your keyboard to compare the enlarged image with its _Autofix copy.

Although the automatic adjustments have brightened the photo and increased its contrast, the result still appears flat, and the sky has become over-exposed, lacking in color and detail. This image is a good candidate for some selective editing.

2   Make sure that you are viewing the original, un-edited photo; then, click the arrow on the Fix tab and choose Full Photo Edit from the menu. In Full Edit mode, click the Reset Panels button (![icon]) at the top of the workspace. Hide the grouped Effects and Content panels, and the Project Bin, by double-clicking their header bars; then, choose View > Fit On Screen.

3   Select the Smart Brush (![icon]) from the toolbox. If the Smart Brush presets picker doesn't open automatically, click the white triangle beside the small square thumbnail in the tool options bar above the Edit pane.

**4** Drag the Smart Brush adjustment presets picker away from the tool options bar to float in a position where it won't obstruct your view of the image while you work. Click the categories menu at the top of the floating Smart Brush presets picker and take note of the categories available. Choose the category Nature. Scroll down in the picker to see the collection of presets in this category; then, select the Blue Skies preset.

**5** In the tool options bar, open the Brush Picker and set the brush diameter to **20** px (pixels). To close the Brush Picker, click elsewhere in the tool options bar, or use the Esc key on your keyboard. Starting in the upper right corner of the photo, drag across the sky. Don't worry if your selection expands to include parts of the buildings; to subtract these areas from the selection, hold down the Alt / Option key and paint over them carefully.

▶ **Tip:** Press the left bracket key ( [ ) to decrease the brush size, and the right bracket key ( ] ) to increase it. While you're fine-tuning the selection, use a small brush and make slow, short strokes.

**6** Choose Select > Deselect. Click the categories menu at the top of the Smart Brush presets picker and choose the category Lighting. Select the Contrast High preset. Drag across the buildings in the photo, staying a little below the roof line, and then work back in the other direction, keeping just above the waterline.

**7** Choose Select > Deselect. From the Lighting category in the Smart Brush presets picker, choose the Brighter preset. Drag across the water area, holding down the Alt / Option key and moving slowly to paint out any over-selections.

**8** Inspect the Layers panel. Each Smart Brush edit occupies its own adjustment layer, where it remains active—so you can add to or subtract from the selection, change the way the adjustment is being applied, or even change which preset is applied at any time, without permanently affecting your original image.

**9** Each adjustment shows a *pin*: a square, colored marker that identifies a Smart Brush edit whenever the tool is active, located near the point that you first clicked with the Smart Brush. Right-click / Control-click the pin for the Brighter adjustment on the water area, and then choose Change Adjustment Settings from the context menu.

**10** The Adjustments panel opens in the Panel Bin. The controls presented will vary from one Smart Paint preset to another, depending on the combination of adjustments that make up each preset. Use the sliders, or type in the text boxes, to increase the Brightness value to 55, and the Contrast setting to 50, noting the changes in the image.

The Blue Skies adjustment looks somewhat overdone. Rather than modifying the effect with the adjustment controls, you can use a different technique.

11 Collapse the Adjustments panel by double-clicking its header bar. If necessary, use the same method to expand the Layers panel. In the layers panel, select the layer **Blue Skies 1** by clicking the layer name—not either of the thumbnails. Use the menu at the top of the Layers panel to change the blending mode from Color Burn to Soft Light. Increase the layer opacity from 75% to 100%.

12 Chose File > Save As. Activate the Include In The Organizer option and disable Save In Version Set With Original. Name the file **DSC_8492_SmartBrush** and save it to your My CIB Work folder in Photoshop format with Layers activated. Close the file.

You can use the Smart Brush on the same area in an image as many times as you wish. If you re-apply the same preset the effects are usually cumulative, applying different presets to the same image area combines their effects.

Original image

Blue Skies preset
Soft Light mode
100% Opacity
+
Cloud Contrast preset
Overlay mode
40% Opacity
+
Dark Sky preset
Multiply mode
75% Opacity

# Working with the image canvas

You can think of the image canvas as the equivalent of the paper on which a photo is printed. While you're working with a digital photo, image data may temporarily lie outside the canvas space, but it will be clipped to the canvas boundary as soon as the image is flattened. To extend our limited analogy just a little further, think of the layer data as the image projected by a photographic enlarger in the darkroom. Although the projected image may be offset or enlarged so that it falls outside the borders of the paper, the data still exists; you can continue to work with it right up until the moment that the photographic paper is exposed.

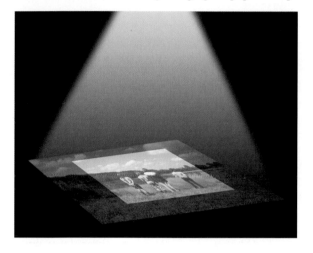

## Adding a border to a photo

By default, the canvas is the same size as the image (if you increase the size of the image file, the canvas is enlarged automatically) and is therefore not visible. However, you can also enlarge the canvas independently of the image size, effectively adding a border around your photo—just as if you printed a photo on a sheet of paper larger than the image.

By default, the extended canvas, and therefore the border, takes on the Background color as set in the color swatches at the bottom of the toolbox.

1   In the Organizer, select the image DSC_1678.jpg from the Lesson 6 images in the Media Browser, making sure not to confuse it with the _Autofix copy. Click the arrow on the Fix tab and Choose Full Photo Edit from the menu.

2   Choose View > Fit On Screen; then, hide the Project Bin by double-clicking its header bar. Hide the Panels Bin by un-checking its name in the Window menu.

3   If you don't see a reasonable amount of blank canvas surrounding the image, hold down the Ctrl / Command key and press the Minus key (-) on your keyboard or choose View > Zoom Out.

**4** Choose Image > Resize > Canvas Size. Move the Canvas Size dialog box, if necessary, so that you can see at least the left half of the image.

**5** Set the Canvas Size dialog box as shown in the illustration below:

- Choose Inches from the units menus. Type **0.5** for both Width and Height.

- Activate the Relative option.

- Leave the Anchor control at the default centered setting.

- Choose Black from the Canvas Extension Color menu.

**6** Click OK.

The new black border appears around the photo in the image window. For the purposes of this exercise, we'll take it one step further, and extend the canvas again to turn the border into an asymmetrical frame.

**7** Choose Image > Resize > Canvas Size. In the Canvas Size dialog box, confirm that the Relative check box is still activated. Leave the Width value at **0** and set the Height to **1 inch**. In the Anchor control grid diagram, click the center square in the top row. At this setting, the height increase will result in the canvas being extended by one inch only at the bottom of the frame. Leave the Canvas Extension Color setting unchanged and click OK.

**8** If you can't see all of the border framing the image, double-click the Hand tool or choose View > Fit On Screen.

The extended border gives you space to add text to the image, making it an easy and effective way to create a postcard, a stylish cover page for a printed document, or a title screen for a slideshow presentation.

9   In the toolbox, select the Horizontal Type tool (**T**).

10  Set up the tool options bar as shown in the illustration below. Choose Lithos Pro from the Font Family menu and Regular from the Font Style menu. In the Font Size text box, type **80 pt**, and then press Enter / Return on your keyboard. Choose Center Text (🗐) from the paragraph alignment options. Click the text color swatch to open the color picker.

**Note:** Photoshop Elements includes several variants of the Type tool. Throughout the remainder of this lesson, the term Type tool will always refer to the Horizontal Type tool, which is the default variant.

11  Move the color picker, if necessary, so that you can see the four monks. Move the pointer over the image; the cursor becomes an eyedropper tool. Sample the brightest orange you can find from the second monk's robe. Click OK.

12  With the Type tool, click below the center of the black space beneath the photo and type **CAMBODIA**.

13  Swipe to select the letter O; then, click the text color swatch to open the color picker. Sample the brightest red you can find in the robe of the monk on the left. Move the pointer over the large color field in the color picker and choose a lighter, bolder shade of the sampled color, and then click OK.

**14** Click the Move tool in the toolbar and drag the text to center it. Choose File > Save As. Activate Include In The Organizer and disable Save In Version Set With Original. Name the file **CAMBODIA** and save it to your My CIB Work folder in Photoshop format with Layers activated. Choose File > Close.

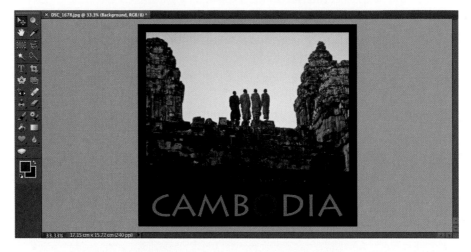

## Adding a quick border

When precision isn't an issue, you can quickly add a border to an image by using the Crop tool, rather than increasing the size of the canvas.

**1** Zoom out far enough so that you can see some of the blank art-board surrounding the image in the edit window.

**2** Use the crop tool to drag a cropping rectangle right around the image.

**3** Drag the corner handles of the crop marquee outside the image area onto the art-board to define the size and shape of border that you wish to create.

**4** When you're satisfied, click the Commit button in the lower right corner of the image. The canvas expands to fill the cropping rectangle, taking on the background color set in the color swatch at the bottom of the toolbox.

# Review questions

1 What are the key differences between adjusting images in Full Edit mode, Quick Edit mode and Guided Edit mode?

2 Can you apply automatic fixes when you are in Full Edit mode?

3 What is the purpose of the Project Bin?

4 Can you float panels and other interface elements in any Edit mode?

5 What is the Smart Brush tool?

# Review answers

1 Full Edit provides the most flexible and powerful image correction environment. Full Edit offers lighting and color correction commands and tools for fixing image defects, making selections, adding text, and painting on your images. Quick Fix provides easy access to a range of basic image editing controls for quickly making common adjustments and corrections. If you're new to digital photography, Guided Edit is the best place to start—stepping you through each procedure to help you get professional-looking results.

2 Yes; the Enhance menu contains commands that are equivalent to the Auto buttons in the Quick Fix panel: Auto Smart Fix, Auto Levels, Auto Contrast, Auto Color Correction, as well as Auto Red Eye Fix. The Enhance menu also provides an Adjust Smart Fix command, which opens a dialog box in which you can specify settings for automatic adjustments.

3 The Project Bin provides easy access to the photos you want to work with, without needing to leave the Editor workspace. You can set the Project Bin to display all the photos that are currently selected in the Media Browser, just those images that are open in the Editor (helpful when some of the open images are hidden behind the front window), or the entire contents of any album in your catalog.

4 No; you can rearrange the workspace only in Full Edit mode.

5 The Smart Brush is both a selection tool and an image adjustment tool—it creates a selection based on similarities in color and texture, through which your choice of editing preset is applied. You can choose from close to seventy Smart Brush presets, each of which can be customized, applied repeatedly for a cumulative effect, or layered with other adjustment presets to produce an almost infinite variety of results.

# 7 ADJUSTING COLOR IN IMAGES

## Lesson Overview

Photoshop Elements delivers a broad range of tools and options for working with color. Whether you want to make corrections for unusual lighting conditions, remove red eye effects, or brighten a smile, you'll find a range of solutions from one-click Auto Fixes to options that give you precise control of the adjustments you apply.

This lesson introduces you to a variety of tools and techniques for fixing color problems in your photos:

* Using automatic options to correct color

* Tweaking automatic color adjustments

* Using Color Variations to correct color balance

* Adjusting skin tones

* Whitening yellowed teeth

* Removing red eye effects

* Using the selection tools and saving selections

* Changing the color of a pictured object

* Replacing a color throughout an image

* Working with color management

 You'll probably need about two hours to complete this lesson.

Explore the many powerful and versatile tools and options available in Photoshop Elements for correcting color problems in your photos. Start with a few of the easy-to-use, one-step image correction features, and then experiment with some of the more advanced photo editing features and techniques that can be mastered easily.

**Note:** Before you start working on this lesson, make sure that you've installed the software on your computer from the application CD (see the Photoshop Elements 10 documentation) and that you have correctly copied the Lessons folder from the CD in the back of this book onto your computer's hard disk (see "Copying the Classroom in a Book files" on page 2). You should also have created a working catalog (see "Creating a new catalog" on page 8).

# Getting started

You'll begin by importing the sample images for this lesson to the CIB Catalog that you created at the beginning of Lesson 1.

1  Start Photoshop Elements and click Organize in the Welcome Screen. When the Organizer opens, make sure that your CIB Catalog is loaded (if you need to refresh your memory, refer to step 2 in the Getting Started section in Lesson 5).

2  Choose File > Get Photos And Video > From Files And Folders. In the Get Photos And Videos From Files And Folders dialog box, locate and select your Lesson07 folder. Activate the option Get Photos From Subfolders and disable the automatic processing options; then, click Get Media.

3  In the Import Attached Keyword Tags dialog box, select the Lesson 07 tag, and then click OK. Click OK to close any other alert dialog box.

## Batch-processing the lesson files

As you discovered in Lesson 6, the batch-processing command lets you apply automatic adjustments to an entire folder of image files at once.

Before you start this lesson, you can follow the steps in "Fixing files automatically in batches" and "Adding the auto-corrected files to your catalog" on page 151 to set up automatic processing for the lesson 7 images. At the end of each of the exercises to follow, you can compare the automatic fixes to the results you achieve using various other techniques.

# Correcting color problems

Color casts are one of the most common of image problems, affecting every color in a photo as if the entire image is overlaid by a colored film. Artificial light sources, unusual shooting conditions, and incorrect camera exposure settings can all result in an unwelcome color cast.

For some images your color problem may be more specific, such as red eyes in a photo taken with a flash, or a portrait spoiled by yellow-looking teeth. Even when a photo is technically perfect, you may still wish to adjust the color—either across the entire image, or just for a particular area or object—in order to create an effect.

You'll begin this lesson by revisiting, and comparing, some of the tools and techniques for making quick and easy adjustments using the simple controls in the Quick Edit mode and the step-by-step editing tasks in Guided Edit mode.

Later in the lesson you'll explore methods for dealing with red eyes and yellow teeth, and learn how to use the selection tools—an essential skill for performing sophisticated, localized edits in Full Edit mode.

## Comparing methods of fixing color

The automatic correction features in Photoshop Elements do an excellent job of bringing out the best in most photographs, but each image—and each image problem—is unique. Some photographs don't respond well to automatic fixes and require a more hands-on approach to color correction. Photoshop Elements offers many ways to adjust color; the more techniques you master, the more likely that you'll be able to meet the challenge presented by a difficult photograph.

In the next exercises you'll compare three different techniques for correcting the same color problem, so you'll need three copies of the original photograph.

1   Select the image 07_01.jpg in the Media Browser, taking care not to confuse the original with the Autofix copy. Click the arrow on the Fix tab at the top of the Task Pane, and choose Quick Photo Edit.

2   Click the Reset Panels button ( ) at the top of the workspace, and then double-click the Hand tool in the toolbox, or choose View > Fit On Screen.

3   Right-click / Control-click the thumbnail in the Project Bin and choose Duplicate from the context menu. In the Duplicate Image dialog box, click OK to accept the default name 07_01 copy.jpg. Repeat the process to create two more duplicates, 07_01 copy 2.jpg and 07_01 copy 3.jpg.

This photo exhibits the overly warm, yellow-orange cast common to many images taken in standard tungsten—or incandescent—lighting. Fluorescent lighting often causes a flat, cold green-blue cast.

Although you can view only one image at a time in the Edit pane while you're in Quick Edit mode, you can easily see which files are open by checking the Project Bin. The name of each image in the Project Bin appears as a tooltip when you hold the pointer over the thumbnail. Alternatively, right-click / Control-click anywhere inside the Project Bin and choose Show File Names from the context menu.

In the Project Bin, a highlighted frame surrounds the active, image—the photo that is currently visible in the Edit pane.

4   Double click the original image 07_01.jpg—the thumbnail at the left—to make it the active photo. Close the file by choosing File > Close, or clicking the Close button (x) in the upper right corner of the Edit pane.

## Correcting color automatically

When you batch-processed the sample files at the start of this lesson, you applied all four automatic Quick Fix options. In this exercise, you'll apply just the Quick Fix color adjustment, so that you can assess the result unaffected by other settings.

1   In the Project Bin, double-click 07_01 copy.jpg—to make it the active file; then, choose Before & After - Vertical from the View menu below the Edit pane. Use the Hand tool and the Zoom slider below the preview to focus on the faces.

2   In the Quick Fix panel, click the Auto button in the Color pane. Compare the Before and After views. There is a marked improvement; the Auto Color fix has corrected the worst of the orange color cast. Skin tones are slightly cooler, clothing colors a little brighter, but the tonal range is still somewhat flat.

▶ **Tip:** If you can't find the My CIB Work folder, refer to "Creating a work folder" on page 3.

3   Choose File > Save. Make sure that Include In The Elements Organizer is activated and the Save In Version Set With Original option is disabled. Name the file **07_01_AutoColor** and save it to your My CIB Work folder in JPEG format. Click Save; then, click OK in the JPEG Options dialog box.

## Adjusting the results of an automatic fix manually

An automatic fix can serve as a good starting point for some manual fine-tuning.

1   In the Project Bin, double-click the image 07_01 copy 2.jpg to make it active. In the Quick Fix panel, click the Auto button in the Color pane.

▶ **Tip:** When you move a slider, the numerical value for the setting is displayed in a tooltip.

2   A slight orange cast can still be detected in the skin tones and the white back-lit panels in the background. In the Balance pane, reduce the Temperature setting to 40 and set the Tint to a value of 10 to give the color a more natural tone.

**3** In the Lighting pane, click the Auto Levels button; then, use the sliders to set the Shadows value to 5 and the Midtones to 15. Click the Commit button (✓) at the top of the Lighting pane.

The contrast has improved, the colors are intensified, and the skin tones have lost the "fake tan" look common in photos captured without a flash in tungsten lighting.

**4** Choose File > Save. Make sure that Include In The Elements Organizer is activated and the Save In Version Set With Original option is disabled. Name the file **07_01_ColorBalanceLighting** and save it to your My CIB Work folder in JPEG format. Click Save; then, click OK in the JPEG Options dialog box.

## Tweaking an automatic fix using Color Variations

The first five commands listed in the Enhance menu apply the same automatic image adjustments as do the various Auto buttons in the Quick Fix panel. These Enhance menu commands are available in both the Quick Edit and Full Edit modes, but not in Guided Edit.

Both the Quick Edit and Full Edit modes also offer other methods of enhancing color that give you finer control over the results. These are the commands in the lower half of the Enhance menu. In this exercise, you'll use one of these options to tweak the adjustments applied by the Auto Color fix button.

**1** In the Project bin, double-click the image 07_01 copy 3.jpg to make it active.

**2** In the Color pane, click the Auto button to apply the Quick Fix color correction; then, choose Enhance > Adjust Color > Color Variations to open the Color Variations dialog box.

**3** In the lower left area of the Color Variations dialog box, make sure that Midtones is selected, and then move the Amount slider one stop to the left of center. Click the Decrease Red and Lighten thumbnails twice each, and click the Decrease Green thumbnail once.

**4** Change the settings from Midtones to Shadows and click the Decrease Red and Decrease Green thumbnails once each, and the Darken thumbnail twice.

**5** Change the setting to Highlights and click the Decrease Red thumbnail once and the Lighten thumbnail four times; then click OK. The Color Variations adjustments have made the colors warmer and more vivid, reduced the yellow-orange color cast, and improved the tonal range.

**6** Choose File > Save. Make sure that Include In The Elements Organizer is activated and the Save In Version Set With Original option is disabled. Name the file **07_01_ColorVariations** and save it to your My CIB Work folder in JPEG format. Click Save; then, click OK in the JPEG Options dialog box.

## Comparing results

In the Project bin, you can see that all three of your saved work files are still open in the Editor. Let's compare them to the batch-processed Autofix file.

**1** Choose File > Open. Locate and open your My CIB Work folder. Select the file 07_01_Autofix, and then click Open. At the top of the Edit tab in the Task pane, click Full to switch to Full edit mode.

**2** Choose Preferences > General from the Edit / Photoshop Elements Editor menu. Activate Allow Floating Documents In Full Edit Mode, and then click OK.

Once you've activated the option to allow floating document windows, this becomes the default for any image opened in Full Edit mode. Throughout the rest of this book however, it will be assumed that you are working with tabbed image windows that are docked (consolidated) in the Edit pane, unless otherwise specified. When you complete this exercise you'll disable floating document windows so that it'll be easier for you to follow the exercise steps as written.

**3** Hide the Project Bin by double-clicking its header bar; then, choose Window > Images > Tile. Use the Zoom and Hand tools to see an area of interest in one of the images, and then choose Window > Images > Match Zoom and Window > Images > Match Location. These commands are also accessible by clicking the Arrange button (⊞) at the top of the workspace and choosing from the menu.

▶ **Tip:** At any given time there is only one active image window. Look at the text in the title bars of the open image windows; the file name and image details are dimmed in the title bars of all but the active image window.

4   Use the Zoom and Hand tools to inspect different areas of the image.
    For each of these tools respectively, activate the Zoom All Windows or Scroll All Windows option in the tool options bar as you compare the four images.

5   Make your favorite the active image and choose Window > Images > Float In Window. Choose View > Fit On Screen. You can cycle through all the open image windows by pressing Ctrl-Tab or Ctrl-Shift-Tab.

6   Choose File > Close All. From the Edit / Photoshop Elements Editor menu, choose Preferences > General and disable floating documents. Click OK.

## Adjusting skin tones

When your primary concern is the people in your photo, you can correct a color cast across the entire image by concentrate on achieving natural, good-looking skin tones. Photoshop Elements offers tools to do just that in all three Edit modes.

1   Choose File > Open. Navigate to and open your Lesson07 folder; then, select the image 07_01.jpg and click Open. Use the Zoom and Hand tools to focus on the faces of the mother and the two daughters that are sitting closest to her.

2   Choose Enhance > Adjust Color > Adjust Color For Skin Tone. In the Adjust Color For Skin Tone dialog box, make sure the Preview option is activated.

**3** As you move the pointer over the image, the cursor changes to an eyedropper tool. With the eyedropper tool, click the lightly shaded area of skin to the right of center on the youngest sister's forehead. The color balance of the entire photo is adjusted using the sampled skin tone as a reference.

**4** Move the Tan, Blush, and Temperature sliders to achieve the skin tones you want, and then click OK. Choose File > Save As. Name the file **07_01_Skin** and save it to your My CIB Work folder with the usual options. Choose File > Close.

## Removing a color cast with one click

▶ **Tip:** The Color Cast Eyedropper tool can be accessed in Guided Edit mode's Remove A Color Cast procedure (as illustrated below), or by choosing Enhance > Adjust Color > Remove Color Cast in Full Edit and Quick Edit modes.

The Color Cast Eyedropper tool provides yet another solution to your color problem that is also available in all three Edit modes.

Use the Color Cast Eyedropper to define a color that should appear temperature-neutral—neither warm nor cool—and the color balance is re-calculated around it. The best choice is a mid gray, though black or white can also work. Choosing the right color can take a little practice. In the photo below, for example, the zippered jacket that appears to be a neutral gray in the before image actually contains a lot of cool blue. In this case, we sampled the brightest point on the lily in the foreground.

# Brightening a smile

Sometimes a photo can be spoiled by a color problem as simple as yellow-looking teeth. As with the red eye effect, Photoshop Elements offers an easy solution that's available in all three Edit modes.

The Whiten Teeth tool, like the Blue Sky and Black And White Touch Up tools, is a variant of the Smart Brush. As such, it is both a selection tool and an image adjustment tool. You can use the Whiten Teeth tool to paint and edit a selection—exactly as you would with the Quick Selection tool—through which the preset tooth whitening adjustment is applied. While the selection is active, you can still add to it or subtract from it, without re-applying the adjustment.

The Whiten Teeth selection and adjustment is made on a new layer separate from the original image in the background layer. The edit remains active on its own adjustment layer—so you can return to alter the selection area or the way the adjustment is applied at any time. You can use the tool more than once on the same area, building up multiple layers that you can then blend for a natural effect.

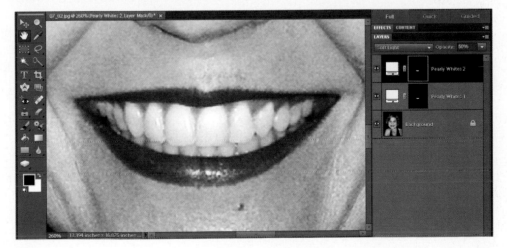

# Working with red eye

The red eye effect occurs when a camera flash is reflected off the retina at the back of the eye so that the dark pupil looks bright red. As you learned in Lesson 2, you can have Photoshop Elements apply an automatic red eye fix during the import process, so the problem is corrected before your images even reach the Organizer. However, the automatic solution is not effective for every photo. In the lesson image chosen for this exercise, the red eye effect is not particularly dramatic, obvious, or well-defined, which makes it a great test case for manual techniques.

## Using the automatic Red Eye Fix

1   In the Organizer, use the Lesson 07 keyword tag, if needed, to locate the file 07_02.jpg. Select the image in the Media Browser; then, click the small arrow on the Fix tab above the Task Pane and choose Quick Photo Edit.

2   Hide the Project Bin and choose Before & After - Horizontal from the View menu below the Edit pane. Use the Zoom and Hand tools to focus on the face of the girl on the right; then, choose Enhance > Auto Red Eye Fix.

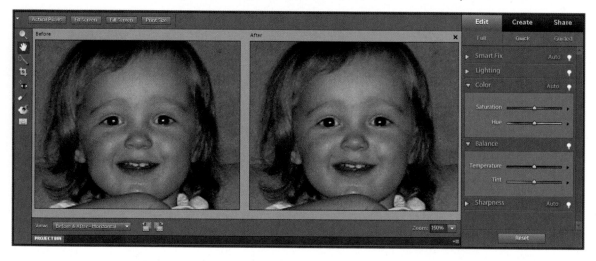

As you can see, the automatic red eye correction does a great job for this little girl. Unfortunately, it hasn't worked for her sisters.

3   Use the Zoom and Hand tools to check the eyes of the other two girls; the automatic fix had no effect for either. In both these cases, the red eye effect may be less pronounced or well-defined, but it's also more difficult to remove.

4   Click the Reset button at the bottom of the Quick Fix panel to clear the Auto Red Eye Fix. Keep the file open for the next exercise.

The automatic red eye removal feature works well for most images, but when you want more control you need to use the Red Eye Removal tool.

## Using the Red Eye Removal tool

For stubborn red eye problems that don't respond well to the automatic fix, the Red Eye Removal tool (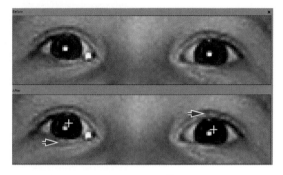), which can be found in both the Full Edit and Quick Edit toolbox, is an easy-to-use and efficient solution.

1  Zoom and pan the photo to focus the view on the eyes of the girl in the center.

2  Select the Red Eye Removal tool ( ) from the tool-box. Click the small white triangle at the far left of the tool options bar and choose Reset Tool from the menu. In the After image, click once in each eye, just outside the upper right corner of the white highlight.

The Red Eye Removal tool over-extends the correction, unevenly blackening portions of the iris and even spilling onto the skin around the eye. Fortunately you can customize the tool to deal with such difficult cases.

3  Choose Edit > Revert. In the Red Eye Removal tool settings in the tool options bar, reduce the Pupil Size to 15% and the Darken Amount to 40%. You can either use the slider controls, type the new values in the text fields, or simply drag left or right over the Pupil Size and Darken Amount values.

4  In the After image, click at the same points you used in step 2. If the effect is off-center, undo and click a slightly different spot.

The red is removed from both eyes. The darkened areas are somewhat shapeless and blurry, giving no real definition to the pupils, but we'll accept that for now.

5  Use the Zoom and Hand tools to position the image so that you can focus on the eyes of the girl on the left of the photo.

6  Make sure the Red Eye Removal tool is still selected. In the tool options bar, reduce the Pupil Size to 10% and the Darken Amount to 20%; then, drag a marquee rectangle around each eye in turn.

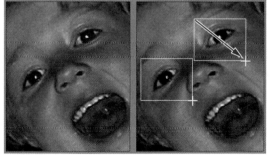

Experiment with the size and placement of the rectangle around each eye to get the best results. If you're not satisfied, just undo and try again. Hold down the Alt / Option key to draw the rectangle from its center.

7  To re-instate the Auto Red Eye Fix for the little girl on the right, zoom out so that you can see all three faces, and then choose Enhance > Auto Red Eye Fix.

8  Choose File > Save As. Set the options to include the file in the Organizer, but not in a Version Set. Name the file **07_02_RedEye**, to be saved to your My CIB Work folder in JPEG format. Click Save, leaving all other options in the Save and JPEG Options dialog boxes unchanged, and then choose File > Close.

# Making selections

By default, the entire area of an image layer is active—any adjustments you make are applied across the whole photo. If you want to edit a specific area or object within the image, you first need to make a selection. Once you've made a selection it becomes the only active area of the image; the rest of the image layer is protected.

Typically, the boundaries of a selection are indicated by a selection marquee: a flashing border of dashed black and white lines, sometimes likened to marching ants. Selections can be geometric in shape or free form, with crisp borders or soft edges. They can be created manually with the pointer, or calculated automatically by Photoshop Elements, based on similarity in color and texture within the image.

You can save a selection, and then re-use it or edit it later, which can save you time when you're building up a complicated selection, or when you need to use the same selection more than once.

Perhaps the simplest, most effective way to create a selection is to "paint" it onto your image. This exercise focuses on the use of two selection tools in Photoshop Elements that let you do just that: the Selection Brush and the Quick Selection tool.

**Note:** The lesson image has been saved in Photoshop file format and not as a JPEG file. The Photoshop format can store additional information together with the image data. In this case, a selection has been made previously, and then saved with the file.

1 In the Organizer, use the Lesson 07 tag to locate the file 07_03.psd. Select the file in the Media Browser, taking care not to confuse the original file with the Autofix copy; then, click the arrow on the Fix tab and choose Full Photo Edit.

2 Hide the Panel Bin by choosing its name from the Window menu; then, hide the Project Bin by double-clicking its header bar. Double-click the Hand tool or choose View > Fit On Screen.

3 Choose Select > Load Selection. In the Load Selection dialog box, choose the saved selection "petals" from the Source menu. In the Operation settings, activate the New Selection option, and then click OK.

The saved selection is loaded. The left half of the flower is now surrounded by a flashing selection marquee, indicating that it has become the active portion of the image.

The petals at the right need to be added to make the selection complete. In the next exercise, you'll modify the saved selection to include the missing petals.

4 Choose Select > Deselect to clear the current selection.

5 In the toolbox, the Selection Brush is grouped with the Quick Selection tool. Right-click / Control-click the Quick Selection tool and choose the Selection Brush from the menu.

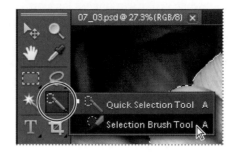

## Using the Selection Brush

The Selection Brush tool has two modes: the default Selection mode, where you paint over the area you want to select for editing, and Mask mode, which lets you brush a semi-opaque overlay onto the areas you want to protect from editing.

1 In the tool options bar, make sure that the Add To Selection button at the far left is activated (*see below*); then, set the brush Size to 100 px (pixels), choose Selection from the Mode menu, and set the brush Hardness value to 100%.

2 Drag with the Selection Brush to paint a live selection over the interior of the petals in the right half of the flower, as in the illustration below. Don't try to paint all the way to the edges; you'll do that in the next step.

▶ **Tip:** While you paint your selection onto the image, release the mouse button every second or two so that you don't have to repeat too much work if you need to undo a stroke.

Now you need to reduce your brush size to paint around the edges of the petals, adding to your selection. You could move the Size slider to change your brush size, but while you're working it's far more convenient to press the open bracket key ([) to reduce the brush size in increments and the close bracket key (]) to enlarge it.

**Tip:** When you need to make a difficult or detailed selection, use the Zoom tool to magnify the area of interest. To remove an area from the selection, hold down the Alt / Option key as you paint.

3   Press the left bracket key ([) to reduce the Selection Brush size to 25 pixels. Paint the selection to the edges of the petals. Use the bracket keys to change the brush size as needed, until the selection outline completely surrounds the petals in the right half of the flower. Make sure the selection extends just a little into the yellow center of the bloom.

If you found it tedious using the Selection Brush tool, you'll appreciate learning about the Quick Selection tool later in this lesson. You'll also learn that both tools have their uses. But first, you'll make use of your hard work and save the results.

## Editing a saved selection

**Note:** The New Selection setting replaces the saved selection with the current selection. The Subtract from Selection setting subtracts the current selection from the saved selection. Intersect with Selection replaces the saved selection with the intersection between the current selection and the saved selection.

In this exercise you'll add your live selection to the one that was saved with the file. You can modify a saved selection by replacing it, adding to it, or subtracting from it.

1   With your new selection still active, choose Select > Load Selection.

2   In the Load Selection dialog box, choose the saved selection "petals" as the Source Selection. Under Operation, activate the option Add To Selection; this setting will combine your current selection with the saved selection of the rest of the flower. Click OK.

You should now see a selection border entirely surrounding all the flower's petals.

**Tip:** If you've missed a spot, simply paint it in with the Selection Brush tool. If you've selected too much, simply set an appropriate brush size, switch to Subtract From Selection mode in the tool options bar, or hold Alt / Option, and paint out your mistakes.

**3** Choose Select > Save Selection. In the Save Selection dialog box, choose petals as the Selection name, activate Replace Selection in the Operation options, and then click OK. Choose Select > Deselect.

## Using the Quick Selection tool

The Quick Selection tool enables you to select an area in the image by simply drawing, scribbling, or clicking on the area you want to select. You don't need to be precise, because while you're drawing, Photoshop Elements automatically expands the selection border based on similarities in color and texture.

In this exercise, you'll use the Quick Selection tool to select everything *but* the flower, and then switch the selected and un-selected areas in the photo to establish the selection you want. This technique can be a real time-saver in situations where it proves difficult to select a complex object directly.

**1** In the toolbox, right-click / Control-click to select the Quick Selection tool (🖊️), which is grouped in the toolbox with the Selection Brush you used earlier.

**2** In the tool options bar, make sure the New Selection mode button on the far left is activated. Set a brush diameter in the Brush picker. For the purposes of this exercise, you can use the default brush diameter of 30 px (pixels).

**3** Scribble over the area to the right if the flower, making sure to draw through black areas, lighter and darker greens, as well as the petals at the right edge of the photo, as shown in the illustration at the right. Release the pointer once or twice to see the result. As you draw, Photoshop Elements automatically expands the selection to areas adjacent to your stroke that have similarities in color and texture.

**4** With an active selection already in place, the Quick Selection tool defaults to Add To Selection mode. Scribble over, or click into, un-selected areas around the flower until everything is selected but the flower itself. Hold down the Alt / Option key as you drag to subtract an area from your selection.

**5** Finally, turn the selection inside out by choosing Select > Inverse, thereby masking the background and selecting the flower—ready for the next exercise.

## Working with selections

Now that you have an active selection outline around the sunflower, you can apply any adjustment you like and only the flower will be affected.

1  Choose Enhance > Adjust Color > Adjust Hue/Saturation.

2  In the Hue/Saturation dialog box, drag the Hue and Saturation sliders to change the color of the flower.

3  Hold down the Alt / Option key; the Cancel button changes to the Reset button. Click Reset to clear your changes.

4  Experiment with applying changes to the Master channel, as well as to the different color channels separately.

Notice that the flower changes color, but the background does not. Only the pixels inside a live selection are affected by edits or adjustments.

5  Click Cancel in the Hue/Saturation dialog box to discard your changes.

By inverting the selection, you could apply changes to the background of the photo instead of the flower.

6  With the flower still selected, choose Select > Inverse.

7  Choose Enhance > Convert To Black And White.

8  Under Select A Style in the Convert To Black And White dialog box, experiment with the different styles to see the effects on the image. Use the Adjustment Intensity sliders to vary the amount of change for red, green, blue, and contrast.

Click Undo if you make an adjustments you don't like. Click Reset to discard all your adjustments and start again.

9 When you're done, click Cancel to discard your changes and dismiss the Convert To Black And White dialog box.

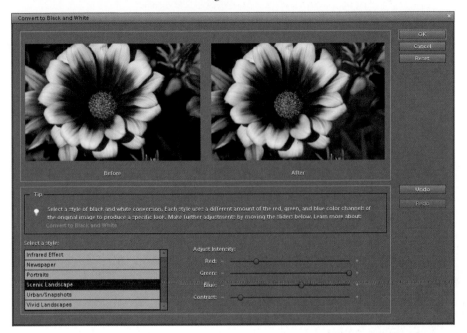

10 Choose Select > Inverse to select the flower again. With the Quick Selection tool still active, old down the Alt / Option key and try to remove all of the center parts of the flower from the selection, including the dark bronze-colored bases of the petals.

You can see that it's very difficult to control the results in this situation—especially when it comes to the shadowed areas where petals overlap. This is precisely the kind of situation where the Selection Brush comes into its own.

11 Swap the Quick Selection tool for its toolbox partner, the Selection Brush. Work at high magnification while you use the Selection Brush together with the Alt / Option key to remove the central disc and its ring of darker petal bases from the selection. When you're satisfied, choose Select > Save Selection. Name the new selection **petals quick select**, activate the New Selection option under Operation, and then click OK.

12 Choose File > Save As. Make sure that the image will be included in the Organizer, but not in a Version Set. Name the file **07_03_SavedSelections**, to be saved to your My CIB Work folder, in Photoshop format. Click Save, and then choose File > Close.

# Why won't Photoshop Elements do what I tell it to do?

In some situations, the changes you try to apply to an image may not seem to work. You may hear a beep, indicating that you're trying to do something that's not allowed. The following list offers explanations and solutions for common issues that might be blocking your progress.

**Commit is required**

Several tools, including the Type tool require you to click the Commit button before you can move on to another task. The same is true when you crop with the Crop tool or resize a layer or selection with the Move tool.

**Cancel is required**

The Undo command isn't available while you have uncommitted changes made with some tools—for example, the Type tool, Move tool, and Crop tool. If you want to undo these edits, click the Cancel button instead of using the Undo command or shortcut.

**Edits are restricted by an active selection**

When you create a selection (using a marquee tool, the Quick Selection tool, or the Selection Brush tool, for example), you limit the active area of the image. Any edits you make will apply only within the selected area. If you try to make changes to an area outside the selection, nothing happens. Edits are restricted by an active selection. If you want to deactivate a selection, choose Select > Deselect, and then you can work on any area of the image.

**Move tool is required**

When you drag a selection, the selection marquee moves, not the image within the selection marquee. If you want to move a selected part of the image or an entire layer, use the Move tool.

# Why won't Photoshop Elements do what I tell it to do? *(continued)*

**Background layer is selected**

Many changes cannot be applied to the Background layer. For example, you can't erase, delete, change the opacity, or drag the Background layer to a higher level in the layer stack. If you need to apply changes to the Background layer, double-click it and rename it (or accept the default name, Layer 0).

**Active layer is hidden**

In most cases, the edits you make apply to only the currently selected layer—the one highlighted in the Layers palette. If an eye icon does not appear beside that layer in the Layers palette, then the layer is hidden and you cannot edit it. Or, if the image on the selected layer is not visible because it is blocked by opacity on an upper layer, you will actually be changing that layer, but you won't see the changes in the image window.

The active layer is hidden, the view is blocked by opacity on an upper layer, or the active layer is locked.

**Active layer is locked**

If you lock a layer by selecting the layer and then clicking the Lock in the Layers palette, the lock prevents the layer from changing. To unlock a layer, select the layer, and then click the Lock at the bottom of the Layers palette to remove the Lock.

**Wrong layer is selected (for editing text)**

If you want to make changes to a text layer, be sure that layer is selected in the Layers palette before you start. If a non-text layer is selected when you click the Type tool in the image window, Photoshop Elements creates a new text layer instead of placing the cursor in the existing text layer.

# Replacing the color of a pictured object

Photoshop Elements offers two very different methods for switching colors in an image: the Color Replacement tool and the Replace Color dialog box. As with the Selection Brush and the Quick Selection tool, the color replacement method that will be most effective depends on the characteristics of the photo you're working with and the extent of the change you wish to make.

## Using the Color Replacement tool

The Color Replacement tool enables you to replace specific colors in your image by painting over a targeted color with another. You can use the Color Replacement tool either for localized color correction, or for creative purposes.

1   In the Organizer, use the Lesson 07 keyword tag to isolate the images for this lesson. In the Media Browser, right-click / Control-click the image 07_04.jpg, taking care not to confuse it with the Autofix copy, and choose Edit With Photoshop Elements Editor from the context menu.

2   In the Editor, click Window > Reset Panels or click the Reset Panels button (⟳) at the top of the workspace. Hide the Project Bin by double-clicking its header bar, and then hide the Panel Bin by un-checking its name in the Window menu. Double-click the Hand tool or choose View > Fit On Screen.

3   Click the foreground color swatch below the tools in the Toolbar to open the Color Picker. In the Color Picker, type new values in the text boxes to set the Hue (H), Saturation (S), and Brightness (B) to **325**, **75**, and **100** respectively. Click OK to close the Color Picker.

4   Right-click / Control-click to select the Color Replacement tool (🖌), which is grouped in the toolbox with the Brush tool, the Impressionist Brush tool, and the Pencil tool.

5   Click the small white arrow at the far left of the tool options bar and choose Reset Tool; then, use the Brush Picker to set the brush Diameter to 80 px. You can leave all the other options for this tool at the default settings.

You'll use the new foreground color to brighten up the dark gray parka worn by the girl on the right, but first you need to know how the Color Replacement tool works.

The cursor for the Color Replacement tool consists of a set of cross-hairs at the center of a circle indicating the brush size. When you drag in the image, the foreground color is applied to any pixel falling inside the cursor's circle that matches the color under the cross-hairs, within the tolerance value specified in the tool options bar.

What this means is that you can be very relaxed as you paint; as long as you keep the cross-hairs inside the area of color that you wish to replace, the circle can overlap the neighboring area without changing the color, making it easy to paint right up to the edge. Only pixels inside the circle that match the sampled color under the cross-hairs are affected.

6   Paint over the dark parka, moving slowly around the edges and always keeping the cross-hairs over the gray fabric. Stop every few seconds so that you can undo a mistake without losing too much work. For now, avoid the edge of the hood around the girl's face and the shadowed underside of her arm, where it rests against her sister's orange jacket. Take extra care with the deeper seams and folds in the fabric, making sure that the cursor cross-hairs make contact with the darker shades in these areas. Work carefully, sometimes simply clicking rather than stroking, or reduce the brush size as you work by pressing the left bracket key ( [ ). You may need to paint over some areas twice to apply the color evenly.

7   In the tool options bar, reduce the brush diameter to 10 px, and the Tolerance value to 10%. Zoom in close to work around the edge of the hood and the lower edge of the arm, keeping the cross-hairs inside the area you wish to re-color.

8   You can now adjust the new color to better match the de-saturated tones in this image. Use the Quick Selection tool ( ) to isolate the re-colored parka, and then choose Enhance > Adjust Color > Adjust Hue/Saturation. Set the Saturation to **-15** and the Lightness to **+15**; then, click OK.

9   Choose Enhance > Adjust Lighting > Levels. Under the Input Levels graph, move the black stop to the right to a value of 40; then, drag the grey stop to the left to a value of 1.30. Click OK and choose Select > Deselect.

10  Choose Save As. Make sure that the image will be included in the Organizer, but not grouped in a Version Set. Name the file **07_04_ReplaceColor** and save it to your My CIB Work folder in JPEG format. Click Save. Click Ok to accept the JPEG options, and then close the file.

## Replacing a color throughout an image

Using the Replace Color dialog box is often faster than painting with the Color Replacement tool, though it can be hard to control when the color of the object you want to change is present in other areas. Even for a difficult case, you can achieve a good result by using the Replace Color dialog box in conjunction with a selection.

In the following exercises, you'll repaint a red toy car. You'll make your changes on a duplicate of the Background layer, enabling you to easily compare the finished project to the original picture. First, you'll work on the entire image, which will give you an indication of where—and how much—the color change will affect the rest of the photo. In the second stage, you'll use a selection to restrict the changes.

1 In the Organizer, use the Lesson 07 keyword tag to isolate the images for this lesson. Right-click / Control-click the image 07_05.jpg (not the Autofix copy), and choose Edit With Photoshop Elements Editor from the context menu.

2 In the Editor, click Window > Reset Panels or click the Reset Panels button (⟳) at the top of the workspace. Hide the Project Bin and the grouped Effects and Content panels by double-clicking their header bars; then, double-click the Hand tool or choose View > Fit On Screen.

3 In the Editor, choose Layer > Duplicate Layer and accept the default name. Alternatively, you can drag the Background layer to the New Layer button (⬜) at the bottom of the Layers panel. By duplicating the layer, you'll have an original to fall back on should you need it.

4 With the Background copy layer still selected in the Layers panel, choose Enhance > Adjust Color > Replace Color.

5 In the Replace Color dialog box, make sure that the Eyedropper tool—the left-most of the three eyedropper buttons—is activated, and that Fuzziness is set to the default value of 40. Activate the Image option below the preview thumbnail, and make sure that the Preview option is activated so that you'll be able to see the results of your adjustments in the Edit pane as you work.

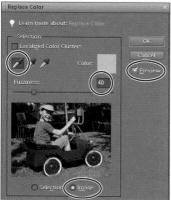

6 Move the pointer over the thumbnail preview in the Replace Color dialog box and click once with the eyedropper on the sunlit side of the toy car. Change the preview option from Image to Selection, so that you can see the extent of the color selection you just made indicated as white areas on a black background.

**7** Below the selection preview, either use the sliders or type in the text boxes to set the Hue, Saturation, and Lightness values to **–160**, **+50**, and **+5** respectively.

**8** To adjust the area of selected color—or color-application area—start by clicking the second of the three eyedropper buttons to switch the Eyedropper tool to Add To Sample mode, and then click in the main image window in a few areas where the paint on the car still appears red.

**9** Use the Add To Sample eyedropper again, if necessary, and then drag the Fuzziness slider left and right and until you have full coverage on the car. In both the Edit pane and the black and white selection preview, you can see that it's not possible to change the color of the car using this technique without affecting much of the background, and even the girl's skin.

**10** Click Cancel to close the Replace Color dialog box.

## Replacing a color in a limited area of an image

In this exercise you'll limit the color change to a selected area of the photograph.

**1** Make sure the Background copy layer is still selected in the Layers panel. In the toolbox, select the Rectangular Marquee tool and drag a rectangular selection marquee just big enough to surround the car.

**2** In the toolbox, switch to the Quick Selection tool (). In the tool options bar, click the tool variant at the right to set the Quick Selection tool to Subtract From Selection mode. In the Brush picker, set the brush diameter to 50 pixels.

**3** Use the Quick Selection tool to subtract the girl's clothing and leg from the rectangular selection. Trim away the red chair legs in the upper left corner and as much of the sunlit grass around the car as possible. Subtract the portion of the girl's foot that's visible beneath the car. If you go too far and need to add areas back into the selection, simply hold down the Shift key as you work to switch the Quick Selection tool temporarily to Add To Selection mode.

▶ **Tip:** Don't be too concerned about the small amount of grass overlapping the car's wheels; within the constraints of our exercise, there's not a lot we can do about it.

4  Choose Enhance > Adjust Color > Replace Color. Using the techniques and settings you used in steps 5 to 9 of the previous exercise, change the color of the car. Be sure to follow the steps in order; you need to sample the original red before setting hue, saturation, and brightness to define the replacement color.

5  When you're satisfied with the results, click OK to close the Replace Color dialog box; then choose Select > Deselect, or press Ctrl+D / Command+D.

6  To compare the edited image with the original, toggle the visibility of the Background copy layer by clicking the eye icon beside the layer thumbnail. When you're done, be sure to leave the visibility for the new layer switched on.

**7**  Right-click / Control-click the Background copy layer and choose Flatten Image from the context menu. Alternately, you could choose the Flatten Image command from the Layers panel Options menu at the right of the panel's header bar. The image is flattened to a single layer; the layer you edited replaces the original background layer.

**8**  Choose File > Save As. Name the file **07_05_ReplaceColor** and save it to your My CIB Work folder in JPEG format. Make sure that the image will be included in the Organizer, but not grouped in a Version Set. Click Save, accept the JPEG Options settings, and then close the file.

# About printing color pictures

Color problems in your photos can result from a variety of causes, such as incorrect exposure, the quality of the camera, artificial lighting, or even weather conditions. If an image is flawed, you can usually improve it by editing it with Photoshop Elements, as you did with the images in this lesson. Sometimes, however, pictures that look great on your computer don't turn out so well when you print them; fortunately, there are things you can do to make sure that what you get from the printer is as close as possible to what you see on screen.

Firstly, it's important that you calibrate your monitor regularly, so that it's set to display the range of color in your photographs accurately. However, even with a correctly calibrated display, your prints may still look disappointing if your printer interprets color information differently from your computer. You can correct this problem by activating the appropriate type of color management.

## Working with color management

Moving a photo from your camera to your monitor and from there to a printer can cause an apparent shift in the colors in the image. This shift occurs because every device has a different *color gamut* or *color space*—the range of colors that the device is capable of interpreting and reproducing.

To achieve consistent color between digital cameras, scanners, computer monitors, and printers, you need to use color management. Color management software acts as an interpreter, translating colors so that each device can reproduce them in the same way. This software knows how each device and program understands color, and adjusts colors so that what you see on screen is similar to the colors in your printed image. It should be noted, however, that not all colors may match exactly.

Color management software calls on device-specific color profiles: mathematical descriptions of each device's color space. If these profiles are compliant with the standards of the ICC (International Color Consortium), they will help you maintain consistent color. When you save a file, activate Embed Color Profile in the Save As dialog box. In Photoshop Elements, you can access the color management controls from the Edit menu in both the Organizer and the Editor.

## Setting up color management

1   Choose Edit > Color Settings; then, select one of these color management options in the Color Settings dialog box:

- **No Color Management** uses your monitor profile as the working color space. It removes any embedded profiles when opening images, and does not apply a profile when saving.

- **Always Optimize Colors For Computer Screens** uses sRGB as the working color space, preserves embedded profiles, and assigns sRGB when opening untagged files.

- **Always Optimize For Printing** uses Adobe RGB as the working color space, preserves embedded profiles, and assigns Adobe RGB when opening untagged files.

- **Allow Me To Choose** lets you choose whether to assign sRGB (the default) or Adobe RGB when opening untagged files.

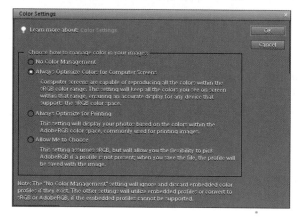

2   Click OK to close the Color Settings dialog box.

Further information on color management, including monitor calibration, can be found in a series of topics in Photoshop Elements Help.

Congratulations, you've completed another exercise. You've learned a wide variety of techniques for working with color in your photos—from tweaking automatic corrections to switching the color of a pictured object. You've gained a lot of experience in all three Edit modes and honed your selection skills—essential for many sophisticated and creative color edits. Now, take a minute to refresh your knowledge by reading through the review questions and answers on the following page.

# Review questions

1  How does the Color Variations command help you correct color problems in a photo?

2  What makes selections so important for adjusting color?

3  Name at least two selection tools and describe how they work.

4  How does the Color Replacement tool work?

# Review answers

1  The Color Variations command provides a very visual, intuitive approach to color correction—making it especially useful when you know that you don't like the color in your photo, but are unsure of what you need to do to fix it. The Color Variations dialog box includes a before and after preview, and an array of image thumbnails that show you just how your image will look if you tweak one color component or another. You can set the controls to deal with saturation, shadows, midtones, or highlights.

2  A selection defines an area as the only part of a layer that can be altered. The areas outside the selection are protected from change for as long as the selection is active. This enables you make adjustments selectively, targeting specific areas or objects.

3  The first selection tool you used in this lesson is the Selection Brush tool, which works like a paintbrush. The Quick Selection tool is similar, but is in most cases a faster, more flexible option. There are more selection tools than are discussed in this lesson: The Magic Wand tool selects areas with the same color as that on which you click. The Rectangular Marquee tool and the Elliptical Marquee tool make selections of a fixed geometric shape. The Lasso tool lets you draw free-form selections, and the Magnetic Lasso tool helps to draw complicated selections around even irregular object edges. The Polygonal Lasso tool is the tool of choice for selecting straight-sided objects.

4  The Color Replacement tool samples the color under the pointer and replaces it with any color that you choose. The cursor for the Color Replacement tool consists of cross-hairs at the center of a circle indicating the brush size. When you drag in the image, the color under the cross-hairs is sampled continuously and the foreground color is applied to any pixel inside the circle that matches the sampled color, within the tolerance value specified in the tool options bar. As long as you keep the cross-hairs inside the area of color that you wish to replace, you can overlap the adjacent area without changing the color, making it easy to paint right up to the edge.

# 8 FIXING EXPOSURE PROBLEMS

## Lesson Overview

Photoshop Elements makes it easy to fix images that are too dark or too light and rescue photos that are dull, flat, or simply fading away.

Start with Quick Fix and Guided Edit and work up to Full Edit as you learn how to make the most of poorly exposed images, retrieve detail from photos that are too dark and liven up images that look flat and washed-out. Photoshop elements delivers powerful, easy-to-use tools for correcting exposure and lighting problems in all three Edit modes.

In this lesson you'll be introduced to a variety of techniques for dealing with a range of common exposure problems:

- Brightening underexposed photographs
- Correcting parts of an image selectively
- Saving selection shapes to reuse in later sessions
- Working with adjustment layers and layer masks
- Choosing layer blending modes
- Using layer opacity settings
- Adjusting lighting controls manually
- Enhancing overexposed and faded photographs

 You'll probably need about one and a half hours to complete this lesson.

Learn how to make the most of images that were
captured in unusual lighting conditions, retrieving
detail from overly dark photos and putting the spark
back into images that look dull or washed-out.
Find out how Photoshop Elements can help you save
those faded memories—no matter what your level
of experience—with a suite of powerful, easy-to-use
tools and the versatility of three Edit modes.

195

● **Note:** Before you start working on this lesson, make sure that you've installed the software on your computer from the application CD (see the Photoshop Elements 10 documentation) and that you have correctly copied the Lessons folder from the CD in the back of this book onto your computer's hard disk (see "Copying the Classroom in a Book files" on page 2). You should also have created a working catalog (see "Creating a new catalog" on page 8).

# Getting started

To start, you'll import the sample images for this lesson to the CIB Catalog that you created at the beginning of Lesson 1.

1   Start Photoshop Elements and click Organize in the Welcome Screen. When the Organizer opens, make sure that your CIB Catalog is loaded (if you need to refresh your memory, refer to step 2 in the Getting Started section in Lesson 5).

2   Choose File > Get Photos And Video > From Files And Folders. In the Get Photos And Videos From Files And Folders dialog box, locate and select your Lesson08 folder. Activate the option Get Photos From Subfolders and disable the automatic processing options; then, click Get Media.

3   In the Import Attached Keyword Tags dialog box, select the Lesson 08 tag, and then click OK. Click OK to close any other alert dialog box.

## Batch-processing the lesson files

As you discovered in Lesson 6, the batch-processing command lets you apply automatic adjustments to an entire folder of image files at once.

Before you start this lesson, you can follow the steps in "Fixing files automatically in batches" and "Adding the auto-corrected files to your catalog" on page 151 to set up automatic processing for the lesson 8 images. At the end of each of the exercises to follow, you can compare the automatic fixes to the results you achieve using various other techniques.

# Adjusting images for tonal balance

Most image problems fall into two basic categories: color or exposure. In some photos, the two issues can be inter-related, and there is also some overlap in the tools and techniques you'll use to correct them.

In the previous lesson, you gained experience recognizing and dealing with color deficiencies in your photos. This lesson will focus on exposure and lighting: issues that effect the *tonal balance* of your image.

Ideally, an image should have a good spread of tonal values from dark to light; any imbalance can result in a photo that is too dark or too light, has too little contrast or too much, or is lacking detail in the shadows, the mid-tones, or the highlights.

As with color correction, Photoshop Elements offers a range of tools for adjusting exposure that are available in all three Edit modes. In the exercises to follow, you'll look at a variety of ways to get the best from poorly exposed images, retrieve detail from photos that are too dark, and liven up images that look flat and washed-out.

# Brightening an underexposed image

Underexposed photographs tend to look dull and flat, or too dark—often across the entire image, but sometimes in just part of it. While the lighting auto-fix feature does a good job with most images, this exercise will teach you techniques that will give you more control for correcting exposure in problem photos.

## Applying Quick Fix adjustments

The first technique you'll learn makes use of the Quick Edit mode.

1  Use the Lesson 08 tag to isolate the lesson images, if needed; then, select the file ghent_ghirls.jpg. Click the arrow on the Fix tab and choose Quick Photo Edit.

2  Click the Smart Fix Auto button at the top of the Quick Fix panel. The photo becomes a little brighter overall, but the skin tones remain quite dark and flat. Drag the Shadows, Midtones, and Highlights sliders in turn to set a value of 20 for each. As you lighten the shadows, note the detail retrieved in the dress of the second girl from the left. Watch the girls' hair as you darken the highlights.

> ▶ **Tip:** Use the View menu below the Edit pane to switch between the After Only view and the Before & After views to help you assess the results of your adjustments as you work.

You've improved the image substantially with just a few clicks. However, although the skin tones have been lightened, they are still a little cool.

**3** In the Color and Balance panes, drag both the Hue and Temperature sliders just fractionally to the right. Take care not to make the image too pink or overly yellow; we set Hue and Temperature values of 4 and 54 respectively.

**4** Commit the changes by clicking the Commit button ( ✓ ) in the header bar of the pane in which you made your most recent adjustment.

Original image       Auto Smart Fix and Lighting sliders       Temperature and Hue tweaked

▶ **Tip:** If you can't find the My CIB Work folder, refer to "Creating a work folder" on page 3.

**5** Choose File > Save. Make sure that Include In The Elements Organizer is activated and disable Save In Version Set With Original. Name the new file **ghent_ghirls_Quick**, to be saved to your My CIB Work folder in JPEG format. Click Save. In the JPEG Options dialog box, use the slider to set the Quality to 9, and then click OK. Choose File > Close.

## Adjusting exposure in Guided Edit mode

When you're not sure exactly what adjustments a poorly exposed image needs, the Guided Edit mode offers three procedures for correcting lighting and exposure: Lighten Or Darken, Brightness And Contrast, and Adjust Levels—each with easy-to-follow prompts and instructions that make it easy for even a novice to get great results. You can improve your photos quickly, at the same time as learning image correction concepts and techniques that you can apply even in Full Edit mode.

**1** In the media browser, select the image ghent_ghirls.jpg; then, click the arrow on the Fix tab and choose Guided Photo Edit. In the guided tasks menu, expand the Color And Lighting group, if necessary; then, click Lighten Or Darken.

**2** Click the Auto button at the upper right of the Lighten Or Darken A Photo pane. For this image, the result is barely noticeable. Whether you use the Auto button or not, you can adjust the lighting controls manually. Drag the sliders to set the Lighten Shadows control to a value of 40, Darken Highlights to 20, and Midtone Contrast to 30; then click Done.

**3** Choose File > Save. Make sure that Include In The Elements Organizer is activated and disable Save In Version Set With Original. Name the new file **ghent_ghirls_Guided** and choose the JPEG format. Click Save, and then click OK in the JPEG Options dialog box to accept the quality setting carried over from the previous exercise. Choose File > Close.

Once again, the adjusted image looks considerably better than the original; however, it would be ideal if we could treat the mother and daughters in the foreground separately from the city background, which still looks a little dull and flat.

## Fixing exposure in Full Edit mode

Underexposure problems can often be caused by your camera automatically cutting down exposure to compensate for backlighting. In our example, the bright highlights edging our subjects may contribute to the problem in this way; their backs are obviously well lit, while the lighting on their faces and in the background is low and indirect. It's also possible that the camera's exposure settings were incorrect.

If your photo is a difficult case, more elaborate methods than those you've used in the Quick and Guided Edit modes might be necessary to achieve the best results. In Full Edit mode you can work with multiple layers and blending modes, and also make selections to isolate specific parts of an image for special treatment.

## Using blending modes

In a multiple-layered image file, each layer has its own blending mode that defines the way it will interact with the layers below it in the stacking order. By default, a newly created layer uses the Normal blending mode: it will not blend with the layer below except where it contains transparency or when the opacity for the layer is set to less than 100%. The Darken and Lighten blending modes will blend a layer with the layers below it only where the result will darken or lighten the lower layers. Other blending modes produce more complex results.

> **Tip:** For information on the effects produced by the different layer blending modes, please refer to Photoshop Elements Help.

If a photo is too dark, applying the Screen blending mode to an overlaid duplicate of the background layer may correct the problem. If your photo is overexposed, an overlaid duplicate with the Multiply blending mode can be a solution. You can adjust the opacity of the overlaid layer to control the intensity of the effect.

**1** In the Media Browser, right-click / Control-click the image ghent_ghirls.jpg, taking care not to confuse the original file with the edited copies, and choose Edit With Photoshop Elements Editor from the context menu.

**2** In Full Edit mode, choose Window > Reset Panels or click the Reset Panels button (⟳) at the top of the workspace. Hide the Project Bin and the grouped Effects and Content panels by double-clicking their header bars. Double-click the Hand tool in the toolbox, or choose View > Fit On Screen.

▶ **Tip:** You can also duplicate a selected layer by choosing Duplicate Layer, either from the Layer menu or from the selected layer's context menu.

**3** In the Layers panel you can see that the image has only one layer: the Background. Duplicate the Background layer by dragging it onto the New Layer button (▢) at the lower left corner of the Layers panel.

The new layer, Background copy, is high-lighted in the Layers panel, indicating that it's currently the selected—or active—layer.

▶ **Tip:** If the layer blending mode menu is disabled, make sure that you have the copy layer—not the original Background—selected in the Layers panel.

**4** With the Background copy layer selected, choose Screen from the blending mode menu at the top of the Layers panel. The image becomes much brighter overall, but the girls still look underexposed. Duplicate the layer Background copy with it's Screen blending mode by dragging it onto the New Layer button. At the top of the Layers panel, set the second duplicate layer's opacity to 50%.

**5** Choose File > Save. Make sure that Include In The Elements Organizer is activated and disable Save In Version Set With Original. Name the new file **ghent_ghirls_Screen** and choose the Photoshop (PSD) format. Make sure the Layers option is activated, and then click Save. If the Format Options dialog box appears, activate Maximize Compatibility and click OK.

**6** To quickly compare the adjusted image to the original, toggle the visibility of the Background Copy layers by clicking the eye icon beside the layer thumbnails. When you're done, close the file without saving.

In this exercise you've seen how using a blending mode can brighten a dull image. For many photos, however, applying a blending mode over the entire image can adversely affect areas that were OK to begin with. In this example, there has been no really "destructive" effect on the background—as there may have been had the buildings been brightly lit by sunlight—but the background does have a somewhat washed-out look and seems to compete for attention with the foreground elements.

## About adjustment layers

An adjustment layer is like an overlay or lens filter over the underlying layers, perhaps darkening the photo, perhaps making it appear pale and faded, or intensifying its hues—but remaining separate from the image itself. Effects applied on an adjustment layer can be easily revised, or even removed, because the pixels of the image layers are not permanently modified. You can even copy an adjustment layer from one photo and paste it on top of the image layers in another—a real time-saver when you wish to apply the same treatment to several similar images.

## Using adjustment layers to correct lighting

In this exercise you'll work with the same underexposed photo that you used for the last series of exercises, but this time you'll open the image from the Editor.

**1** In Full Edit mode, choose File > Open Recently Edited File and choose the file ghent_ghirls.jpg from the menu.

**2** Click the Create New Fill Or Adjustment Layer button (●) at the bottom of the Layers panel and choose Brightness/Contrast from the menu. The Adjustments panel opens to give you easy access to the Brightness and Contrast controls. Drag the sliders or type in the text boxes to set Brightness and Contrast values of **100** and **-50** respectively.

**Note:** A new adjustment layer always appears immediately above the layer that was active when the adjustment layer was created. For our image, the Background is the only layer, so it's active (selected) by default.

**3** Click the Create New Fill Or Adjustment Layer button again, this time choosing Levels from the menu. Notice the new Levels 1 adjustment layer in the Layers panel. The Adjustments panel is updated to present the Levels controls.

**4** In the Levels controls, drag the gray midtones stop under the center of the tonal distribution graph to adjust the mid-tones, until the tonal balance looks right to you. We set a value of 1.10.

**Tip:** The Levels controls provide a very effective and versatile method for adjusting tonal deficiencies, and can also help to correct color imbalances.

**5**  Choose File > Save. Make sure that Include In The Elements Organizer is activated and disable Save In Version Set With Original. Name the new file **ghent_ghirls_Adjustment** and choose the Photoshop (PSD) format. Make sure the Layers option is activated, and then click Save. If the Format Options dialog box appears, activate Maximize Compatibility and click OK.

**6**  To quickly assess the effect of the adjustment layers, toggle the visibility of each layer by clicking the eye icon beside its thumbnail in the Layers panel. When you're done, close the file without saving.

The beauty of adjustment layers is that you can return to adjust your settings at any time, as long as you save the file in the Photoshop format, preserving the layers. If you reopen the file that you just closed and click the Brightness/Contrast layer, the Adjustments panel will show the Brightness and Contrast values set just as you left them. The adjustment is still live and can be refined; if necessary, you could even revert to the original image by either hiding or deleting the adjustment layers.

# Correcting parts of an image selectively

Although our adjustment layers brought out color and image detail from the overly dark original photo, the background is now overexposed and lacking in tonal depth. So far in this lesson, all the corrections you've made have been applied to the entire image; in the next exercise you'll adjust just part of the image selectively.

## Creating a selection

In this exercise you'll isolate our subjects in the foreground from the city backdrop so that you can treat these two areas of the image separately. To start, you'll select the combined silhouette of the mother and her daughters and save the selection.

You've already explored some of the many ways to make a selection in Lesson 7. The choice of selection tool depends on the picture. With experience, you'll learn to assess the characteristics of the area or object you wish to select, as well as those of the surrounding area. We'll start with the Quick Selection tool, which automatically determines selection borders based on similarity in color and texture.

**1**  Open the original image file ghent_ghirls.jpg once again.

**2**  In the toolbox, select the Quick Selection tool (🖌), which is grouped with the Selection Brush tool.

**3**  In the tool options bar, make sure that the New Selection mode is activated for the Quick Selection tool. Set a brush diameter of around 100 px (pixels).

**4** Place the cursor just inside the hair-line above the woman's forehead and drag a line down the face and body of the girl in front of her, and then to the left across the three younger sisters. The active selection automatically expands to surround the combined silhouette of our subjects; not bad for a quick first pass.

Next you need to refine the border to capture the silhouette as closely as possible. You'll need to deselect a very small area of background between the hips of the two girls at the left, add the railing on which the group is leaning, and pay attention to the hair and highlight areas.

To refine your selection, you'll alternate between the Add To Selection (🖌) and Subtract From Selection (🖌) modes of the Quick Selection tool. Buttons for these modes are located in the tool options bar.

**5** Choose the Subtract From Selection (🖌) mode for the Quick Selection tool from the tool options bar. Keeping the Quick Selection tool active, focus the view on the space between hips of the two sisters at the far left. Hold down the Ctrl / Command key and press the plus sign (+) to zoom in to the image. Hold the spacebar and to drag pan the image as required.

▶ **Tip:** You can also use the Shift key and the Alt / Option key to switch between the Add To Selection and Subtract From Selection modes. Use the left and right bracket keys ( [ , ] ) to reduce or increase the brush size as you work, without stopping to open the Brush Picker.

**6** Press the left bracket key ( [ ) on your keyboard repeatedly to reduce the brush size to 10 px and then drag in the fragment of background. The selection contracts to exclude the area. Alternate between the Add To Selection (🖌) and Subtract From Selection (🖌) modes and use a combination of clicks and very short strokes to refine the selection border around the deselected area.

**7** Without being overly fussy, use the same techniques as you continue to refine the selection around the subjects' heads and any highlighted edges. Your work will be much simpler if you use the keyboard shortcuts detailed in step 5 and in the margin Tip above to navigate in the image and adjust the tool settings.

**8** Finally, pay attention to the highlighted areas on the arm and hand of the girl at the right, then add the other foreground element—the railing—to the selection, taking care to exclude the background areas framed by its uprights.

**9** To soften the hard edges of the selection, you can smooth and feather the outline. Click Refine Edge in the tool options bar.

**10** In the Refine Edge dialog box, accept the default settings. Move the pointer over each slider in turn to see a description of its action at the bottom of the dialog box. Notice that the Refine Edge dialog box has its own Zoom and Hand tools to help you get a better view of the details of your selection.

**11** While you're working on refining your selection, you can preview the results against a variety of backgrounds, each helpful in different circumstances. Move the pointer over each of the five preview mode buttons below the sliders to see the description, then click on each in turn to see the result in the Edit window.

**12** Click OK to apply the default edge refinement to your selection; then, choose Select > Save Selection. In the Save Selection dialog box, choose New from the Selection menu, type **Girls** for the selection name, and then click OK. Once a selection is saved, you can always re-use it—after assessing your adjustments you can reload the selection to modify them. Choose Select > Deselect.

## Using layer masks to isolate parts of an image

Now that you've created a selection including only the figures in the foreground, you can adjust the exposure and lighting for the subjects and the background independently. You could use your selection (even at a later date, now that you've saved it) to temporarily isolate part of the image for editing. Instead you'll use the saved selection to create separate layer masks for the different areas in the image.

A layer mask can be permanently linked to a particular layer in an image, so that any modification made to that layer will be applied only through the mask. The parts of the layer protected by the layer mask are hidden from view when it's blended with the other layers in your image. Layer masks can be edited by painting and erasing, so you can add to or subtract from a layer mask (and thereby, add to or subtract from the area that will be modified by an editing operation) without affecting the image pixels on the layer to which the mask is attached.

**1** Duplicate the Background layer by dragging it onto the New Layer button ( ) at the lower left corner of the Layers panel.

**2** Click the menu icon ( ) at the right of the Layers panel's header to open the Layers panel Options menu; then, choose Panel Options. In the Layers Panel Options dialog box, select either large or medium thumbnails—seeing the layer thumbnails can help you visualize the layers you're working with. Click OK. If necessary, choose View > Fit On Screen or, if the Zoom tool is active, click the Fit Screen button in the tool options bar so that you can see the entire image.

**3** Choose Select > Load Selection. Choose the saved selection Girls from the Source Selection menu, click the check box to activate the Invert option and choose New Selection under Operation; then click OK.

**4** Make sure the layer Background copy is still selected, and then click the Add Layer Mask button () at the bottom of the Layers panel.

A mask thumbnail appears on the Background copy layer, showing that your active selection in the image window has been converted to a layer mask on that layer. The white frame around the mask thumbnail indicates that the mask is currently selected—any change you make right now will modify the mask, not the image pixels on this layer. To edit the image instead, you first need to click the image thumbnail.

**5** Alt-click / Option-click the layer mask thumbnail to make the mask visible in the Edit window. With the mask selected, as it is now, you can edit it using painting and selection tools—or even the Text tool. Alt-click / Option-click the layer mask thumbnail again to hide the mask.

**6** Click the image thumbnail on the masked layer; then click the eye icon beside the image thumbnail on the original Background layer to make the layer temporarily invisible. You can see that the protected areas of the masked layer are actually hidden from view. Make the Background layer visible again.

While this layer mask is active, any change made to the original Background layer will be visible only in the figures in the foreground; any change you make to the masked layer will be applied only the backdrop around them.

**7** Make another copy of the original Background layer by dragging it onto the New Layer button () at the lower left corner of the Layers panel. Choose Select > Load Selection. Accept your saved selection as the Source Selection, but this time, leave the Invert option disabled. Choose New Selection under Operation; then click OK.

**8** Make sure the new layer, Background copy 2 is still selected, and then click the Add Layer Mask button () at the bottom of the Layers panel. Repeat steps 5 and 6 for the new mask layer.

If you keep the layer masks linked to the Background copy layers as they are now, they will remain editable. For the purposes of this exercise however, we've already refined our selection, and we have no other reason to keep the mask active.

**9** Right-click / Control-click each black and white layer mask thumbnail in turn and choose Apply Layer Mask from the context menu.

The layer masks can no longer be edited; they have been applied to their respective layers permanently. The layer mask thumbnails have disappeared and the image thumbnails now show areas of transparency.

> **Tip:** Edits made on a masked layer will be applied at full strength through the white parts of the mask; black areas in the mask represent the parts of your image that are completely protected. A gray area will allow a modification to be applied at a strength equivalent to the percentage of white present; a layer mask containing a gradient from white to black can be a great way to fade one image into another.

**10** You'll find it much easier to deal with layers—especially when you're working with many of them—if you give your layers descriptive names in the Layers panel. Double-click the name text of Background copy 2 and type **Girls** as the new name for the layer. Change the name of Background copy to **Ghent**.

## Correcting underexposed areas

We can now apply the most effective brightening technique from the earlier exercises to the subjects of our photo selectively.

**1** In the Layers panel, make sure that the Background layer is visible; then, select the layer Girls and choose Screen from the blending menu.

**2** Duplicate the Girls layer and set the opacity for the new copy to 25%. The figures are brighter and clearer, while the Ghent layer remains unchanged.

## Adding more intensity

Now that the figures in the foreground look so much better, the shaded buildings behind them need to be adjusted to appear less dull and murky.

With the foreground and background isolated on separate masked layers, you're free to apply whatever modifications you choose. There are no hard-and-fast rules; you might decide to emphasise the figures by making the background bright and pale (along the lines of the effect you achieved with ghent_ghirls_Screen.psd), or by making it even darker and more dramatic. For the purposes of this exercise, we'll simply boost the contrast to increase the clarity of the architectural detail without really interfering with the lighting dynamics of the original image.

1   In the Layers panel, select the layer Ghent. Choose Enhance > Adjust Lighting > Brightness/Contrast. Leave the Brightness setting unchanged, but increase the Contrast setting to a value of 50. Click OK. The buildings look clearer and more vibrant—without competing too much with the figures in the foreground.

With these few adjustments to the separate layers, the photograph now looks far more lively. There are still possibilities for improving the separated areas of the image; for example you could apply a Gaussian blur to the background to create a depth-of-field effect. There's also more you could do with blending modes and layer opacity—you'll learn more of those techniques as you work through this book.

2   Choose File > Save. Make sure that Include In The Elements Organizer is activated and disable Save In Version Set With Original. Name the new file **ghent_ghirls_Layers** and choose the Photoshop (PSD) format. Make sure the Layers option is activated, and then click Save. If the Format Options dialog box appears, activate Maximize Compatibility and click OK. Close the file.

3   In Lesson 7 you learned how to tile the image windows to best compare the results of different correction methods. Use that technique now to compare the six adjusted and saved versions of this photograph before moving on.

# Improving faded or overexposed images

In this exercise, you'll work with the scan of an old photograph—an image that could represent a valuable and treasured record of personal history, well worth preserving for posterity. An extreme case, this photo is not only overexposed, but also badly faded and in danger of being lost forever. The automatic fixes you applied to a copy of the image at the beginning of this lesson improved the photo markedly; in this project, you'll try to do even better using other techniques.

1  If you're in the Organizer, switch to Full Edit mode in the Editor by clicking the arrow on the Fix tab and choosing Full Photo Edit from the menu. Choose Preferences > General from the Edit / Photoshop Elements Editor menu. Activate the option Allow Floating Documents In Full Edit Mode; then, click OK.

2  Choose File > Open. Navigate to and open your Lesson08 folder, select the image frida&mina.jpg, and then click Open.

3  Click the Reset Panels button (⊙) at the top of the Full Edit workspace, and then double-click the Hand tool in the toolbox or choose View > Fit On Screen. Hide the grouped Effects and Content panels by double-clicking the header bar. If you don't see the filename beneath the photo's thumbnail in the Project Bin, right-click / Control-click the thumbnail and choose Show Filenames.

## Creating a set of duplicate files

You'll compare a variety of editing techniques during the course of this project. You can begin by creating a separate file to test each method, named for the technique it will demonstrate.

1  Right-click / Control-click the thumbnail image in the Project Bin and choose Duplicate from the context menu. In the Duplicate Image dialog box, name the new file **frida&mina_Shad_High**, and then click OK.

2  Perform step 2 twice more, naming the duplicates **frida&mina_Bright_Con** and **frida&mina_Levels**.

3  In the Project Bin, double-click the thumbnail frida&mina.jpg to make that image active and bring its image window to the front. If you can't see the whole of a filename under a thumbnail in the Project Bin, hold the pointer over the thumbnail; the name of the file is displayed as a Tooltip.

4  Choose File > Save As. Select your My CIB Work folder as the destination for the new file, then activate Include In The Elements Organizer and disable the option Save In Version Set With Original. Type **frida&mina_Blend_Mode** as the new filename and select Photoshop (PSD) from the Format menu.

▶ **Tip:** While you're working in the Editor, the Project Bin lets you see which images are open, even when a single active photo fills the edit window. When you can see more than one photo in the edit window, you can identify the active image by the un-dimmed text in its title bar or name tab, and the highlighting surrounding its thumbnail in the Project Bin.

**5**  Click Save. Click OK to accept the default settings in any dialog boxes or messages that appear. Leave all four images open for the rest of this project.

**6**  Choose Window > Images > Consolidate All To Tabs.

**7**  Choose Window > Images > Tile.

**8**  Make sure that frida&mina_Blend_Mode.psd is the active image, and then click the Arrange button (⊞) at the top of the workspace. Choose Match Zoom And Location. Many of the commands in this menu are also available in the Window > Images menu.

## Using blending modes to fix a faded image

A layer's blending mode can cause it to interact with the layers beneath it in a variety of ways. The Multiply mode intensifies or darkens pixels in an image. The Overlay mode tends to brighten the image while preserving its tonal range.

**1**  Make sure that frida&mina_Blend_Mode.psd is still the active image. If necessary, double-click its thumbnail in the Project Bin to make it active. In the Layers panel right-click / Control-click the Background layer and choose Duplicate Layer from the context menu. Click OK in the Duplicate Layer dialog box, accepting the default name "Background copy."

**2**  In the Layers panel, choose Multiply from the layer blending mode menu. Note the effect in the image window.

**3**  Drag the Background copy layer with its Multiply blend mode onto the New Layer button (▢) at the bottom of the Layers panel to create a copy of the Background copy layer.

**4**  In the Layers panel, change the blending mode for the layer Background copy 2 from Multiply to Overlay, watching the effect of the new blending mode on the image. Set the layer's Opacity value to **25**%, either by dragging the Opacity slider or by typing the new value in the text field.

Adding a layer with the Multiply blending mode made the image bolder and the third layer in Overlay mode brightened it considerably. Taken together, our changes have made the detail in the photo clearer, but the contrast in parts of the image, particularly in the clothing, is still unimpressive.

**5**  Choose File > Save to save the file in your My CIB Work folder, leaving the file open. If a message appears about maximizing compatibility, click OK to close it, or follow the instructions in the message to prevent it from appearing again.

## Adjusting shadows and highlights manually

Although both the Auto-fix and blending modes do a good job of correcting many fading images, some of your own photos may be more challenging. You'll try three more techniques in the exercises to follow. The first involves manually adjusting the Shadows, Highlights, and Midtone Contrast of the image.

▶ **Tip:** If you can't see the whole of the filename in the Project Bin, hold the pointer over the thumbnail; the name of the file is displayed as a Tooltip.

1   In the Project Bin, double-click the thumbnail frida&mina_Shad_High to make it the active window. Choose Window > Images > Float In Window; then double-click the Hand tool or choose View > Fit On Screen.

2   Choose Enhance > Adjust Lighting > Shadows/Highlights. If necessary, move the Shadows/Highlights dialog box so that it doesn't obscure the image window. Make sure that the Preview option is activated.

By default, the Lighten Shadows setting is 25%. You can see the effect on the image by toggling the Preview option on and off in the Shadows/Highlights dialog box.

3   In the Shadows/Highlights dialog box, set the Darken Highlights value to **25%**, and the Midtone Contrast value to **+50%**.

▶ **Tip:** The controls you are using to make the adjustments for this technique are also available in the Lighting panel in Quick Fix mode.

4   Adjust the three settings as needed until you think the image is as good as it can be. When you're done, click OK to close the Shadows/Highlights dialog box.

5   Choose File > Save and save the file as frida&mina_Shad_High to your My CIB Work folder, in JPEG format. Make sure that the image will be included in the Organizer, but not in a Version Set. Click OK in the JPEG Options dialog box and leave the file open. Choose Window > Images > Tile.

## Adjusting brightness and contrast manually

The next approach you'll take to fixing an exposure problem makes use of another option from the Enhance > Adjust Lighting menu.

1   In the Project Bin, double-click the image frida&mina_Bright_Con to make it active. Choose Window > Images > Float In Window; then click the Arrange button (⊞) at the top of the workspace and choose Fit On Screen.

**2**  Choose Enhance > Adjust Lighting > Brightness/Contrast. Make sure that the Preview option is activated in the Brightness/Contrast dialog box. If necessary, position the dialog box so that it doesn't block your view.

**3**  Drag the Brightness slider to –70, or type **–70** in the text field, being careful to include the minus sign when you type. Set the Contrast to 70.

**4**  Adjust the Brightness and Contrast settings until you are happy with the look of the image. Click OK to close the Brightness/Contrast dialog box.

**5**  Choose File > Save and save the file as frida&mina_Bright_Con to your My CIB Work folder, in JPEG format. Make sure that the image will be included in the Organizer, but not in a Version Set; then, click Save. Click OK in the JPEG Options dialog box, but keep the file open. Choose Window > Images > Tile.

## Adjusting levels

The Levels controls affect the distribution of tonal values in an image—the range of tones from dark to light, regardless of color. In this exercise, you'll enhance the image by shifting the reference points that define the spread of those tonal values.

**1**  In the Project Bin, double-click the image frida&mina_Levels to make it active. Choose Window > Images > Float In Window; then double-click the Hand tool.

**2**  Choose Enhance > Adjust Lighting > Levels. Activate the Preview option in the Levels dialog box, if it is not already active. If necessary, drag the Levels dialog box aside so that you can also see most of the image window.

The Levels graph represents the distribution of tonal values across all the pixels in the image, from darkest at the left to lightest at the right. A trough (or gap) in the curve indicates that there are few (or no) pixels mapped to that part of the range; a peak shows the opposite.

As you can see from the graph, this image has no black pixels, very few tones of less than 50% brightness, and far too much information clustered at the light end of the scale.

**3** In the Levels dialog box, drag the black triangle below the left end of the graph to the right; the value in the first Input Levels box should be approximately 105. Drag the white marker from the right side of the graph until the value in the third Input Levels box is approximately 250. Drag the gray marker to set the mid-tone value to approximately 0.85. Click OK to close the Levels dialog box.

**4** Choose File > Save and save the file to your My CIB Work folder in JPEG format as frida&mina_Levels. Make sure that the image will be included in the Organizer, but not in a Version Set. Click Save; then, click OK in the JPEG Options dialog box and leave the file open.

## Comparing results

You can now compare the six versions of the image: the original file, the four files you edited, and the image that was fixed automatically at the start of this lesson.

**1** Choose File > Open. Locate and open the file frida&mina_Autofix.jpg from the My CIB Work folder; then repeat the process for the original file from your Lesson08 folder, frida&mina.jpg. The Project Bin should show six open files.

**2** Hide the Panel Bin and the Project Bin by un-checking their names in the Window menu; then, choose Window > Images > Tile.

> **Tip:** You can also access The Match Zoom and Match Location commands by clicking the Arrange button (⊞) at the upper left of the workspace.

**3** Select the Zoom tool; then, in the tool options bar, activate Zoom All Windows. Click in any of the image windows so that you can see enough of the photo to enable you to compare the different results. Choose Window > Images > Match Zoom and Window > Images > Match Location; then, compare the six versions.

**4** Choose Preferences > General from the Edit / Photoshop Elements Editor menu. Disable floating documents, and then click OK. Choose File > Close All. Save any changes to your CIB Work folder if you're prompted to do so.

Congratulations! You've finished another lesson. Before you move on to the next chapter, take a few moments to review what you've learned by reading through the questions and answers on the next page.

# Review questions

1  How can you create an exact copy of an existing layer?

2  Where can you find the controls for adjusting the lighting in a photograph?

3  How do you change the arrangement of image windows in the work area?

4  What is an adjustment layer and what are its unique advantages?

# Review answers

1  You must be in Full Edit mode to copy a layer. Select a layer in the Layers panel and choose Layer > Duplicate Layer. You can access the same command in the Layers panel Options menu or by right-clicking / Control-clicking the layer in the Layers panel. Alternatively, drag the layer to the New Layer button. Whichever method you use, you get two layers identical in all but their names, stacked one above the other.

2  You can adjust the lighting for a photo in Full Edit, Guided Edit, and Quick Edit mode. In Full Edit, you can use the Enhance > Adjust Lighting menu to open various dialog boxes that contain the controls. Alternatively, you can choose Enhance > Auto Levels, Enhance > Auto Contrast, or Enhance > Adjust Color > Adjust Color Curves. In Guided Edit mode, choose operations from the Lighting and Exposure pane. In Quick Edit mode, you can use the Lighting pane in the Quick Fix panel.

3  You cannot rearrange image windows in Quick Edit and Guided Edit modes, which display only one photograph at a time. In the Full Edit workspace, there are several ways you can arrange them. Choose Window > Images, and select one of the choices listed there—you can access the same options and more by clicking the Arrange button ( ▦ ). Another method is to drag the image window title bar to move an image window, and drag a corner to resize it (provided Maximize mode is not active).

4  An adjustment layer does not contain an image; instead, it modifies some quality of all the layers below it in the Layer panel. For example, a Brightness/Contrast layer will alter the brightness and contrast of any underlying layers. One advantage of using an adjustment layer instead of adjusting an existing layer directly is that adjustment layers can be easily modified or even removed. Toggle the eye icon for the adjustment layer to remove or restore the edit instantly. You can change a setting in an adjustment layer at any time—even after the file has been saved. An adjustment layer can also be copied and pasted into another image to apply the same settings there.

# 9 REPAIRING, RETOUCHING, AND RECOMPOSING IMAGES

## Lesson Overview

For some images you'll need to deal with flaws other than color or exposure problems. A picture that was taken hurriedly might be spoiled by being tilted or poorly composed. Perhaps you have an antique photograph that is creased and worn or a scanned image marked by dust and scratches.

Sometimes the problem has nothing to do with the photograph itself, such as an extraneous object that clutters an otherwise striking composition or even just spots and blemishes on a portrait subject's skin.

In this lesson, you'll learn a range of techniques for restoring, retouching, and rearranging the composition of such flawed images:

- Using the Straighten tool
- Customizing the Crop tool
- Re-framing an image to improve composition
- Improving the impact of an image with the Recompose tool
- Retouching skin with the Healing Brush tool
- Working with opacity and blending modes in layers
- Removing unwanted objects with content-aware healing

You'll probably need about one and a half hours to complete this lesson.

Not every image problem is a result of incorrect camera settings. Learn how to straighten a tilted photo, rearrange an image's composition, and retouch spots and blemishes on your subject's skin. The same tools, techniques and tricks used to remove spots or repair creases and tears when you're restoring a treasured keepsake can also be used creatively to manipulate reality and produce exactly the image you want.

**Note:** Before you start working on this lesson, make sure that you've installed the software on your computer from the application CD (see the Photoshop Elements 10 documentation) and that you have correctly copied the Lessons folder from the CD in the back of this book onto your computer's hard disk (see "Copying the Classroom in a Book files" on page 2). You should also have created a working catalog (see "Creating a new catalog" on page 8).

# Getting started

You'll begin by importing the sample images for this lesson to the CIB Catalog that you created at the beginning of Lesson 1.

1   Start Photoshop Elements and click Organize in the Welcome Screen. When the Organizer opens, make sure that your CIB Catalog is loaded (if you need to refresh your memory, refer to step 2 in the Getting Started section in Lesson 5).

2   Choose File > Get Photos And Video > From Files And Folders. In the Get Photos And Videos From Files And Folders dialog box, locate and select your Lesson09 folder. Activate the option Get Photos From Subfolders and disable the automatic processing options; then, click Get Media. In the Import Attached Keyword Tags dialog box, select the Lesson 09 tag, and then click OK. Click OK to close any other alert dialog box.

3   The lesson images appear in the Media Browser. If you don't see filenames below the thumbnails, choose View > Show File Names.

# Improving the composition of a photo

When you're hurried, distracted by movement, or shooting in awkward conditions, the result is often a photo that *could* have been great—if only it had been framed better. In the Full Edit mode toolbox, the Crop tool and the Straighten tool will help you turn the shot you got into the photo you *should* have captured.

The Crop tool can be customized, offering a range of preset aspect ratios, and a choice of cropping overlays to help you bring out the visual potential of your image.

Sometimes you're just too busy fitting everyone into frame to notice a crooked horizon. The Straighten tool makes it easy to quickly correct a tilted image.

## Using the Straighten tool

With the Straighten tool you can draw a line in your crooked photo to be used as either a horizontal or vertical reference. Photoshop Elements rotates the image to straighten it in relation to your reference line.

1   Select the file 09_01.jpg in the Media Browser; then, click the arrow on the Fix tab above the Task Pane and choose Full Photo Edit. Alternately, you could select the file and choose Edit > Edit With Photoshop Elements Editor.

2   Click the Reset Panels button (![icon]) at the top of the Editor workspace. Hide the Project Bin by double-clicking its header bar or by un-checking its name in the Window menu. Hide the Panel bin by un-checking its name in the Window menu, and then double-click the Hand tool or choose View > Fit On Screen.

**3** Select the Straighten tool (![straighten icon]). In the tool options bar, make sure that Canvas Options is set to Grow Or Shrink Canvas To Fit. As there are no truly straight lines in the sculpture in the foreground, and no reliable horizon, our best reference for a true level in this photo is the old building in the background. Drag a line along the ledge between the first and second stories.

**Tip:** For this image we chose the Straighten tool option Grow Or Shrink Canvas To Fit because we wish to have manual control over cropping. When this is not an issue, try the options Crop To Remove Background and Crop To Original Size, which are also available from the Canvas Options menu in the tool options for the Straighten tool.

**4** When you release the mouse button, Photoshop Elements straightens the image relative to the line you've just drawn. Choose Fit On Screen from the View menu or the menu on the Arrange button (![arrange icon]) so that you can see all of the newly enlarged canvas surrounding the rotated image.

**5** In the toolbox, select the Crop tool (![crop icon]). From the Aspect Ratio menu in the tool options bar, choose Use Photo Ratio; this will constrain the cropping rectangle to the original proportions. Drag a cropping rectangle inside the image, which is now displayed at an angle—being careful not to include any of the blank area around the photo. When you're satisfied with the crop, click the green Commit button in the lower right corner of the cropping rectangle. The straightened and cropped image is much more comfortable to look at than the tilted original.

**Tip:** If you can't find the My CIB Work folder, refer to "Creating a work folder" on page 3.

**Tip:** In some cases, you can achieve good results by choosing either Straighten Image, or Straighten And Crop Image from the Image > Rotate > menu. Both of these commands perform straightening functions automatically.

6 Choose File > Save As. Make sure the new file will be included in the Organizer, but not in a Version Set. Name the file **09_01_Straight.jpg** to be saved to your My CIB Work folder in JPEG format. Click Save; then, click OK to dismiss the JPEG Options dialog box. Keep the file open for now.

7 Staying in the Editor, choose File > Open; then, navigate to and open your Lesson09 folder, select the file 09_02.jpg, and click Open.

In this photo, the horizon is hidden, the river bank is irregular, and the horizontal lines of the building in the background are angled by perspective—so your best option is to use one of the vertical lines in the large apartment building. By default, the Straighten tool is set for a horizontal reference; to designate a vertical reference you need to use the tool together with the Ctrl / Command key.

8 Select the Straighten tool (⬚). In the tool options bar, make sure that Canvas Options is set to Grow Or Shrink Canvas To Fit. Click and hold down the mouse button on a point at the top of a vertical lines in the apartment building; then, press the Ctrl / Command key and drag a line down your vertical reference. Release the mouse button, and then the Ctrl / Command key.

9 Select the Crop tool (⊐). In the tool options bar, set the cropping aspect ratio to No Restriction. Drag a rectangle inside the rotated photo, retaining as much of the image as possible without including any of the blank canvas surrounding it. When you're satisfied with your crop, click the Commit button in the lower right corner of the cropping rectangle.

10 Choose File > Save As. Make sure the new file will be included in the Organizer, but not in a Version Set. Name the file **09_02_Straight.jpg**, to be saved to your My CIB Work folder in JPEG format. Click Save; then, click OK to close the JPEG Options dialog box. Choose File > Close to close the file.

## Re-framing a photo with the Crop tool

Composing your photo well can make the difference between an ordinary snapshot and a striking, memorable image. Unfortunately, in practice, there's often just not enough time to frame your photo carefully.

Framing too much irrelevant detail can diminish the impact of your photo by detracting from your intended focus, and an awkward arrangement of forms within the frame can make your picture appear unbalanced. The Crop tool can be customized to achieve exactly the crop you want, and offers a choice of overlays to guide you in framing a balanced composition.

1   With the image 09_01_Straight.jpg open in the Edit window, select the Crop tool (⊡). Click the white triangle at the far left of the tool options bar and choose Reset Tool from the menu. From the Aspect Ratio menu, choose Use Photo Ratio; this will produce a crop of the same proportions as the original image. By default, the Overlay option is set to Rule Of Thirds. According to this rule, objects look more interesting and balanced when aligned with the lines and intersections of the grid. Drag a rectangle around the girl on the sculpture so that the lines intersect on her face.

2   Click the Cancel button at the lower right of the cropping rectangle. From the Overlay menu in the tool options bar, choose Golden Ratio. This guide is based on a formula that has been used to create appealing compositions in painting and architecture through the ages. The Aspect Ratio menu is now disabled; the Golden Ratio works within a rectangle of set proportions. Inside the rectangle, the intersection of two diagonals defines a focus.

3   Drag a small rectangle anywhere in the image; then, drag the lower right handle of the cropping box upwards and to the left to flip the orientation of the Golden Ratio guides.

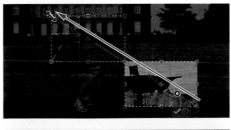

4   Adjust the cropping rectangle to define a pleasing crop, with the focus of the Golden Ratio centered on the girl's face. Click the Commit button to execute the crop.

5   Choose File > Save As. Make sure the new file will be included in the Organizer, but not in a Version Set. Name the file **09_01_GoldenCrop.jpg**, to be saved to your My CIB Work folder in JPEG format. Click Save; then, click OK to close the JPEG Options dialog box. Choose File > Close.

## Recomposing an image within its frame

▶ **Tip:** As with the Healing brushes and the Clone Stamp tool that are covered later in this chapter, and the Photomerge tools that you'll use in Lesson 10, the Recompose tool is also a lot of fun to use creatively, letting you manipulate reality to produce exactly the image you want.

Do you have a group shot where you wish the group had stood a little closer together? Or a photo where a walk-on extra draws attention away from the stars and the main story? With the Recompose tool you can fix these and other image composition problems in a few easy steps.

Essentially, the Recompose tool enables you to crop your photo from the *inside*, rather than at the edges. Whether you want to bring people closer together, fit a horizontal image to a vertical space, or remove extraneous elements that spoil the composition, the Recompose tool puts image editing magic at your fingertips.

In this exercise, you'll use the Recompose tool to tighten the arrangement of this group portrait and re-frame the landscape format image as a square composition.

1   If you're still in the Editor from the previous exercise, switch to the Organizer now by clicking the Organizer button (▦) at the top right of the Editor workspace. In the Keyword Tags panel, click the Find box beside the Lesson 09 tag, if necessary, to isolate the images for this lesson.

2   In the Media Browser, right-click / Control-click the image 09_03.jpg and choose Edit With Photoshop Elements Editor from the context menu.

3   If you don't already see some gray space around the edge of the photo in the Edit window, press Ctrl / Command together with the minus sign key (–) to zoom out a little.

4   In the toolbox, right-click / Control-click the Crop tool (🄴) and select the Recompose tool (🔲). A message appears with quick instructions on using the Recompose tool, including a link to a video tutorial. For now, click OK to dismiss the message.

The image is now surrounded by a live bounding box, with control handles at the corners and at the mid-point of each side. For simple recomposing operations, all you need to do is drag the handles; the Recompose tool makes use of content-aware scaling technology that distinguishes people and other featured objects and attempts to prevent them being distorted as the background is compressed around them. For this exercise, however, we'll use the special Recompose brushes instead. For more complex images, this generally produces better results.

5   Select the green Mark For Protection brush in the tool options bar. Either type in the brush size text box or use the slider to increase the brush size to about 150 px.

As its name suggests, you can use this brush to define those areas in the image that you want protected from any scaling operation.

**6** Paint roughly over the girl on the left side of the photo, making sure that her extended left arm and hand are well protected. As she is already very close to the edge of the image, cover the area between the girl and the left edge of the photo—including her shadow—to mark it for protection. If you find that you've over-painted, use the green eraser (), right beside the protection brush in the tool options bar, to modify your strokes. You can decrease or increase the size of the eraser as you work by pressing the left and right bracket keys ( [ , ] ).

**7** Right-click / Control-click the image and change the mode for the brush from the default Use Normal Highlight to Use Quick Highlight. In the default mode, you need to paint over the entire area you wish to protect. In Quick Highlight mode you mark an area for protection by simply drawing a line to surround it.

**8** Set the brush size to 50 px; then, draw a rough outline to surround the girls at the right, together with their shadows. You don't need to protect all of the jacket carried by the girl at the far right. Release the mouse button; the area you outlined is marked for protection automatically. Right-click / Control-click the image again and switch back to Normal Highlight mode.

**9** In the tool options bar, select the red Mark For Removal brush. Set the brush size to 100 px. You can use this brush to define any areas that you wish the Recompose tool to remove from the image. Click once on each of the dead leaves on the grass in the foreground. You can also mark the sky, as shown in the illustration below, so that the Recompose tool will remove that area before compressing the adjacent areas. This will help to minimize distortion in the trees at the top of the image.

**10** Alternate between the red Mark For Removal brush and its associated eraser, using the bracket keys ( [ , ] ) to decrease or increase the brush size as you work.

**11** Now for the fun part! Move the pointer over the handle on the right side of the bounding box and, when the double-arrow cursor appears, drag the handle slowly in towards the center of the photo. Watch the photo as you drag; some areas of the image are removed while others are compressed and merged with their surroundings. As the proportions of the image become closer to a square, keep an eye on the width (W) and height (H) values in the Tool options bar; stop dragging and release the mouse button when the two values are equal.

► **Tip:** As this was a rather extreme opera-tion, you may find some seam artifacts, espe-cially near the edges of areas that were removed or protected. If these are noticeable enough to worry you, a few strokes with the Clone Stamp tool or the Healing Brush tool will fix the problem. You'll learn more about those tools later in this lesson. Use the Zoom tool to inspect the area where the wedge of sky was removed. Experiment with recomposing the original image in differ-ent ways; try removing slices of foliage instead of the sky area.

**12** Click the green Commit button at the lower right of the recomposed photo or press Enter / Return to accept and render the new composition.

**13** Choose Image > Crop. A cropping box appears on the image; drag the handles to crop the file to the new square format, trimming away the transparent area. The edges of the cropping box snap to the edges of the image to make the operation very easy. Click the green Commit button or press Enter / Return.

**14** Choose File > Save As. Make sure the new file will be included in the Organizer, but not in a Version Set. Name the new image **09_03_Recompose.jpg**, to be saved to your My CIB Work folder in JPEG format. Click Save; then click OK to accept the default JPEG Options settings. Choose File > Close.

The Recompose tool is as easy to use as it is powerful—with creative possibilities that are virtually limitless. Play with as many pictures as you can; you'll learn how content-aware scaling works and what to expect from different types of image as you have fun finding creative new ways to make the most of your photos.

# Removing wrinkles and spots

In this exercise, you'll explore several techniques for retouching skin flaws and blemishes to improve a portrait photograph. Retouching skin can be a real art, but luckily Photoshop Elements provides several tools that make it easy to smooth out lines and wrinkles, remove blemishes, and blend skin tones—even for a novice.

1   If you're still in the Editor, switch to the Organizer. Use the Lesson 09 tag, if necessary, to isolate the images for this lesson. Right-click / Control-click the image 09_04.jpg and choose Edit With Photoshop Elements Editor.

2   In the Editor, click the Reset Panels button (![icon]) at the top of the workspace. Drag the Layers panel out of the Panel Bin by its header bar, and then hide the Panel Bin and the Project Bin by un-checking their names in the Window menu.

3   Drag the Background layer to the New Layer button (![icon]) at the bottom of the Layers panel to create another layer, named "Background copy" by default. Drag the new Background copy layer to the New Layer button to create a third layer. If necessary, resize the Layers panel by dragging its lower right corner. You only need the panel to be just big enough to show your three layers.

4   Use the Zoom tool to zoom in on the upper half of the photo, as you'll be retouching the skin around the woman's eyes first.

This photo is quite a challenging candidate for retouching; the harsh flash lighting has caused strong reflections on the skin that only serve to accentuate the wrinkles. You'll begin the retouching process using the Healing Brush tool in botox mode.

# Fixing blemishes

There are three main tools in Photoshop Elements for fixing flaws in your photos:

**The Spot Healing Brush tool**

The Spot Healing Brush is the easiest way to remove wrinkles in skin and other small imperfections in your photos. Either click once on a blemish or click and drag to smooth it away. By blending the information of the surrounding area into the problem spot, imperfections are made indistinguishable.

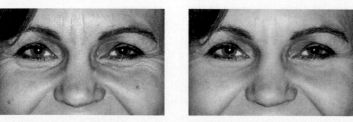

**The Healing Brush tool**

The Healing Brush can fix larger imperfections with ease. You can define one part of your photo as a source to be sampled and blended into another area. The Healing Brush is so flexible you can even remove large objects from a uniform background—such as a person in a wheat field.

**The Clone Stamp tool**

Rather than blending the source and target areas, the Clone Stamp tool paints directly with a sample of an image. You can use the Clone Stamp tool to remove or duplicate objects in your photo. This tool is great for getting rid of garbage, power lines, or a signpost that may be spoiling a view.

## Using the Healing Brush tool

1  Make sure that the top layer, Background copy 2, is still active, and then right-click / Control-click to select the Healing Brush tool ( ) which is grouped together in the toolbox with the Spot Healing Brush tool.

2  In the tool options bar, click the small arrow to open the Brush Picker and set the Diameter to **20** px. Set the brush Mode to Normal and Source to Sampled. Make sure that the options Aligned and Sample All Layers are disabled.

3  Alt-click / Option-click a smooth area on the left cheek to define the area sampled as a reference texture. Note that if you switch to another tool and then back to the Healing Brush, you'll need to repeat this step.

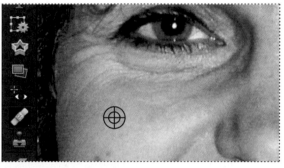

4  Draw a short horizontal stroke under the left eye. As you drag, it may look as if you're creating a strange effect, but when you release the mouse button, the color will be blended and natural skin tones will fill the area.

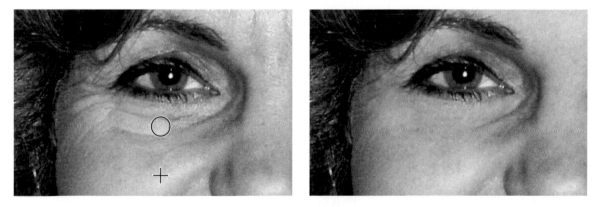

5  Continue to smooth the skin on the face with the Healing Brush. Avoid areas very close to the eyes, shadowed areas, and the hair-line. You can also reduce the worst of the shine caused by the harsh flash. As you work, re-establish the reference area occasionally by Alt-clicking / Option-clicking in new areas of the face to sample appropriate skin tone and texture. Press the left and right bracket keys ( [ , ] ) to decrease or increase the brush size as you work. Be sure to remove the moles on the woman's right cheek and the spots on her left cheek and just below the lower lip. You can use the same techniques on the neck.

▶ **Tip:** Use short brush strokes. Try just clicking rather than dragging, taking care to overlap your clicks to avoid a spotty effect. If you see results you don't like, check that the Aligned option is disabled in the tool options bar.

Long strokes may produce unacceptable results—especially near shaded areas where the darker tones may spread. If that happens, choose Edit > Undo Healing Brush. Try setting the brush to a smaller size or reversing the direction of your strokes. If the problem is related to the shadowed areas beside the nose or at the sides of the face, try stroking towards the shadows rather than away from them, or temporarily changing the mode for the Healing Brush tool from Normal to Lighten in the tool options bar.

6   Choose Window > Undo History. You can use the Undo History panel to quickly undo a series of steps. Every action you perform is recorded in chronological order from the earliest at the top to the most recent at the bottom of the panel. To restore the file to an earlier state, simply select an earlier (higher) action in the Undo History list.

As long as you have not made any further changes to the file, you can still return the image to a more recent state by selecting a step lower in the list. Once you've used the Undo History panel to restore a photo to an earlier state, any change you make to the image will replace all the actions in the more recent history.

The Healing Brush tool copies *texture* from the source area, not color. It samples the colors in the target area—the area you're brushing—and arranges those colors according to the texture of the reference area. Consequently, the Healing Brush tool appears to be smoothing the skin. So far however, the results are not convincingly realistic; you'll work to improve that in the next exercise.

## Refining the Healing Brush results

In this exercise, you'll make your retouching work look a little more natural by altering the opacity of the layer you've been working on, and then use another of the texture tools to refine the resulting blend.

1   Choose Window > Navigator. In the Navigator panel, use the zoom slider and drag the red frame in the Navigator preview to focus the view in the image window on the area around the woman's eyes and mouth.

Extensive retouching can leave skin looking artificially smooth, looking a little like molded plastic. Reducing the opacity of the retouched layer will give the skin a more realistic look by allowing some of the wrinkles on the un-edited Background layer to show through.

2   In the Layers panel, change the Opacity of the layer "Background copy 2" to about 50%, using your own judgment to set the exact percentage.

We opted for quite a low setting, wishing a fairly natural look for this photo of a friend, but the opacity value you set will depend on the extent of your retouching and the purpose for which the edited image is intended.

The opacity change restores some realism, but three noticeable blemishes have also made a reappearance—one on each cheek and one just below the lower lip.

3   Select the layer "Background copy" to make it the active layer.

4   Set the brush size for the Healing Brush tool to 20 px and click once or twice on each blemish. Gone!

5   In the toolbox, select the Blur tool (⬤). In the tool options bar, set the brush diameter to approximately 13 px and set the Blur tool's Strength to 50%.

6   With the layer "Background copy" still active, drag the Blur tool over some of the deeper lines around the eyes and brow. Use the Navigator panel to change the zoom level and shift the focus as needed. Reduce the Blur tool brush diameter to 7 px and smooth the lips a little, avoiding the edges.

**Tip:** To remove spots and small blemishes in your photo, try the Spot Healing Brush in Proximity Match mode as an alternative to the Healing Brush. With the Spot Healing Brush, you can either click or drag to smooth away imperfections without needing to set a reference point.

Compare your results to those below—the original, the version retouched with the Healing Brush, and final refined version. Toggle the visibility of your retouched layers to compare the original image in your Background layer with the edited results.

Original                    Healing Brush 100% Opacity          Healing Brush 50% Opacity over Blur tool

7   Choose File > Save As. Make sure that the new file will be included in the Organizer, but not in a Version Set. Name the edited image **09_04_Retouch**, to be saved to your My CIB Work folder in Photoshop (PSD) format.

8   Make sure that the Layers option is activated, and then click Save.

9   Choose File > Close.

In this exercise, you've learned how to set an appropriate source for the Healing Brush tool, and to sample the texture of the source area to repair flaws in another part of the photograph. You also used the Blur tool to smooth textures, and an opacity change to achieve a more realistic look. You've also gained a little experience in working with both the Undo History and Navigator panels.

**Tip:** For a quick and easy solution to portrait retouching, try the Perfect Portrait procedure listed under Fun Edits in the Guided Edit mode, where you'll be stepped through smoothing skin, removing spots, fixing red eye, increasing definition in facial features, whitening teeth, and even slimming your subject!

# Removing unwanted objects from images

The impact of a photo can easily be spoiled by an unwanted object in the frame. In the modern world, it's often impossible to photograph even a remote landscape without capturing a fence, power lines, satellite dishes, or litter—mundane clutter that can reduce the drama of an otherwise perfect shot.

Photoshop Elements offers several tools to help you improve an image by getting rid of extraneous detail. As you've seen, the Recompose tool lets you remove areas as you scale a photo. In this set of exercises you'll use the Spot Healing Brush tool to remove an object *without* altering the overall composition.

1  If you're still in the Editor, switch to the Organizer. Use the Lesson 09 tag, if necessary, to isolate the images for this lesson. Ctrl-click / Command-click to select the photos 09_05.jpg and 09_06.jpg; then, right-click / Control-click either selected image and choose Edit With Photoshop Elements Editor.

2  In the Editor, either choose Window > Reset Panels or click the Reset Panels button (⟳) at the top of the workspace. In the Project Bin, double-click the photo of the two girls to make it the active image and bring its image window to the front in the Edit pane.

3  Select the Zoom tool; then, check the tool settings right above the toolbox to make sure that the Zoom In Mode is activated. In the Edit pane, drag a marquee with the Zoom tool to closely surround the lower half of the photo.

4  Press Shift+Tab on your keyboard to hide everything but the image window and the toolbox.

## Using the Content-Aware healing feature

In the last project, you may have used the Spot Healing Brush in Proximity Match mode to help smooth skin blemishes in a portrait photo. In this exercise you'll set the Spot Healing Brush to Content-Aware mode.

In Content-Aware mode, the Spot Healing Brush tool compares nearby image content to fill the area under the pointer, seamlessly maintaining detail such as shadows, object edges, and even perspective, as shown in the illustration above.

1   Right-click / Control-click to select the Spot Healing Brush tool ( ), which is grouped together in the toolbox with the Healing Brush tool. In the tool options bar, make sure that the Content-Aware option is activated. Type in the text box to set a brush diameter of **330** pixels.

2   Position the circular cursor so that it completely surrounds the yellow plastic package and its shadow; then click once.

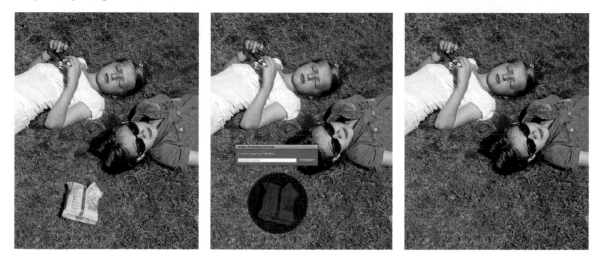

3   If you notice any image artefacts such as blurring or obvious repetition of detail, reduce the brush size to 50 pixels and click a few points to break up the effect.

4   Choose File > Save As. Make sure that the new file will be included in the Organizer, but not in a Version Set Name the new file **09_05_Remove**, to be saved to your My CIB Work folder in JPEG format, and then click Save. Click OK to accept the JPEG Options settings; then, close the file.

# 10 COMBINING IMAGES

## Lesson Overview

Although you can do a lot to improve a photo with tonal adjustments, color corrections and retouching, sometimes the best way to produce the perfect image is simply to fake it!

Photoshop Elements delivers powerful tools that will enable you to do just that by combining images. Merge ordinary scenic photos into stunning panoramas that truly recapture the feel of the location or combine a series of shots to produce the perfect group photo where everybody is smiling and there are no closed eyes. Deal with difficult lighting conditions by blending differently exposed pictures.

In this lesson you'll learn some of the tricks you'll need for combining images to create that perfect shot that you didn't actually get:

- Merging a series of photos into a panorama
- Assembling the perfect group shot
- Removing unwanted elements
- Blending differently exposed photographs
- Combining images using layers
- Resizing and repositioning selections
- Creating a gradient clipping mask
- Defringing a selection

 You'll probably need between one and two hours to complete this lesson.

If you're ready to go beyond fixing pictures in conventional ways, this lesson is for you. Why settle for that scenic photo that just doesn't capture the way it really looked? Or that group portrait where Dad's looking away and Mom's eyes are closed? Combine images to produce the perfect shot. Merge photos to make a stunning panorama, remove obstructions from the view, and even get little Jimmy to stop making faces.

**Note:** Before you start working on this lesson, make sure that you've installed the software on your computer from the application CD (see the Photoshop Elements 10 documentation) and that you have correctly copied the Lessons folder from the CD in the back of this book onto your computer's hard disk (see "Copying the Classroom in a Book files" on page 2). You should also have created a working catalog (see "Creating a new catalog" on page 8).

# Getting started

To start, you'll import the sample images for this lesson to the CIB Catalog that you created at the beginning of Lesson 1.

1  Start Photoshop Elements and click Organize in the Welcome Screen. When the Organizer opens, make sure that your CIB Catalog is loaded (if you need to refresh your memory, refer to step 2 in the Getting Started section in Lesson 5).

2  Choose File > Get Photos And Video > From Files And Folders. In the Get Photos And Videos From Files And Folders dialog box, locate and select your Lesson10 folder. Activate the option Get Photos From Subfolders and disable the automatic processing options; then, click Get Media.

3  In the Import Attached Keyword Tags dialog box, select the Lesson 10 tag, and then click OK. Click OK to close any other alert dialog box.

4  Click the Show All button in the Find bar. In the Keyword Tags panel, expand the Imported Keyword Tags category, and then click the find box beside the Lesson 10 tag to isolate the images for the projects in this lesson.

5  If you don't see filenames below the thumbnails in the Media Browser, choose View > Show File Names.

# Combining images automatically

The Photomerge tools offer a variety of ways to combine photos. These tools not only deliver effective solutions to some tricky photographic problems, but are also great fun to use creatively, enabling you to generate striking and unusual images.

In this lesson, you'll use the Photomerge Exposure tool to combine exposures made in difficult lighting conditions into a composite image that would have been virtually impossible to capture in a single shot. You'll compose a group photo from three single-subject images with the Photomerge Group Shot tool, combine photos from a busy scene to produce an unobstructed view using the Photomerge Scene Cleaner, and blend a series of scenic photographs into a dramatic panorama.

## Merging photos into a panorama

A common problem for many of us when taking photos at a scenic location is that standard lenses do not have a wide enough angle to capture the entire scene. The Photomerge Panorama tool provides the solution: you can capture a series of overlapping shots, and then merge them to create a panorama. In the following pages you'll learn how to have Photoshop Elements do most of the work for you.

You could start the Photomerge Panorama process from the Organizer, but for this exercise, you'll open the lesson photos in the Editor and set up the workspace.

1   In the Organizer, Ctrl-click / Command-click to select the images 10_01a.jpg through 10_01e.jpg in the Media Browser; then, right-click / Control-click any of the selected thumbnails and choose Edit With Photoshop Elements Editor.

2   In the Editor, click the Reset Panels button () at the top of the workspace, or choose Window > Reset Panels. Drag the Layers panel out of the Panel Bin, and then hide the Panel Bin by un-checking its name in the Window menu. Drag the lower right corner of the Layers panel to make it large enough to show five layers; then, position the panel at the lower right of the workspace.

3   Choose File > New > Photomerge Panorama to open the Photomerge dialog box.

## Setting up the Photomerge Panorama options

In the Photomerge dialog box you have the option to select individual source files or the entire contents of a specified folder, and a choice of layout methods that will affect the way the source images will be stitched together to create your panorama.

1   In the Photomerge dialog box, choose Spherical from the layout options at the left. Under Source Files, select Files from the Use menu. Click Add Open Files.

> **Tip:** To add more images to the source files selection, click Browse. To remove a photo from the source list, select the file, and then click Remove. To use all the photos from a specific folder on your hard disk as source files for a panorama, select Folder from the Use menu rather than Files, and then click Browse.

Not all of the panorama Layout options—methods for matching, aligning, and blending your source images—will work for every series of photos. Experiment with your own photos to get a feel for what will work. Before you go on with the exercise, take a moment to read the layout descriptions on the next two pages.

# Photomerge Panorama layout options

**Auto**  Analyzes the source images and applies either a Perspective or Cylindrical layout, depending on which produces a better photomerge.

**Perspective**  Creates a consistent composition by designating one of the source images (by default, the middle image—or images, in this case) as a reference. The other images are then repositioned, stretched, or skewed as necessary, so that overlapping content is matched.

**Cylindrical**  Reduces the "bow-tie" distortion that can occur with the Perspective layout by displaying individual images as on an unfolded cylinder. Overlapping content is still matched. The reference image is placed at the center. This is best suited for creating wide panoramas.

**Spherical**  Aligns and transforms images as if mapped to the inside of a sphere. This is particularly effective for a set of images that cover 360 degrees, but can also produce great results in other cases. For the images used here, there is noticeable distortion in the horizontal line of the river-bank.

**Collage**   Aligns images and matches overlapping content by rotating and scaling the source photos.

**Reposition**   Aligns the images and matches overlapping content without scaling, skewing, or stretching any of the source photos. In our example, there has been a problem with matching the construction crane at the junction of the two photos on the right. You can often fix this kind of problem very easily with the Clone Stamp tool or the Spot Healing Brush.

**Interactive Layout**   A message will appear on screen when Photoshop Elements can't align photos automatically. This may happen when Photomerge can't identify specific detail to match, often in photos without man-made structures. You can then choose the Interactive Layout option to open the Photomerge dialog box where you'll find the tools you need to position the source images manually.

**▶ Tip:** If the Blend Images Together option is disabled, a simple rectangular blend is applied. You may prefer this if you intend to retouch the layer blending masks manually.

**2** In the Photomerge dialog box, make sure that the Blend Images Together option is activated below the source files list. This option calculates the optimal borders between overlapping photos, and also color-matches the images. Click OK.

**3** Watch the Layers panel while Photoshop Elements creates a new file for the panorama, and places each source image on its own layer. Photomerge calculates the overlapping areas, adds a blending mask to each image layer accordingly, and then color-matches adjacent images as it blends the seams. When the Clean Edges dialog box appears, drag it aside so that you can see the edges of all the source images, and the checker-board transparency around them.

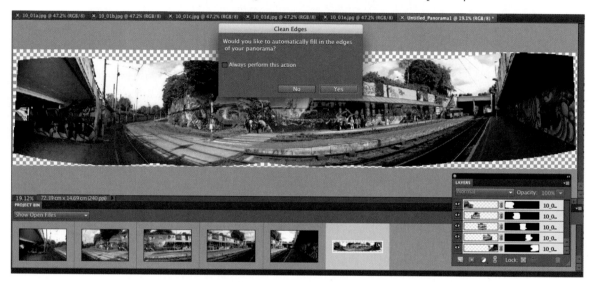

You can see that for this particular combination of photos, with the Spherical panorama layout applied, cropping away the transparent areas would not result in the loss of any significant detail at the top of the merged image, but would remove a substantial strip across the bottom. Photoshop Elements 10 can help you solve this problem, by using content-aware healing to fill in the missing detail.

**4** In the Clean Edges dialog box, click Yes.

The content-aware fill usually does a great job with non-specific or organic content, such as foliage, clouds, or water—and even with regular patterns like brickwork, but cannot deal with too much mechanical detail. Let's check over the results.

**5** Press Ctrl+Z / Command+Z. This will not undo the healing operation—only the last step in the process, the de-selection of the area that was filled. Use the Zoom and Hand tools to examine the extended image in detail; the re-instated selection will help you to look in the right places to spot the anomalies.

The content-aware fill has produced artefacts right across the top of the merged image, but the results at the sides and along the bottom are very good, with the exception of the missing segment of steel track in the center of the lower edge.

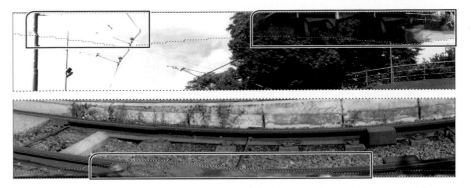

**6** (Optional) It would not take a lot of work with the Spot Healing Brush and the Clone Stamp to remove the unwelcome artefacts; even the blurred track is manageable. If you choose, you can retouch these areas before moving on.

**7** When you're done, press Ctrl+D / Command+D, or choose Select > Deselect.

Now let's have a closer look at how well Photoshop Elements matched the overlapping areas between the source images.

**8** In the Layers panel, click the eye icon (👁) beside the top layer—Layer 1, the content-aware fill—to hide it. Use the Zoom and Hand tools, if necessary, to focus on the right half of the panorama. Hold down Alt+Shift / Option+Shift and click the layer mask thumbnail on the bottom layer.

▶ **Tip:** Depending on the source files you use for a panorama, you may notice small edge artefacts—problem areas along the blended seams between images. When this occurs, you can either try a different layout option for the Photomerge operation, or manually retouch the layer blending masks.

In the edit window, the mask associated with this layer appears as a semi-transparent overlay, enabling you to see which part of the image in the lower layer has contributed to the panorama. The unused portion is hidden by the layer mask.

► **Tip:** If you wished to edit any portion of the seam between images, you could alternate between these two views of the layer mask to adjust the blend by painting (or erasing) directly onto the mask. If you do this with a panorama extended by content-aware fill, you'll need to erase the corresponding area of the top layer, creating a "window" so that your changes to the lower layers are visible.

**9** Click the image thumbnail for the bottom layer; then, Alt-click / Option-click the layer mask thumbnail.

The layer mask is displayed in opaque black and white; black represents masked portions of the layer and white represents areas that have contributed to the blend.

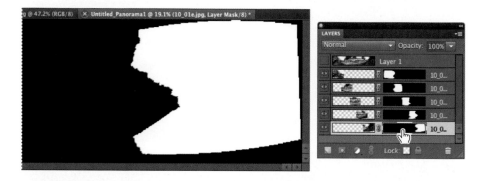

**10** Use the same technique to inspect the blended seams between the other source layers. When you're done, make the top layer visible once more.

**11** Choose View > Fit On Screen, and then choose Image > Crop. Drag the handles of the cropping rectangle to make it as large as possible without including the blurred track at the lower edge or the artefacts across the top of the image; then, click the Commit button in the lower right corner of the cropping rectangle.

► **Tip:** If you can't find the My CIB Work folder, refer to "Creating a work folder" on page 3.

**12** Choose File > Save. Name the merged image **10_01_Panorama**, to be saved to your My CIB Work folder in Photoshop format with Layers activated. Saving your file in Photoshop format enables you to preserve the layers, so that you can always return to adjust them if necessary. If you saved in JPEG format the image would be flattened and layer information lost. Make sure that the file will be included in the Organizer. Click Save; then, choose File > Close All.

## Creating a composite group shot

Shooting the perfect group photo is a difficult task, especially if you have a large family of squirmy kids. Fortunately, Photoshop Elements offers a solution: a powerful photo blending tool called Photomerge Group Shot. This exercise will show you how multiple photos can be blended together into one with amazing precision.

No longer do you need to put up with family photos where someone has their eyes closed, someone else has looked away at the wrong moment, and you-know-who has just made an even odder facial expression than usual. Photomerge Group Shot lets you merge the best parts of several images into the perfect group photo.

Typically, you'd use the Photomerge Group Shot feature to create a merged image from a series of very similar source images such as you might capture with your camera's burst mode, as was the case with the photos in the illustration above.

For this exercise however, you'll work with just three distinctly different images to make it easier for you to learn the technique.

1  If you're still in the Editor, switch to the Organizer now. Use the Lesson 10 tag to isolate the files for this lesson; then, Ctrl-click / Command-click to select the images 10_02a.jpg, 10_02b.jpg, and 10_02c.jpg in the Media Browser.

2  Choose File > New > Photomerge Group Shot.

3  Photoshop Elements has automatically designated the first image as the source image and placed it in the pane on the left. To replace it, click the second thumbnail in the Project Bin (10_02b.jpg). Drag the first thumbnail (10_02a.jpg) from the Project Bin and drop it into the Final image pane on the right.

As a rule, you would make the best image in a series the Final image, and then use each of the other photos as sources for those elements you would like to replace. We chose the image 10_02a.jpg as the Final (target) image because it includes more of the wooden decking than the other photos. As the girl in the photo is sitting fur-ther forward than the girls on the chairs, it's preferable that we retain the decking around her rather than try to blend it to either of the other photos.

4  Use the Zoom and Hand tools to magnify and position the image so you can see all of the girl in the Source pane and at least part of the girl in the Final image.

**5**  In the Photomerge Group Shot panel at the right of the workspace, select the Pencil tool (  ). Make sure that the Show Strokes option is activated, and the Show Regions option is disabled.

**6**  With the Pencil tool (  ), draw one stroke in the Source image, from the top of the girl's head to the hem of her dress, as shown in the illustration below. Allow the edges of your stroke to just slightly overlap the window and wall behind the girl's head. Extend the end of the stroke just far enough onto the wooden decking to pick up the shadow beneath the light-colored fabric.

When you release the mouse button, Photoshop Elements merges the girl from the Source image into the Final image—including the shadow below her skirts.

Click with the Pencil tool to add any part of the subject that was not copied from the source. Use the Eraser tool (  ) to delete part of a stroke drawn with the Pencil tool; the area copied to the Final image will be adjusted accordingly.

Sometimes it can be a little tricky to make the perfect selection—especially when you're working with a more complex source image than our example. You may find you are copying more of the source image than you want. If you've switched several times between the Pencil and Eraser tools and you still can't get the selection right, click the Reset button below the Photomerge Group Shot controls and start again. Try modifying the shape that you're drawing with the Pencil tool, reducing the brush size, changing the direction of the stroke, or making shorter strokes.

**7** Double-click the green framed image (10_02c.jpg) in the Project Bin to make it the Source image. Use the Zoom and Hand tools to move the Source image in its frame so you can see all of the girl in the pink dress; then, use the Pencil tool to add her to the Final image. Be sure to include the shadow below her left foot.

**8** Double-click the Hand tool so that you can see the areas that are still missing from the Final image. With the Pencil tool, drag a line through the right side of the Source image as shown in the illustration below.

**9** In the Project Bin, click the thumbnail with the yellow border to make it the source image once more; then, drag with the Pencil tool through the upper left corner of the image in the Source pane.

**10** To see which part of each of the three source images was used for the merged composition, first click the Fit Screen button above the Edit pane so that you can see the entire image, and then activate the Show Regions option in the Photomerge Group Shot panel. The regions in the Final image are color coded to correspond to the borders of the thumbnails in the Project Bin.

**11** Select the Hand tool; then click the Actual Pixels button above the edit pane. Position the image so that you can see a boundary between colored regions.

**12** Toggle Show Regions off and on while you look for imperfections along the region boundaries in the merged image. If necessary, use the Pencil and Eraser tools to add to or subtract from the portions of the source images that are being merged to the Final image. When you're satisfied with the result, click Done.

**13** The merged image needs to be cropped slightly. Choose Image > Crop to place a cropping rectangle on the image, and then drag the handles of the cropping rectangle to trim off the empty corners of the photo.

**14** Click the Commit button at the bottom right of the cropping rectangle; then, choose File > Save and save the merged image to your My CIB Work folder as **10_02_Composite**, in Photoshop (PSD) format. Make sure that the Layers option is activated and that the new file will be included in the Organizer. Click Save, and then choose File > Close All.

▶ **Tip:** The Photo-merge Faces feature works similarly to the Photomerge Group Shot tool, except that it's specialized for working with faces. You can have a lot of fun merging different faces into one. Try merging parts of a picture of your own face with one of your spouse to predict the possible appearance of future offspring. Choose File > New > Photomerge Faces, or click the Faces button in the Photomerge panel In Guided Edit mode to create your own Frankenface.

# Removing unwelcome intruders

The Photomerge Scene Cleaner helps you improve a photo by removing passing cars, tourists, and other unwanted elements. The Scene Cleaner works best when you have several shots of the same scene, so that you can combine the unobstructed areas from each source picture to produce a photograph free of traffic and tourists.

You can use up to ten images in a single Scene Cleaner operation; the more source images, the more chance that you'll produce a perfect result. In this exercise, you'll do the best you can with just two photos.

▶ **Tip:** When you're sightseeing, it's a great idea to take extra shots of any busy scene so that later you can use the Scene Cleaner to put together an uncluttered image. It's not necessary to use a tripod; as long as your photos were shot from roughly the same viewpoint, Photoshop Elements will align the static content in the images automatically. Sequences shot with burst mode are ideal.

1   Ctrl-click / Command-click to select the images 10_03a.jpg and 10_03b.jpg in the Media Browser. Choose File > New > Photomerge Scene Cleaner.

2   Photoshop Elements analyzes and aligns the images. By default, the first image in the Project Bin, 10_03a.jpg (framed in blue), has been loaded as the Source image. Drag 10_03b.jpg (framed in yellow) from the Project Bin to the Final pane. This is the photo you will "clean"—the base image for your composite.

3   If necessary, scroll down in the Photomerge Scene Cleaner panel at the right, to select the Pencil tool (✐); then, set the brush size to **30** px in the tool options bar. In the Final image, draw a line through the girl in the foreground.

You can see that the Source image has some information across the top and down the right hand side of the photo that is missing from the Final image.

▶ **Tip:** Hold down the Shift key as you drag with the Pencil tool to constrain your movement to a straight line.

4   Make sure the Pencil tool is selected, and then drag a line down the right side of either image. Release the mouse button; then, drag a line from right to left across the top of either image. Toggle the Show Regions option to see which part of each source image has contributed to the blended result.

5   Working with only two images, there's not a lot more we can do. Click Done in the Photomerge Scene Cleaner panel, and then choose View > Fit On Screen.

6   You can see that there are small empty patches in both the top left corner and the bottom right of the photo. You can crop the image to remedy that. Choose Image > Crop and drag the corner handles of the cropping rectangle to trim the blank area at the bottom right and exclude the group of tourists at the left. When you're done, click the Commit button in the corner of the bounding box.

7   Choose File > Save. Name the file **10_03_Depopulated** and save it to your My CIB Work folder, in Photoshop (PSD) format. Activate Layers and make sure the file will be included in the Organizer. Click Save, and then close all three files.

## Blending differently exposed photos

There are many common situations where we (or our cameras in automatic mode) are forced to choose between properly exposing the foreground or the background.

Interior shots often feature overexposed window views where the scene outside is washed-out or lost completely. Subjects posing in front of a brightly lit scene or backlit by a window are often underexposed, and therefore appear dull and dark.

A person posing in front of a city skyline at night is another classic example of this kind of exposure problem; we need to use a flash to make the most of our subject in the foreground, but the background is better exposed without it.

Photomerge Exposure provides a great new way to deal with photos captured in difficult lighting conditions, enabling you to combine the best-lit areas from two or more images to make the perfect shot.

1   If you're still in the Editor from the last exercise, switch to the Organizer now by clicking the Organizer button (⊞) at the top right of the Editor workspace.

2   In the Organizer, activate the Find box beside the Lesson 10 tag in the Keyword Tags panel, if necessary, to isolate the images for this lesson.

3   Ctrl-click / Command-click to select the images 10_04a.jpg and 10_04b.jpg, two different exposures of the same stained-glass window.

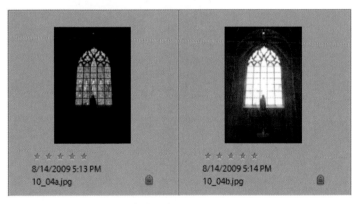

4   Click the small white arrow on the Fix tab above the Task Pane and choose Full Photo Edit.

## Using the Photomerge Exposure tool

When you're faced with difficult lighting conditions, you can simply take two or more photos at different exposure settings and let the Photomerge Exposure tool align them and blend them together.

Photoshop Elements can detect whether the images you've chosen to blend with the Photomerge Exposure tool were captured with the exposure bracketing feature on your camera, and whether they were taken with or without flash.

The Photomerge Exposure tool has two working modes; it will default to Automatic mode for exposure-bracketed shots, or open in Manual mode for a set of photos captured with and without flash.

## Merging exposures automatically

For this exercise you'll work with two interior shots of a stained-glass window captured with exposure bracketing.

One shot has been correctly exposed to capture the dimly lit interior, but the window appears "burnt out" so that all color and detail have been lost. The other photo is exposed perfectly to capture the glowing colors in the stained glass, but has failed to register any detail in the church walls and vaulted ceiling.

1   Ctrl-click / Command-click to select both photos in the Photo Bin, and then choose File > New > Photomerge Exposure. Wait while Photoshop Elements aligns the content in the source photos and creates the composite image.

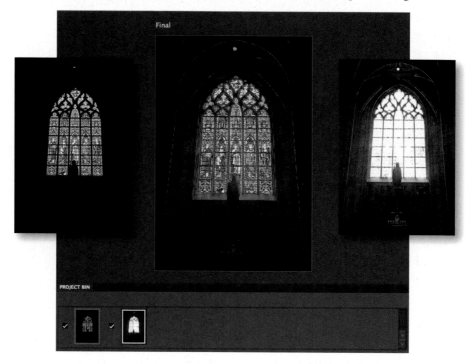

Photomerge Exposure has defaulted to Automatic mode for these exposure bracketed shots, and has successfully combined the differently exposed areas to produce an image that looks like what we actually saw but couldn't capture in a single shot.

2   Use the Zoom and Hand tools to inspect the merged image.

## Adjusting the automatically merged image

Even in Automatic mode, Photomerge Exposure provides you with controls to fine-tune the way the source images are combined.

**1** If necessary, click the Fit Screen button above the Edit pane or double-click the Hand tool so that you can see the entire image.

**2** To increase the contrast in the blended image, drag the Shadows slider in the Photomerge Exposure panel to the left to set a Shadows value of –50.

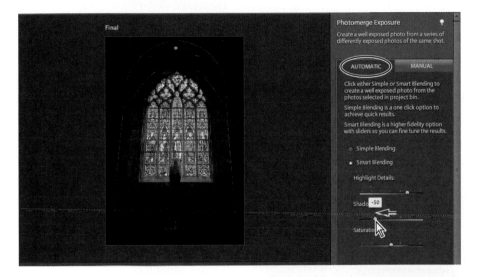

**3** Use the Zoom tool to zoom in on the stained-glass window. Increase the Highlight Details value to 100 and the Saturation value to 10.

**4** Click Done, and then wait while the merged image file is generated.

**5** Choose File > Save. Name the file **10_04_Leadlight** and save it to your My CIB Work folder, in the default Photoshop (PSD) format with the Layers option activated. You know the drill.

**6** Choose File > Close All.

# Merging exposures manually

Photomerge Exposure does a great job of merging your exposure bracketed shots automatically, producing good results in Automatic mode for most backlit situations. When Photoshop Elements detects shots taken with Flash / No Flash, Photomerge Exposure defaults to Manual mode.

Select two or more images in the Photo Bin, and then choose File > New > Photomerge Exposure. Depending on your photos, Photomerge Exposure may open in Manual or Automatic mode.

You can easily switch modes by clicking the Manual and Automatic tabs in the Photomerge Exposure panel.

On the Manual tab you'll find basic instructions together with the Selection (Pencil) tool—for identifying the areas you wish to copy from the Foreground (source) image—and the Eraser tool for modifying your selection.

There are also controls for showing or hiding Selection tool strokes and the color-coded regions indicating the areas being contributed to the blend by each source image.

Activating the Edge Blending option will smooth the edges between merged regions and the Transparency slider lets you fine tune the way each source photo is blended into the final composite image.

For more detail on using the Photomerge Exposure feature, please refer to Photoshop Elements Help.

# Using layers to combine photographs

In this project, you'll use layers to combine three photos. You'll apply a clipping mask to one photo in order to blend it smoothly into the background image; then, you'll add a selection from another photo and learn how to remove the colored fringe that is often visible surrounding such a selection. Your finished work file will retain the original pixel information from all three source images, so you can go back and make adjustments to any of them at any time.

1   In the Organizer, use the Lesson 10 tag, if necessary, to isolate the images for this lesson. Ctrl-click / Command-click to select the images 10_05b.jpg and 10_05c.jpg, a scenic view of an alpine valley and a photo of a sunlit paraglider.

2   Click the arrow on the Fix tab above the Task Pane and choose Full Photo Edit.

## Arranging the image layers

In the first exercise, you'll place these two images on separate layers and blend them to create a composite background.

1   Click the Arrange button (▣) at the top of the workspace and choose the layout at the right of the top row, Tile All Horizontally.

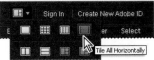

2   Click the title tab of the image 10_05c.jpg (the paraglider) to make it the active window. Select the Move tool (▸⊕) and hold down the Shift key as you drag the paraglider onto the alpine view. Release the mouse button, and then the Shift key. Holding the Shift key as you drag a layer to another file ensures that the image appears in the same position in the target file as it occupies in the source.

**3** Close the image 10_05c.jpg, and then double-click the Hand tool or choose View > Fit On Screen. In the Layers panel, select Layer 1 (the paraglider) to make it active. Choose Image > Resize > Scale. In the tool options bar, make sure Constrain Proportions is activated, and then type **50%** in the W (width) field. Click the Commit button in the lower right corner of the bounding box.

**4** With the Move tool, drag the paraglider into the upper right corner; then, drag the lower left handle of the bounding box upwards and to the right to reduce the image further. As you drag, keep your eye on the width (W) and height (H) values in the tool options bar; stop when the width and height reach 80%.

**5** Click the Commit button on the bounding box to accept the changes.

# Creating a gradient layer mask

A layer mask allows only part of the image on a layer to show and hides the rest by making it transparent. Layers lower in the stacking order will be visible through the transparent areas in the masked layer.

In the next steps you'll create a gradient that fades from opaque to transparent, and then use this gradient to create a soft-edged mask. This will make it easy to blend the images together without a visible edge.

1 With Layer 1 selected as the active layer, click the Add Layer Mask button (⬚) at the bottom of the Layers panel to add a new, blank layer mask.

2 In the toolbox, select the Gradient tool (▬); then, click the Default Foreground And Background Colors button beside the foreground and background color swatches, or press the D key on your keyboard.

3 In the tool options bar, click the Radial Gradient (⬤) button, the second in the row of gradient type options, and then click the Edit button to the left.

4 In the Gradient Editor dialog box, drag the left-hand marker below the black and white gradient strip to the right. As you drag the marker, keep an eye on the Location value below the gradient strip; stop dragging when the value reaches 33%. Click OK to close the Gradient Editor.

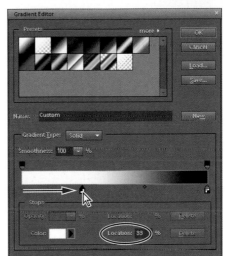

**5** Make sure that Layer 1 is still selected in the Layers panel. Starting from a point between the parachute and the parachutist, drag a line upwards with the Gradient tool. Release the mouse button when you reach the top of the image.

**6** To see the layer mask displayed in the image window as a semi-transparent overlay, hold down the Shift key, and then Alt-click / Option-click the layer mask thumbnail on Layer 1.

As you can see, the central area of the mask is completely clear; the soft edge created by the gradient begins well away from the paraglider. This is a result of the modification that you made in the Gradient Editor dialog box in step 4.

**7** Review step 4 on the previous page. You moved the left color stop marker to a location 33% of the distance from the start to the end of the gradient strip. By doing this, you set the gradient so that the transition from foreground color to background color began one-third of the way along the line you dragged with the Gradient tool in step 6. Had you not made this adjustment to the gradient, the fade would have begun at the point you first clicked, and the paraglider would have been partially masked.

**8** Hold down the Shift key, and then Alt-click / Option-click the layer mask thumbnail again to hide the overlay.

Although your gradient mask blends the image on Layer 1 very smoothly into the layer beneath it, it's obvious that the color in our paraglider image will need to be adjusted to match the background.

# Matching the colors of blended images

Every color-matching problem will have its own solution, but this exercise should at least give you an idea of what kinds of things you can try. In this case you'll use a blending mode together with several different adjustments to color and lighting.

1  In the Layers panel, click the layer thumbnail on Layer 1; then, use the menu at the top of the panel to change the blending mode to Hard Light. Leave the opacity set to 100%.

2  Choose Enhance > Adjust Lighting > Levels. In the Levels dialog box, drag the gray slider beneath the center of the tone graph to the left slightly, or type in the text box, to set a new midtone value of **1.2**; then, click OK.

3  Choose Enhance > Adjust Color > Adjust Hue/Saturation. In the Hue/Saturation dialog box, use the menu above the sliders to switch from the Master channel to the Cyans channel. Set the Saturation value for the Cyans channel to −**90**. Switch to the Blues channel and set the Saturation to −**50**; then click OK.

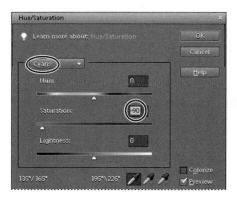 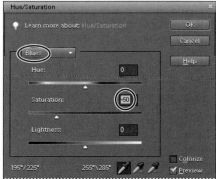

4  Choose Enhance > Adjust Lighting > Brightness/Contrast. Reduce the value for Brightness to −**10**; then, click OK.

As you can see in the before and after illustration to the right, this combination of adjustments has not only matched the colors in the blended images, but has also dimmed the paraglider slightly, helping it to fit in better with the hazy aerial perspective in the background image.

5  Choose File > Save As. Save the file to your work folder, in the Photoshop format with Layers enabled. Make sure that the image will be included in the Organizer, but not in a Version Set. Name the new file **10_05_Composite**, and then click Save. Keep the blended image open for the next exercise.

## Cleaning up selection edges with the Defringe command

Defringing removes the annoying halo of color that often surrounds a selection copied and pasted from one image to another. In this exercise you'll add a foreground image of four sisters, so that they appear to be overlooking our alpine valley. To do this, you'll select and delete the background from the photo of the girls and use the Defringe feature to blend the selection halo into the background.

1   Choose View > Fit On Screen; then, choose File > Open. Navigate to and open your Lesson10 folder. Select the file 10_05a.jpg, and then click Open.

2   With the image 10_05a.jpg selected as the active window in the Edit pane, choose Select > All. Choose Edit > Copy, and then File > Close. In the Layers panel, make sure that Layer 1, the top layer of your composite image, is still selected; then, choose Edit > Paste. The image of the four sisters is placed on a new layer named Layer 2, right above the layer that was selected.

3   With the new layer selected in the Layers panel, select the Move tool (⊕) and drag the photo of the girls to the lower left corner of the image.

4   Choose Image > Resize > Scale. Make sure that Constrain Proportions is activated in the tool options bar, and then drag the upper right handle of the bounding box upwards and to the right, until the wooden rail extends just a little outside the right border of the image. Click the Commit button near the lower right corner of the bounding box to accept the change. Press the left arrow key twice to nudge the content of Layer 2 just a fraction to the left.

**5** Select the Magic Wand tool (✨). In the tool options bar, set the Tolerance to **25**, activate Anti-alias, and disable Contiguous and Sample All Layers. Click on the pink-colored background of the Layer 2 image with the Magic Wand tool. If necessary, hold down the Shift key and click to select any un-selected pink areas in the background.

**6** Zoom in on the faces of the three girls on the right. Small areas in the sun-lit skin of all three faces have become selected. Pick up the Lasso tool (⌀); then, hold down the Alt / Option key and drag around the selected areas in the faces to subtract them from the selection. Zoom in on the right hand of the girl on the left, and then both hands of the girl on the right. Use the same technique to clear the selected areas. Check the pink sweater at the girl's right hip.

**7** Press the Delete key to delete the pink background, and then press Ctrl+D / Command+D, or choose Select > Deselect to clear the selection.

**8** Zoom in to the edge of the left hand and lower arm of the girl in the purple sweater. A pinkish fringe or halo is clearly visible here.

**9** Choose Enhance > Adjust Color > Defringe Layer. In the Defringe dialog box, enter **5** pixels for the width and click OK. Most of the fringe is eliminated.

**10** Double-click the Hand tool in the toolbox, or choose View > Fit On Screen to see the whole image in the edit window.

**11** Select the Magic Wand tool (✨) once more, and click anywhere in the cleared area surrounding the girls. Choose Select > Modify > Border and set a border width of 4 pixels; then, click OK.

**12** Choose Filter > Blur > Blur More, and then repeat the command to soften the harder edges of the pasted image. Press Ctrl+D / Command+D, or choose Select > Deselect to clear the selection.

**13** Choose File > Save, and then close the document.

Congratulations, you've completed the last exercise in this lesson. You've learned how to create a stunning composite panorama, how to merge multiple photos into the perfect group shot, how to remove obstructions from a view, and how to compose several photos into a single image by arranging layers and using a gradient to define a layer mask. You've also gained some experience with solving difficult lighting problems by combining shots taken at different exposures.

Take a moment to work through the lesson review on the next page before you move on to the next chapter, "Advanced Editing Techniques."

# Review questions

1   What does the Photomerge Group Shot tool do?

2   How does the Photomerge Scene Cleaner work?

3   Why is it that sometimes when you think you're finished with a transformation in Photoshop Elements you cannot select another tool or perform other actions?

4   Why does Photomerge Exposure sometimes open in Automatic mode and at other times in Manual mode?

5   What is a fringe and how can you remove it?

6   What are the Photomerge tools that are not covered in this lesson?

# Review answers

1   With the Photomerge Group Shot tool you can pick and choose the best parts of several similar photos, and merge them together to form one perfect picture.

2   The Photomerge Scene Cleaner helps you improve a photo by removing passing cars, tourists, and other unwanted elements. The Scene Cleaner works best when you have several shots of the same scene, so that you can combine the unobstructed areas from each source picture to produce a photograph free of traffic and tourists.

3   Photoshop Elements is waiting for you to confirm the transformation by clicking the Commit button, or by double-clicking inside the transformation boundary.

4   Photomerge Exposure detects whether your source photos were taken with exposure bracketing or with and without flash and defaults to Automatic or Manual mode accordingly. Manual mode works better for source files taken with flash/no flash.

5   A fringe is the annoying halo of color that often surrounds a selection pasted into another image. When the copied area is pasted onto another background color, or the selected background is deleted, pixels of the original background color show around the edges of your selection. The Defringe Layer command (Enhance > Adjust Color > Defringe Layer) blends the halo away so you won't see an artificial-looking edge.

6   The Photomerge Faces and Photomerge Style Match tools are not treated in this lesson. Photomerge Faces works similarly to the Photomerge Group Shot tool, except that it's specialized for working with faces. The Photomerge Style Match tool lets you merge the developing style—the tone and color settings—from one image to another.

# 11 ADVANCED EDITING TECHNIQUES

## Lesson Overview

In this final chapter you'll learn some advanced editing concepts and try some of the innovative tools that Adobe Photoshop Elements delivers to help you improve the quality and clarity of your images.

Discover the benefits of working with raw image files and how the power and simplicity of the Camera Raw plug-in makes it easy for you to achieve professional-looking results with your color corrections and tonal adjustments. Save your raw files in the versatile DNG format and take advantage of Camera Raw's non-destructive editing.

Enjoy the creative possibilities of combining and calibrating multiple filters, creating your own special effects to turn your photos into art.

This lesson will introduce some essential concepts and skills for making the most of your photos:

- Working with raw images
- Converting files to DNG format
- Using the histogram to assess a photo
- Improving the quality of highlights and shadows
- Designing custom effects in the filter gallery
- Creating layer masks
- Using the Type Mask tool

 You'll probably need between one and two hours to complete this lesson.

Discover the advantages of working with raw images in the Camera Raw window, where the easy-to-use controls make it simple to correct and adjust your photos like a professional. Learn how to use the Histogram panel to help you understand what a less-than-perfect picture needs and to give you visual feedback on the solutions you apply. Finally, have some fun putting together your own filter effects.

263

# Getting started

**Note:** Before you start working on this lesson, make sure that you've installed the software on your computer from the application CD (see the Photoshop Elements 10 documentation) and that you have correctly copied the Lessons folder from the CD in the back of this book onto your computer's hard disk (see "Copying the Classroom in a Book files" on page 2). You should also have created a working catalog (see "Creating a new catalog" on page 8).

You can begin by importing the sample images for this lesson to the CIB Catalog that you created at the beginning of Lesson 1.

1   Start Photoshop Elements and click Organize in the Welcome Screen. When the Organizer opens, make sure that your CIB Catalog is loaded (if you need to refresh your memory, refer to step 2 in the Getting Started section in Lesson 5).

2   Choose File > Get Photos And Video > From Files And Folders. In the Get Photos And Videos From Files And Folders dialog box, locate and select your Lesson11 folder. Disable any automatic processing option that is currently active, and then click Get Media.

3   In the Import Attached Keyword Tags dialog box, select the Lesson 11 tag, and then click OK. Click OK to close any other alert dialog box.

# Working with camera raw images

In this first exercise you'll be working with a raw image from a Nikon camera as you explore the correction and adjustment controls in the Camera Raw window.

1   In the Organizer, click the Show All button in the Find bar. Type the word **hat** in the Text Search box, at the left of the bar above the Media Browser. The test search returns a single image: 11_01_SunHat.NEF.

2   Right-click / Control-click the thumbnail in the Media Browser and choose Edit With Photoshop Elements Editor. Photoshop Elements opens the image in the Camera Raw window.

The moment you open a camera raw file for the first time, the Camera Raw plug-in creates what is sometimes referred to as a *sidecar file* in the same folder as the raw image file. The sidecar file takes the name of the raw file, with the extension ".xmp." Any modification that you make to the raw photograph is written to the XMP (Extensible Metadata Platform) file, rather than to the image file itself, which means that the original image data remains intact, while the XMP file records every edit.

3   Use the Windows System Tray (XP), the Notification Area (Vista), or the Dock on Mac OS to switch back to the Elements Organizer.

4   With the image of the girl in the sun hat selected in the Media Browser, click the Display button (▢) at the upper right of the workspace and choose Folder Location from the menu. In the Folders panel at the left of the Media Browser, right-click / Control-click the Lesson11 folder and choose Reveal In Explorer / Reveal In Finder. A Windows Explorer / Finder window opens to show the contents of your Lesson11 folder. The new XMP sidecar file, 11_01_SunHat.XMP, is listed beside the NEF image file. Return to the Editor in Photoshop Elements.

# Getting to know the Camera Raw window

On the right side of the Camera Raw window is a control panel headed by three tabs: Basic, Detail, and Camera Calibration. For this set of exercises you'll work with the Basic tab—the default—which presents controls for making adjustments that are not possible with the standard editing tools in Photoshop Elements.

**Tip:** Click the Detail tab to access controls for sharpening image detail and reducing the grainy digital artefacts known as noise.

1 Make sure that the Preview checkbox above the image window is activated.

2 In the toolbar above the image window, hold the pointer over each of the tools in turn to see a tooltip with the name of the tool and the respective keyboard shortcut. Click the Toggle Full Screen Mode button at the right of the tool bar to switch to full screen mode.

3 Click the menu icon at the right of the Basic tab's header bar to see the choices available from the control panel Options menu. You can apply the same settings that you used for the last image you worked with, have Photoshop Elements revert to the default Camera Raw profile for your camera by choosing Reset Camera Raw Defaults, or save your own custom settings as the new default for the camera that captured this image.

# What is a raw image?

Raw files are referred to as such because, unlike many of the more common image file formats that you may recognize, such as JPEG or GIF, they are unprocessed by the digital camera or image scanner. In other words, a raw file contains all the unprocessed image data captured for every pixel by the camera's sensors, without any software instructions about how that data is to be interpreted and displayed as an image on any particular device.

A limited but basically effective analogy or model for understanding the distinction is the difference between sending a film off for automatic processing by a commercial machine and using your own darkroom where you can control everything from the development of the negative to the way the image is exposed and printed onto paper.

## The benefits of working with a raw image

Raw images are high-quality image files that contain the maximum amount of original image data in a relatively small file size. Though larger than a compressed image such as a JPEG file, a raw image contains more data than a TIFF image and uses less space.

Many types of image processing result in loss of data, effectively degrading the quality of the image. If a camera produces compressed files for instance, some data deemed superfluous is discarded. If a camera maps the whole range of captured image data to a defined color space, the spread of the image data can be narrowed. Processes such as sharpening and white balance correction will also alter the original captured data.

Whether you are an amateur photographer or a professional, it can be difficult to understand all the process settings on your digital camera and just what they mean in terms of data loss and image degradation. One solution is to use the camera's raw setting. Raw images are derived directly from the camera's sensors, prior to any camera data processing. Not all digital cameras have the capability to capture raw images, but many of the newer and more advanced cameras do offer this option.

Capturing your photos in a raw format means you have more flexibility when it comes to producing the image you want. Many of the camera settings such as sharpening, white balance, levels, and color adjustments can be undone when you're working with your image in Photoshop Elements. For instance, automatic adjustments to exposure can be undone and recalculated based on the raw data.

Another advantage is that, with 12 bits of data per pixel, it's possible to extract shadow and highlight detail from a raw image that would have been lost in the 8 bits/channel JPEG or TIFF formats.

Raw files provide an archival image format, much like a digital negative. In much the same way that you could produce a range of vastly different prints from the same film negative in a darkroom, you can reprocess a raw file repeatedly to achieve whatever results you want. Photoshop Elements doesn't save your changes to the original raw file; rather, it saves the settings you used to process it.

Note: Raw filenames have different extensions, depending on the camera used to capture the image. Examples are Canon's CRW and CR2, Epson's ERF, Fuji's RAF, Kodak's KDE and DER, Minolta's MRW, Olympus' ORF, Pentax's PTX and PEF, Panasonic's RAW, and the various flavors of Nikon's NEF.

## Adjusting the white balance

The Camera Raw white balance presets can be helpful when you need to rectify a color cast caused by incorrect camera settings or poor lighting conditions. If your camera was not correctly set up to deal with overcast conditions, for example, you could correct your image by choosing the Cloudy preset from the White Balance menu. Other presets help you to compensate for the deficient color balance caused by different types of artificial lighting. Incandescent lighting typically causes an orange-yellow color cast; fluorescent lighting is notorious for a dull greenish tint.

The As Shot setting reads the embedded metadata that records the camera settings when the image was captured, while the Auto setting recalculates the white balance based on an analysis of the image data.

1   Experiment with some of the presets available in the White Balance menu. Switch the setting back and forth to compare the Auto, Cloudy, and Tungsten preset to the default As Shot setting. In the following pages you'll discover why the appropriate white balance is so important to the overall look of the image.

As Shot

Auto

Tungsten

Cloudy

2   For now, choose As Shot from the White Balance presets menu.

For many photos, the right white balance preset will produce satisfactory results, either used "as is," or as a starting point for manual adjustment. When none of the presets seems to take your image in the right direction, you can use the White Balance tool () to sample a color from the photo to be used as a neutral reference in relation to which Camera Raw will recalculate the white balance.

The ideal sample for this purpose is a light to medium gray that is neither discernibly warm or cool in tone. In some images it can be difficult to identify such a color; in the absence of a definitive visual reference you may sometimes rely on what you know about the photo: that it was taken on a cloudy day, for example, or under fluorescent lighting. It may help to look for references such as white paper, clothing, or paint, and then sample a shaded area. In our sample photo, the weathered wood is a potential reference, but we can probably be more certain that the steel fencing wire in the background is a neutral gray.

3   Zoom into the image by choosing 100% from the Zoom Level menu in the lower left corner of the preview window, or by double-clicking the zoom tool.

4   Select the Hand tool (🖐) and drag the image downwards and to the right so that you can see the thick wire above the left side of the girl's hat.

5   Select the White Balance tool (🖋), right beside the Hand tool in the tool bar. Sample a medium gray from the center of the wire where it crosses a relatively dark area. If you see little effect, click a slightly different point.

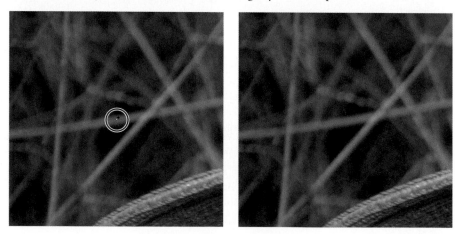

**6** Zoom out by choosing Fit In View from the Zoom Level menu in the lower left corner of the preview window.

The White Balance is now set to Custom and the image has become cooler. The weathered wood in the background is a more neutral gray and the girl's skin is rosier. Her eyes also look clearer, having lost the original yellow-orange cast.

**7** Use the White Balance menu to alternate between your custom settings and the As Shot preset, noting the change in the preview window, as well as the differences in the Temperature and Tint settings.

**8** Repeat step 7 for each of the other white balance presets, comparing the position of the sliders and look of the image to your custom adjustment. When you're done, return the white balance to your custom setting.

## Working with the Temperature and Tint settings

The White Balance tool can accurately remove any color cast or tint from an image but you may still want to tweak the Temperature and Tint settings. In this case, the color temperature seems fine, but the girl's skin still has a slightly sallow look that can be corrected by fine-tuning the green/magenta balance using the Tint control.

1   Use the Zoom tool or the Zoom Level menu in the lower left corner of the preview window to focus closely on the girl's face.

2   Increase the Tint setting to +25 with the slider or type **+25** in the Tint text box. Press Ctrl+Z / Command+Z to toggle between the new Tint setting and the value set with the White Balance tool, comparing the effect.

3   Double-click the Hand tool or by choose Fit In View from the Zoom Level menu. Test the Temperature slider by dragging it from one end of its range to the other. You'll see that the colors of the image become cooler or warmer as you move the slider. In this case, the corrected temperature of the image seemed fine but this slider could help you on other occasions—for warming up the cold underwater tones resulting from fluorescent lighting, for example.

**4** Reset the Temperature control to the corrected value of 3700 either by dragging the slider or typing the value **3700** into the Temperature text box.

**5** Experiment with the extremes of the Tint slider; then, reset the value to +25.

▶ **Tip:** As well as helping to correct color and improve the tonal range, the white balance settings can also be used creatively to achieve dramatic atmospheric effects.

Depending on the subject matter and the effect you wish to achieve, you might actually want a slight, controlled color cast or tint. For example, although technically in need of correction, you might prefer the original overly warm cast in our lesson image (a result of late afternoon sunlight) for its evocative, summery look.

## Camera Raw white balance settings

A digital camera records the white balance at the time of exposure as metadata, which you can see when you open the file in the Camera Raw dialog box. This setting usually yields the correct color temperature. You can adjust it if the white balance is not quite right. The Basic tab in the Photoshop Camera Raw dialog box includes three controls for correcting a color cast in your image:

**White Balance** Balances color in the image to reflect the lighting conditions under which the photo was taken. A white balance preset may produce satisfactory results as is, or you may want to customize the Temperature and Tint settings.

**Temperature** Fine-tunes the white balance to a custom color temperature. Move the slider to the left to correct a photo taken in light of a lower color temperature; the plug-in makes the image colors bluer to compensate for the lower color temperature of yellowish ambient light. Move the slider to the right to correct a photo taken in light of higher color temperature; the plug-in makes the image colors warmer to compensate for the higher color temperature of bluish ambient light.

**Tint** Fine-tunes the white balance to compensate for a green or magenta tint. Move the slider to the left to add green to the photo; move it to the right to add magenta.

To adjust the white balance quickly, click an area in the preview image that should be a neutral gray or white with the White Balance tool. The Temperature and Tint sliders automatically adjust to make the selected color as close to neutral as possible. If you're using a white area to set the white balance, choose a highlight area that contains significant white detail rather than a specular highlight.

—From Photoshop Elements Help

# Using the tone controls on a raw image

The settings for tonal adjustments are located below the White Balance controls on the Basic tab. In this exercise, you'll use these controls to correct exposure, check highlights and shadows, and adjust brightness, contrast, and saturation. Before you adjust any of the settings, you should understand what each of the controls does:

**Exposure** adjusts the lightness or darkness of an image. Underexposed images are too dark and look dull and murky; overexposed images are too light and look washed out. Use the Exposure control to lighten an underexposed image or correct the faded look of an overexposed image.

**Recovery** attempts to recover details from burned-out highlights. The Recovery control can reconstruct some detail in areas where one or two color channels have been clipped to white. Clipping occurs when a pixel's color values are higher or lower than the range that can be represented in the image; over-bright values are clipped to output white, and over-dark values are clipped to output black.

**Fill Light** recovers details from shadows, without brightening blacks. The Fill Light control does something close to the inverse of the Recovery control, reconstructing detail in areas where one or two of the color channels have been clipped to black.

**Blacks** specifies which input levels are mapped to black in the final image. Raising the Blacks value expands the areas that are mapped to black.

**Brightness** adjusts the brightness of the image, much as the Exposure slider does. However, instead of clipping the image in the highlights (areas that are completely white, with no detail) or shadows (areas that are completely black, with no detail), Brightness compresses the highlights and expands the shadows when you move the slider to the right. In general, it's best to use the Brightness slider to adjust the overall brightness after you have set the white and black clipping points with the Exposure and Blacks sliders.

**Contrast** is the amount of difference in brightness between light and dark areas of an image. The Contrast control determines the number of shades in the image, and has the most noticeable effect in the midtones. An image without enough contrast can appear flat or washed out. Use the Contrast slider to adjust the midtone contrast after setting the Exposure, Blacks, and Brightness values.

**Clarity** sharpens the definition of edges in the image. This process helps restore detail and sharpness that tonal adjustments may reduce.

**Vibrance** adjusts the saturation so that clipping is minimized as colors approach full saturation, acting on all lower saturated colors but having less impact on higher saturated colors. Vibrance also prevents skin tones from becoming oversaturated.

**Saturation** is the purity, or strength, of a color. A fully saturated color contains no gray. The Saturation control makes colors more vivid (containing less black or white) or more muted (containing more black or white).

First you'll adjust the Exposure setting, checking for clipping in the brighter areas.

1 Hold down the Alt / Option key as you drag the Exposure slider slowly to the right. Watch the preview in the image window to see which parts of the image will be forced towards white as the highlights are clipped as a result of this adjustment. Set the Exposure to +2.00, where white appears in the preview. You can see the clipping at the right end of the graphed curve in the histogram.

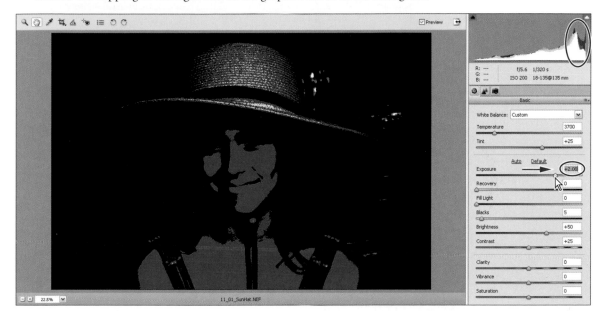

2 Keep holding the mouse button down on the slider control, but release the Alt / Option key to see the effect of the excessive exposure adjustment on the image. Switch between these two views several times to see the correlation between the clipping preview and the over-exposed image. Drag the slider left to set a value of +1.20 and check the clipping preview. At this point the reflected highlights on the beads under the girl's chin and at her shoulders are visible as the last few points of red showing in the highlights clipping preview.

In the histogram, the main body of the distribution curve has moved left—most of the clipping has been resolved. The tail end of the red curve that is still clipped at the right end of the graph represents the tiny reflected highlights in the image.

3 Reduce the Exposure further to set the value to +1.00.

**4** The highlights of the girl's skin, and the brightest-lit areas of her straw hat now look burnt out. Watch the curve in the histogram as you drag the Recovery slider to 70. The clipping is completely corrected. No part of the distribution curve reaches the right end of the graph, which is what we'd expect as there are no areas of pure white in this image.

**5** Hold down the Alt / Option key and drag the Blacks slider to the right to a value of 20. Areas that appear in the clipping preview will be forced to a solid black. Switch between the clipping preview and the image to assess the effect.

**6** Watch the clipping preview as you drag the slider slowly to the left until only the deepest shadows register as black. We set the Blacks value to 10. Click the Brightness slider, and then press the up arrow on the keyboard to increase the value to +60. Click the Contrast slider; then, press the up arrow key on the keyboard to increase the value to +50.

**7** Choose a magnification level of 100% from the Zoom menu at the lower left of the image window. Use the Hand tool to center your view on the girl's face; then, drag the Clarity slider to +50 and set the Vibrance value to +25. Double-click the Hand tool to see the entire image.

**8** Toggle the Preview checkbox at the right of the tool bar on and off to compare the adjusted photo to the raw image.

▶ **Tip:** Remember that everything you do to a raw image in the Camera Raw window is recorded only in the XMP sidecar file, not written to the original image file. This is one advantage of working with raw images: the original data remains absolutely intact. Your adjustments are applied only when you output a copy of the enhanced image in another file format.

The photo looked somewhat dull, muddy, and indistinct, and a little too dark. It now shows a broader range of detail and is more vivid; the colors are brighter and the tones are more realistic. For the sake of clarity in our demonstration however, some of the adjustments you made were quite extreme. If you wish to tone down the corrections to balance the image to your taste, you can do so now.

## Saving the image in the DNG format

Each camera manufacturer has its own proprietary raw format, and not every raw file can be read or edited by software other than that provided with the camera. There is also the possibility that manufacturers might not support every format indefinitely. To help alleviate these problems, Photoshop Elements gives you the option to save raw images in the DNG format, a publicly available archival format for raw images that provides an open standard for files created by different camera models, ensuring that you'll still be able to access your images in the future.

**1** To convert and save the image, click the Save Image button at the lower left of the Camera Raw dialog box. Under Destination in the Save Options dialog box, click Select Folder. Navigate to and open your Lessons folder; then, highlight your My CIB Work folder and click Select.

▶ **Tip:** If you can't find the My CIB Work folder, refer to "Creating a work folder" on page 3.

**2** Under File Naming, leave Document Name selected in the menu on the left. Click the menu on the right and select 1 Digit Serial Number. This will add the number 1 to the end of the file name.

**3** Click Save. The file, together with all your current settings, will be saved in DNG format, which you can reprocess repeatedly without losing the original data.

**4** Click the Open Image button in the right lower corner of the Camera Raw dialog box. Your image will open in a regular image window in Photoshop Elements. Choose File > Save. Navigate to your My CIB Work folder, name the file **11_01_SunHat_Work**, and choose the Photoshop format. Make sure that the new file will be included in the Organizer, but not in a Version Set.

**5** Click Save, and then choose File > Close.

# Workflow overview for raw images

To make use of the raw image editing capabilities in Photoshop Elements, you'll first need to set your camera to save images in its own raw format.

After processing a raw file in the Camera Raw window, you can then open the adjusted image in Photoshop Elements, where you can work with it just as you would with any other photo. When you're done, you can save the results in any format supported by Photoshop Elements.

Photoshop Elements can open only raw files from supported cameras. To see an up-to-date list of the currently supported camera models and file formats, visit the Adobe website or search in Community Help.

Note: The RAW plug-in, used to open raw files from a digital camera, is updated over time as new cameras are added to the list of those supported. You can check for updates and download the latest version of the plug-in at www.adobe.com.

# Using the histogram

In the previous exercise, you referred to the histogram in the Camera Raw window as you learned about clipping in highlights and shadows.

In this part of the lesson, you'll learn how to use the Histogram panel in Full Edit mode—both as a guide to help you understand an image's deficiencies, and also as a source of dynamic feedback as you make changes to improve its quality.

In the following exercises, you'll work on an image that was shot in poor lighting and also has a slight magenta cast. This is quite a common problem—many digital cameras introduce a slight color cast into images.

## About histograms

A histogram is a graph that maps the spread of tonal values present in an image, indicating how much tonal detail an image contains, from the shadows at the left end of the curve, through the midtones, to the highlights at the right of the curve. The histogram can help you to recognize where corrections need to be made, and then to assess how effective an adjustment will be, even as you set it up.

In the histogram below it's very apparent that there is not a good spread of tonal information in this image. The curve is weighted heavily towards the shadows at the left and deficient in the midtones. You can see clearly that the image is overly dark, and has a flat, dullish appearance, lacking in midtone contrast.

Excessive tonal adjustment can degrade image information, causing posterization, or color-banding. The histogram in the illustration below reveals that the image has already lost tonal detail in certain ranges; there are gaps, bands, and anomalous spikes in the curve. Any further adjustment will only degrade the image more.

## Understanding highlights and shadows

In the next part of this lesson, you'll adjust the highlights and shadows and make additional tonal corrections to this photo while keeping an eye on the Histogram.

1  Make sure you are in Full Edit mode. Choose File > Open, navigate to your Lesson11 folder, select the file 11_02.psd and click Open.

2  Choose File > Save As. Name the image **11_02_Work** and save it to your My CIB Work folder in Photoshop (PSD) format, with the usual option settings.

3  If the Histogram panel is not already visible, choose Window > Histogram. From the Channel menu at the top of the Histogram panel, choose RGB.

4  In order to watch the effects of your adjustments more closely, drag the Histogram panel out of the Panel bin and position it beside the image.

The histogram shows that there is a lack of data in the midtone range for this image: it needs more pixels with values in the midtones and less clustered in the shadows at the left end of the distribution curve. You can adjust the tonal range of this photo in the Levels dialog box, which includes its own histogram curve.

## Adjusting levels

1  Choose Enhance > Adjust Lighting > Levels. In the Levels dialog box, make sure that the Preview is option is activated.

You'll use the shadows, midtone, and highlights sliders (left, middle, and right respectively) below the histogram graph in the Levels panel as well as the Set Black Point, Set Gray Point, and Set White Point eyedroppers (left, middle, and right respectively).

Although the midtones are the range most in need of adjustment in this image, it's important to get the highlights and shadows right first. We'll try two slightly different methods for setting the white and black points in the image—both making use of the controls in the Levels dialog box.

2 In the Levels dialog box, hold down the Alt / Option key as you drag the highlights slider to the left to a value of 235—just inside the right-hand end of the tonal curve. The clipping preview shows you where the brightest parts of the image are: principally in the cloud reflections on the water.

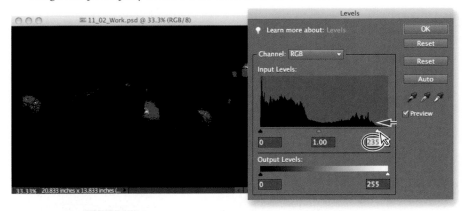

3 Watch the histogram as you release first the Alt / Option key, and then the mouse button. The curve in the histogram shifts—possibly a bit far—to the right. You can see that the right-hand end of the curve has become truncated. Move the highlights slider in the Levels dialog box to a value of 240. The curve in the histogram is adjusted accordingly.

4 In the Levels dialog box, click Reset and we'll try another method for adjusting the highlights. Select the Set White Point Eyedropper tool and watch the histogram as you click in the brightest of the reflections on the water. The white line in the histogram indicates the shape of the curve prior to this adjustment. The result is very similar to the previous method, but it won't be as easy to fine-tune any clipping at the right end of the curve. Now you'll correct the shadows.

▶ **Tip:** If your image has an easily identified neutral grey, neither too warm nor cool, you can quickly remove a color cast using the Set White Point Eyedropper.

**5** Hold down the Alt / Option key and drag the shadow slider to 4. The area below the right ear of the girl at the left shows as a dark patch in the clipping preview. Watch the histogram as you release the mouse button and the Alt / Option key.

**6** In the Levels controls, drag the midtone slider (the gray triangle below the center of the graph) to the left to set the midtone value to 1.35.

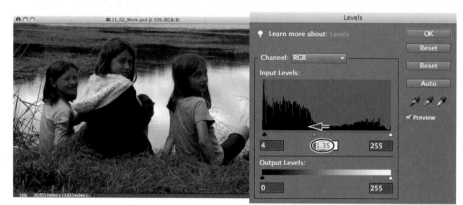

▶ **Tip:** Don't worry about the yellow alert icon in the Histogram panel; you'll deal with that in a moment.

**7** Notice the change in the Histogram. Compare the original data (displayed in white) to the data for the corrections that you have made (displayed in black). The fullest part of the curve has shifted right into the midtones and the highlights are better represented.

The changes have caused some gaps and banding in the distribution curve.

Where possible, you should try to avoid modifications that create large gaps in the histogram; even if the image still looks fine on screen, large gaps may indicate a loss of image data that will be apparent as color banding when the photo is printed.

8   Click OK to close the Levels dialog box. In the Histogram panel, click the yellow alert icon to refresh the histogram display with new, rather than cached data.

9   Select Edit > Undo Levels, or press Ctrl+Z / Command+Z to see how the image looked prior to redistributing the tonal values. Choose Edit > Redo Levels, or Press Ctrl+Y / Command+Y to reinstate your corrections.

10  Chose File > Save, and then close the file.

# Creating effects with filters

● **Note:** Not all filters are available from the Filter Gallery—some are available only individually as Filter menu commands. The Filter Gallery does not include the effects and layer styles that you'll find in the Effects panel.

You can have a lot of fun experimenting with special effects in the Filter Gallery, where you can apply multiple filters to your image and tweak the way they work together, effectively creating new custom effects. Each filter has its own sliders and settings, giving you a great deal of control over the effect it will have on your photo. The possibilities are limitless—it's up to you! Have a look at "About Filters" in Photoshop Elements Help to find out more about the different filters.

You can achieve even more and sophisticated results by applying different combinations of filters to multiple duplicate layers of the same image, and then blending the layers using partial transparency, blending modes, or masks.

Before you start exploring the creative possibilities of the Filter Gallery, you can set up a work file with some extra layers.

1   In the Organizer, use the Lesson 11 tag, if necessary, to isolate the images for this lesson. Right-click / Control-click the image 11_03.jpg in the Media Browser and choose Edit With Photoshop Elements Editor from the context menu. In the Editor, click the Reset Panels button (⟳) at the top of the workspace, or choose Window > Reset Panels.

2   Many filters use the foreground and background colors currently active in the toolbar to create effects, so you should reset them first. Click the Default Foreground And Background Colors button beside the overlapping color swatches at the bottom of the toolbox.

3   Drag the Background layer to the New Layer button (◻) at the bottom of the Layers panel to create another layer, named "Background copy" by default. Drag the new Background copy layer to the New Layer button to create a third layer.

4   Click the the the eye icon (👁) beside the top layer, Background copy 2, to hide it. Click the middle layer, Background copy, to make it active.

5   In the toolbox, select the Quick Selection tool (🖌), which is grouped in the toolbox with the Selection Brush.

**6** With the Quick Selection tool, select the wreath of flowers and leaves on the girl's head, and also her lips. Use the left and right square bracket keys ( [ , ] ) to decrease or increase the brush size as you work. Hold down the Alt / Option key as you paint to subtract from your selection.

**7** When the selection is complete, click Refine Edge in the Tool Options bar. In the Refine Edge dialog box, set the Smooth value to **0**, the Feather amount to **1** px, and the Contract/Expand value to **1**%. This will soften the edges of the selection, without reducing its effective area. Click OK.

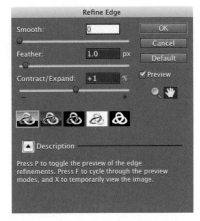

**8** Choose Select > Save Selection. Name the new selection **color details**. Under Operation, activate New Selection; then, click OK. Choose Select > Deselect.

**9** Choose File > Save As. Navigate to your My CIB Work folder, name the file **11_03_Work**, choose the Photoshop format, enable Layers, and then click Save.

## Using the filter gallery

**1** Choose Filter > Filter Gallery. If necessary, use the menu in the lower left corner of the Filter Gallery window to set the magnification level to 100%.

**2** If you can't see the entire photo, drag the image in the preview pane so that you can see most of the girl's face. If you don't see the center pane listing filter categories, click the blue button, to the left of the OK and Cancel buttons.

▶ **Tip:** When you're working with filters, the most reliable way to assess the effects of the filters you apply is to set the zoom level to 100%.

▶ **Tip:** If you try a filter and see little effect, your image may be too big; although many of the filters include a brush size control, or a slider affecting the magnitude at which the filter is applied, if your file has too high a resolution the effect may not be discernible even at the maximum setting. Use the File > Image Size command to create a smaller copy of your file; then, try the filter again.

**3** In the center pane, expand the Artistic filters category by clicking the arrow to the left of the category name, and then choose the Watercolor filter. Experiment with the full range of the control sliders. Set the Brush Detail to **5**, the Shadow Intensity to **3**, and the Texture to **2**.

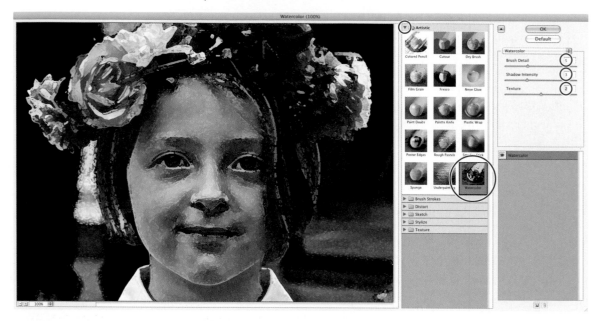

▶ **Tip:** In the Filter Gallery, you can combine as many filters as you wish, building up your own complex custom effects.

**4** Collapse the Artistic category. Click the New Effect layer button (⬜) below the right pane in the Filter Gallery dialog box, expand the Texture category, and choose the Texturizer filter. The Watercolor and Texturizer filters are applied simultaneously. Choose Canvas from the Texture menu; then, set the Scaling value to **100%** and the Relief to **4**. From the Light menu, choose Top Left.

**5** Click OK. The combined Watercolor and Texturizer filters are applied to the Background copy layer. Choose Enhance > Adjust Color > Remove Color; then, choose Enhance > Adjust Lighting > Brightness/Contrast. Increase both the Brightness and Contrast values to **50**, and then click OK.

## Layering filters and effects

In the Filter Gallery, the possibilities are endless for combining different filters at varied settings, but sometimes the best way to get the effect you want is to use the Filter Gallery in tandem with the Layers panel. By using layers and masks, layer opacity, and blending modes, you can achieve even more sophisticated results, and really make the most of the filters and effects.

**1** Click the eye icon beside the layer Background copy 2 to make it visible again; then, click the layer thumbnail to make the layer active. Choose Filter > Filter Gallery. Be careful to choose the second listing for the Filter Gallery—the first listing simply applies the previous settings without opening the Filter Gallery.

**2** The Filter Gallery window opens with your previous filters, and all their settings, exactly as you left them. Click the New Effect Layer button ( ) again. Expand the Distort category and choose the Diffuse Glow filter. Set the Graininess value to **10**, and both the Glow Amount and Clear Amount to **15**. Click OK.

> **Tip:** If you've set up an effect that looks great in the background, but makes the faces of your subjects unrecognizable, use layer masks to separate the subjects from the background, and then apply the same set of filters at different settings—or a different effect—to each layer. Even without separating elements, you can apply different effects to duplicate layers, and then mix them.

> **Note:** The stacking order of filters in the list in the Filter Gallery will alter the way they interact, though this may be more noticeable with some filters than others. You can change the order of the filters by simply dragging them in the list.

**3** In the Layers panel, click to select the layer Background copy. At the top of the panel, decrease the layer's opacity setting to **70%**.

**4** Select the top layer, Background copy 2. Choose Overlay from the Blending Mode menu at the top left of the Layers panel and set the layer opacity to **30%**.

**5** Right-click / Control-click the layer Background copy 2 and choose Duplicate Layer from the context menu. In the Duplicate Layer dialog box, type **color details** as the name for the new layer, and then click OK.

**6** Change the new layer's blending mode to Multiply, and its opacity to **70%**.

**7** Choose Select > Load Selection. The Load Selection dialog box shows your saved selection, color details, ready to be loaded as a new selection. Click OK.

**8** With the saved selection active, and the top layer active in the Layers panel, click the Add Layer Mask button (  ) at the bottom of the panel. The selection is converted to a layer mask.

In the Layers panel, a layer mask icon is added to the top layer, color details, which is now masked so that only the girl's lips and the flowers on her head remain visible.

**9** Toggle the visibility of each layer in turn, watching the effect in the Edit window. Choose File > Save, and then close the file.

# Creative fun with layer masks

There are endless ways to use layer masks to edit, blend, and combine photos. In this exercise you'll paint directly into a layer mask to produce a free-form cutout. Using layer masks in this way offers yet another way to create composite images.

1   In the Organizer, use the Lesson 11 tag, if necessary, to isolate the images for this lesson. Select the image 11_04.jpg in the Media Browser; then, click the arrow on the Fix tab above the Task Pane and choose Full Photo Edit. In the Editor, click the Reset Panels button (⟳) at the top of the workspace, or choose Window > Reset Panels.

2   Right-click / Control-click the image's single layer, the Background layer, and choose Duplicate Layer from the context menu. In the Duplicate Layer dialog box, click OK to accept the default layer name.

3   Click the eye icon beside the Background layer to hide it from view. With the new layer, Background copy, selected in the Layers panel, click the Add Layer Mask button (◻) at the bottom of the panel.

4   Click the new Layer Mask thumbnail on the Background copy layer to make it active for editing, and then choose Edit > Fill Layer. Under Contents in the Fill Layer dialog box, choose Black from the Use menu; then, click OK.

In the image window, you see only the checkerboard pattern that indicates layer transparency; the Background layer is currently invisible, and the black fill in the layer mask hides the image on the Background copy layer completely.

5   Click the box to the left of the Background layer thumbnail to reinstate the eye icon and make the layer visible again. Hold down the Shift key; then, Alt-click / Option-click the layer mask thumbnail to see the mask displayed as a semi-transparent overlay in the image window.

6   Press the E key to select the Eraser tool. In the tool options bar, choose Brush from the Mode menu and make sure that the Opacity is set to 100%.

7   Open the Brush Picker and choose Thick Heavy Brushes from the Brushes menu. The name of each brush appears in a tooltip when you hold the pointer over the swatch. Select the second brush in the set—the Rough Flat Bristle brush: then, press the Esc key to close the Brush Picker. Press the right bracket key ( ] ) repeatedly to increase the brush size to 300 pixels.

**8** With the Eraser tool, scribble a rough line in the image window to quickly clear the red overlay from the faces of all four girls.

**9** Hold down Shift+Alt / Shift+Option and click the layer mask thumbnail to hide the mask overlay; then, hide the Background layer.

**10** As you can see, the Rough Flat Bristle brush is partly transparent. In the image window, make another short stroke or two over each girl's face.

▶ **Tip:** When you wish to make a hard-edged mask, you can use any of the mechanical selection tools (either the Rectangular or Elliptical Marquee tool, or the Polygonal Lasso tool) rather than a brush or an eraser. You could also use any of the bit-mapped Shapes from the Content library as the basis for your clipping mask.

That's all there is to it! By using a layer mask in this way, you've effectively created your own ragged-edged photo frame.

**11** Choose File > Save As. Save the file to your work folder in Photoshop format with layers enabled. Make sure the file will be included in the Organizer without being saved in a Version Set. Name the new file **11_04_BrushMask**, and then click Save. Close the file.

# Creating a type mask

The Type Mask tool (🏊) turns text outlines into a layer mask through which an underlying image is visible, effectively filling the letter shapes with image detail. This can create much visual impact than using plain text filled with a solid color.

● **Note:** The Type Mask tool has one variant for horizontal type and another for vertical type.

1 In the Organizer, click the Show All button in the Find bar, and then type the word **run** in the Text Search box, at the left above the Media Browser. The search returns one image: 11_05_Runners.jpg. Right-click / Control-click the thumbnail image and choose Edit With Photoshop Elements Editor.

2 In the Editor, either choose Window > Reset Panels or click the Reset Panels button (🔁) at the top of the workspace. Drag the Layers and Effects panels out of the Panels Bin by their name tabs and position them at the bottom of the workspace where they won't block your view of the image. Hide the Panels Bin by un-checking its name in the Window menu, and then double-click the Hand tool or choose View > Fit On Screen.

3 Select the Horizontal Type Mask tool (🏊) which you'll find grouped with the other type tools in the tool box.

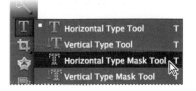

**4** Set up the text attributes in the tool options bar: Choose a font from the Font Family menu. We chose Mercurius CT Std, Black Italic, but if you don't have that font, choose any typeface that's blocky enough to let plenty of the image show through the letter forms. Type a new value of **950** pt for the font Size (you may need to adjust that for a different font). Choose Center Text (▤) from the paragraph alignment options. You don't need to worry about a color for the text; the type will be filled with detail from our marathon image.

**5** Click at a horizontally centered point low in the image and type **RUN!**

**6** Hold down the Ctrl / Command key on your keyboard; a bounding box surrounds the text in the image window. Drag inside the bounding box to reposition the type mask.

**7** If you wish to resize the text, hold down the Ctrl / Command key and drag a corner handle of the bounding box. The operation is automatically constrained so that the text is scaled proportionally. Alternatively, you can double-click the text with the Type Mask tool to select it, and then type a new font size in the tool options bar.

**8** When you're satisfied with the result, click the green Commit button in the tool options bar. The outline of the text becomes an active selection. If you're not happy with the placement of the selection, use the arrow keys on your keyboard to nudge it into place.

**9** Choose Edit > Copy, and then Edit > Paste. In the Layers panel, you can see that the cutout type image has been placed onto a new layer, surrounded by transparency.

**10** Hide the Background layer by clicking the eye icon beside the layer thumbnail.

## Adding impact to a type mask

The text is no longer live—the mask was converted to a selection outline, so it can no longer be edited with a text tool; however, you can still apply a layer style or an effect to enhance it or make it more prominent.

**1** If necessary, select Layer 1 in the Layers panel to make it active. With the Move tool (), drag the type to center it in the image window; then, press the up arrow and right arrow keys eight times each.

**2** Expand the Effects panel, if necessary, and click the Layer Styles button (). Choose the effects category Drop Shadows from the menu.

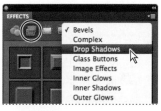

**3** In the Drop Shadows panel, double-click the swatch for the drop-shadow effect named High.

**4** In the Layers panel, select the Background Layer. Make the layer visible; then, choose Image > Rotate > Flip Layer Horizontal. Click OK to confirm the conversion of the background, and then click OK to accept the default name.

**5** Choose Enhance > Adjust Color > Adjust Hue/Saturation. In the Hue/Saturation dialog box, reduce the Saturation value to **–60** and increase the Lightness to **+60**; then, click OK.

**6** In the Layers panel, select the layer with the cut-out type; then, double-click the *fx* icon. In the Style Settings dialog box, set the Lighting Angle to **45°**. Increase the Drop Shadow Size to **40** px, the Distance to **50** px, and the Opacity to **80**%; then, click OK.

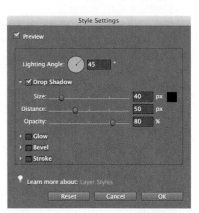

**7** Choose File > Save As. In the Save As dialog box, choose Photoshop (PSD) as the file format, enable layers, and save the file to your My CIB Work folder. Make sure that the new file will be included in the Organizer, but not in a Version Set; then, name the file **runners_mask** and click Save. Close the file.

Congratulations, you've finished this lesson on advanced editing in Photoshop Elements. You discovered how to take advantage of the Camera Raw plug-in and learned to correct images using the Histogram panel as both a diagnostic tool and a dynamic feedback reference. You also found out how to create custom effects using the Filter Gallery and had a little fun while gaining more experience with layer masks. Take a minute or two now to brush up on your new skills by reading through the lesson review on the facing page.

## Learning more

You've picked up some great tricks and techniques—but this book is just a start. You can learn even more by using the Photoshop Elements Help system, which is integrated with the application. Don't forget to look for tutorials, tips, and expert advice in the Inspiration Browser and on the Adobe website, www.adobe.com.

# Review questions

**1** What is a camera raw image, and what are some of its advantages?

**2** How can you correct an image's white balance in the Camera Raw window?

**3** How do you use the Levels controls to correct highlights and shadows?

**4** How do you create a Layer Mask to mask or reveal a specific area of an image?

# Review answers

**1** A raw file is one that is unprocessed by a digital camera, though not all cameras create raw files. One of the advantages of raw images is the flexibility of having detailed control over settings that are usually pre-applied by the camera. Image quality is another plus—because raw formats have 12 bits of available data, it's possible to extract shadow and highlight detail that would have been lost in an 8 bits/channel JPEG or TIFF file. Finally, raw files provide an archival image format, much like a digital negative: you can reprocess the file whenever you want to produce different results, while your original image data remains unchanged.

**2** In the Camera Raw window you can set the white balance in an image automatically by using the White Balance eyedropper. Clicking on a neutral color with the White Balance eyedropper automatically adjusts the Temperature and Tint sliders. Alternatively, you can choose a preset from the White Balance menu. The options include corrections based on a range of common lighting conditions. It's also possible to correct the white balance manually with the Temperature and Tint sliders.

**3** In the Levels dialog box, you can adjust the shadows and highlights in your image by using either the slider controls below the Levels histogram, or the Set Black Point and Set White Point eyedroppers. You can hold down the Alt / Option key as you drag a slider to see a clipping preview, which gives you visual feedback on the location of the darkest and lightest areas of your image. With the Set Black Point and Set White Point eyedroppers you can click directly in the image to define the white and black points, or double-click the eyedroppers to call up the color picker where you can define the values precisely.

**4** Make sure the layer that you wish to mask is selected in the Layers panel. In the Edit window, select the area that you wish to reveal, and then click the Add Layer Mask button at the bottom of the Layers panel.

# INDEX

## W

## Z

# Production Notes

The *Adobe Photoshop Elements 10 Classroom in a Book* was created electronically using Adobe InDesign CS3. Art was produced using Adobe InDesign, Adobe Illustrator, and Adobe Photoshop.

References to company names in the lessons are for demonstration purposes only and are not intended to refer to any actual organization or person.

## Team credits

The following individuals contributed to the development of this edition of the *Adobe Photoshop Elements 10 Classroom in a Book*:

Project coordinators, technical writers: John Evans & Katrin Straub

Production: Manneken Pis Productions (www.manneken.be)

Copyediting & Proofreading: John Evans & Katrin Straub.

Designer: Katrin Straub

Special thanks to Cory Borman, Torsten Buck, Connie Jeung-Mills, Petra Laux, Berenice Seitz and Philipp Meyer, and Christine Yarrow.

## Typefaces used

Adobe Myriad Pro and Adobe Warnock Pro are used throughout the lessons. For more information about OpenType and Adobe fonts, visit www.adobe.com/type/opentype/.

## Photo Credits

Photographic images and illustrations supplied by Torsten Buck, Han Buck, John Evans, Katrin Straub, and Adobe Systems Incorporated. Photos are for use only with the lessons in the book.

# Contributors

 **John Evans** has worked in computer graphics and design for more than 20 years, initially as a graphic designer, and then since 1993 as a multimedia author, software interface designer, and technical writer. His multimedia and digital illustration work associated with Japanese type attracted an award from Apple Computer Australia. His other projects range from music education software for children to interface design for innovative Japanese font design software. As a technical writer his work includes software design specifications, user manuals, and copy editing for *Adobe Photoshop Elements 7 Classroom in a Book*, *Adobe Photoshop Lightroom 2 Classroom in a Book*, and *Adobe Creative Suite 4 Classroom in a Book*. More recently he has authored *Adobe Photoshop Lightroom 3 Classroom in a Book* and several editions of *Adobe Photoshop Elements Classroom in a Book*.

 **Katrin Straub** is an artist, a graphic designer, and author. Her award-winning print, painting, and multimedia work has been exhibited worldwide. With more than 15 years experience in design, Katrin has worked as Design Director for companies such as Landor Associates and Fontworks in the United States, Hong Kong, and Japan. Her work includes packaging, promotional campaigns, multimedia, website design, and internationally recognized corporate and retail identities. She holds degrees from the FH Augsburg, ISIA Urbino, and The New School University in New York. Katrin has authored many books, from the *Adobe Creative Suite Idea Kit* to Classroom in a Book titles for Adobe Photoshop Lightroom 2, Adobe Creative Suite 4, Adobe Soundbooth, and several versions of *Adobe Photoshop Elements Classroom in a Book* and *Adobe Premiere Elements Classroom in a Book*.

 **Tao Buck** and her sisters have been volunteering as photomodels for the last five editions of the Photoshop Elements Classroom in a Book. When she is not riding her unicycle, Tao wants to become a top model or at least as famous as Audrey Hepburn.

 **Zoë Buck** loves to juggle with numbers, play chess, do gymnastics, and at this very moment is considering becoming a biologist.

 **Han Buck** would like to become a rock singer, an architect, a painter (actually, she is one already), or else "work from home and do nothing like her parents."

 **Mia Buck** strives to become a ballerina and great pianist (although she does not believe in practicing).

44.99

# AdobePress

## LEARN BY VIDEO Series

Learn Adobe Photoshop CS5 by Video:
Core Training in Visual Communication
(ISBN 9780321719805)

Learn Adobe Flash Professional CS5 by Video:
Core Training in Rich Media Communication
(ISBN 9780321719829)

Learn Adobe Dreamweaver CS5 by Video:
Core Training in Web Communication
(ISBN 9780321719812)

The **Learn by Video** series from video2brain and Adobe Press is the only Adobe-approved video courseware for the Adobe Certified Associate Level certification, and has quickly established itself as one of the most critically-acclaimed training products available on the fundamentals of Adobe software.

**Learn by Video** offers up to 21 hours of high-quality HD video training presented by experienced trainers, as well as lesson files, assessment quizzes and review materials. The DVD is bundled with a full-color printed book that provides supplemental information as well as a guide to the video topics.

Up to 21 hours of high-quality video training

Tutorials-to-Go! Transfer selected movies to your iPhone, iPod, or compatible cell phone

Table of Contents never more than a click away

Watch-and-Work mode shrinks the video into a small window while you work in the software

Video player remembers which movie you watched last

Lesson files are included on the DVD

## Additional Titles

- **Adobe Photoshop Elements 10: Learn by Video** (ISBN 9780321810816)
- **Introducing Adobe Premiere Elements 10 Learn by Video** (ISBN 9780321812124)
- **Learn Photography Techniques for Adobe Photoshop CS5 by Video** (ISBN 9780321734839)
- **Learn Adobe After Effects CS5 by Video** (ISBN 9780321734860)
- **Learn Adobe Flash Catalyst CS5 by Video** (ISBN 9780321734853)
- **Learn Adobe Illustrator CS5 by Video** (ISBN 9780321734815)
- **Learn Adobe InDesign CS5 by Video** (ISBN 9780321734808)
- **Learn Adobe Premiere Pro CS5 by Video** (ISBN 9780321734816)

For more information go to **www.learnbyvideo.com**

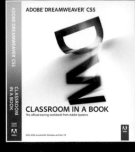
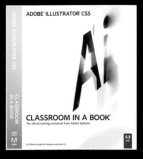
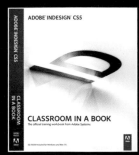

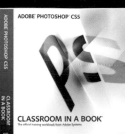